THE
SMART
MAGAZINES

GEORGE H. DOUGLAS

The Smart Magazines

50 Years of Literary Revelry
and High Jinks at
- Vanity Fair -
- The New Yorker -
- Life - Esquire -
and
- The Smart Set -

Archon Books
1991

First Published 1991 as an Archon Book,
an imprint of The Shoe String Press, Inc.,
Hamden, Connecticut 06514

Library of Congress Cataloging-in-Publication Data

Douglas, George H., 1934–
The smart magazines : 50 years of literary revelry and high jinks
at Vanity fair, the New Yorker, Life, Esquire, and the Smart set /
George H. Douglas.
p.   cm.
Includes bibliographical references and index.
1. American periodicals — History — 20th century.
2. United States — Popular culture — History — 20th century.
3. Elite (Social sciences) — United States — History — 20th century.
I. Title
PN4877.D67   1991   91-15036
051′.09041 — dc20
ISBN 0-208-02309-7

Printed in the United States of America

The paper used in this publication meets the minimum requirements
of American National Standard for Information Sciences — Permanence of Paper
for Printed Library Materials, ANSI Z39.48-1984 ∞

Designed by Abigail Johnston

· CONTENTS ·

THE
SMART
MAGAZINES

· Introduction ·

Magazines in
High Style

Τhis book contains a series of historical profiles of some
of the most memorable and delightful magazines ever to
be published in America. They have never been
treated as a group before, but for the sake of convenience they are being called "smart magazines," although other fitting terms might have been chosen instead. Smart magazines are magazines that at least superficially
were designed for smart sets or social elites. At one time in their
history, mostly in their early days, their appeal was to the upper
crust of high society, or to some assumed class of sophisticated
readers. Truth to tell, the better magazines of this sort often
dropped all extravagant pretensions to social snobbery, broadened
their appeal, and often became phenomenally successful with large
audiences far outside the gentry or the "Four Hundred." They
became first-rate magazines, better than many that were adver-

tised to the public as "quality" magazines or "intellectual" magazines. Full
of charm, regularly entertaining on a superior level, their appeal to an "elite"
often became nothing but a mannerism—not necessarily a stale mannerism,
but a mannerism nevertheless.

Each of these magazines had a distinct flavor, a character, a style of its
own. Yet it is clear that they bore a close resemblance to one another in the
beginning. During their best years—for the purposes of this book their best
years were the first four decades of the twentieth century—they shared a
community of talent. A good number of major American writers and artists
appeared in several, or even all of these magazines. The best smart magazines stood out from the commercial mainstream, and this had a powerful
magnetic appeal for some of the most creative talents of the land. This was
not because these magazines were more generous than the commercial giants—some of them were in financial straits and paid their contributors
poorly. But they were magazines that talented people loved to work for.

Strange it may seem, even paradoxical, that some of the best magazines
in an avowedly "egalitarian" American democracy should attempt to make
their primary appeal to the upper crust of society. Perhaps Americans have
always had a love-hate relationship with all forms of elitism. Surely these
magazines were at least partially the result of historical accident. Most of
them made their appearance at a time of prosperity and self-assurance, a
time when class distinctions were mostly not troubling and may have provided
a kind of zesty challenge in an upwardly mobile society. Too, because
"smartness" was often merely a mannerism we find that these magazines were
not merely pandering to social elites at all, and didn't refrain from having a
little fun at their expense. Indeed, a thumb-the-nose attitude or a scoffing at
high society seemed to be a trait of the best of these magazines from the start.
While they may have attempted to ride the coattails of the smart set for
stylish effect, most of these magazines were really neither of, for, nor by,
members of the upper crust. Yes, there were a few top-hatted writers and
artists in the early days, on the old *Vanity Fair*, on the *New Yorker* of Harold
Ross, but more often these were disaffected eccentrics, sardonic castaways,
who wore their top hats at a cockeyed angle. Indeed, it was the strange and
often crooked angle at which these magazines tilted toward smartness that
gave them their distinction.

The smart magazines—the good ones at any rate—were few in number.
Some of the magazines discussed in this book are now defunct; others have
persisted although they may work a different vein, ministering to the needs
of a radically different age. At least one of the magazines discussed herein—

Vanity Fair—disappeared for many years but has been revived in a decidedly different form. That is not necessarily an intent to disparage the reborn child, but merely to point out that the older smart magazines were products of considerable rarity and beauty. We do not have their like today, and doubtless lack the spirit to bring them back in anything like their original vitality.

In a somewhat looser and broader sense, of course, today's newsstand is filled with magazines that seem to make a strong appeal to the affluent, to the sons and daughters of rising commercial and professional classes. There is no lack of aspiring "slick" magazines, and some of them are more than a little successful financially. More often than not, today, we confuse smartness with slickness—there are a great many slickly produced magazines available that seem to make strong appeals to snobbery, manufactured taste, to what Thorstein Veblen liked to call "conspicuous consumption." The typical newsstand or bookstore in your average airport or posh hotel or suburban mall is literally covered with these slick magazines of conspicuous consumption. They pass, stealthily, as magazines for imagined elites, so that their bogus qualities largely go unnoticed.

These magazines are what they might call in the book trade "coffee table magazines." They look beautiful, perhaps they often *are* beautiful. But they seem too often lacking in any real originality or vitality. Their pages are so moist with slickness and with some perfumed essence that they seem to defy separation. Here are gorgeous pictures of women in gowns, pages of advertisements for cognac, for fashionable jewelry stores on Fifth Avenue, yachts, cars (often called motor cars for a nice British touch); here are interviews with some unknown French countess and full-color pictures of her chateau on the Loire. Here are reproductions of impressionistic masterpieces, of modern etchings; here are pictures of handmade dolls, gold coins, spreads of haute cuisine, hotels in the Bahamas and all the rest. Such magazines are a feast for the eye, of course, the kind of thing that one loves to look at momentarily while waiting for a partner to get ready for the cocktail hour. There is the written word here, too, or at least pale ribbons of designer type, but invariably the writing is unmemorable. One sees the article about the French countess, or some new Broadway stars; one glances at the inevitable illustrations that carry the continuity of the whole; one nods agreeably, but without the necessity of activating any brain waves in the process. These magazines are a great tribute to modern print technology and to the noble arts of graphic design; still, few of them rise above the level of ephemera—few are discussed, few reach out to a live audience; they eventually find their way into the scrap pile, or, with phenomenal luck, into a dentist's office where they might well enjoy their happiest uses.

The smart magazines discussed in this book are not of this sort. They may seem to have a kinship with the moist and pallid slicks, but it is a relationship at distant remove. The smart magazines of a half century or more ago were vital, full of bravura, of verve and dash. They were not all sheen and glitter; they possessed sinews, bone marrow, and muscle. Frank Crowninshield, the founding editor of *Vanity Fair*, liked to say that his magazine was a conversation piece in New York society. Yes, *Vanity Fair* was slick by the standards of the day, although probably not by the standards of today. It looked rich, it looked important. But it also had an undoubted seriousness, the power to elicit thought and interest. A coffee table magazine — Crowninshield might actually have liked that term. He wanted to see his magazine on display in salons and drawing rooms — and he usually did. But what really pleased him was that his magazine sparked discussion, interest, charming conversation among those who found it appealing. It was not merely picked up with a glacially indifferent eye; it was read. And so it was with the editors of all the magazines here under discussion. Their product was never merely a sauce or meringue; they never regarded themselves as purveyors of commercially crafted confections; rather they hoped to spark response from witty and intelligent people. If their products could enflame the interest of a large audience, all to the good. But their first obligation was to produce magazines that were intelligent, thought provoking, lighthearted but still substantial — publications that were not standardized, not slavishly predictable. All of these magazines had that ineffable quality we sometimes call personality, a habit and cast of mind that stand out in memory.

This is to say that the smart magazines were top-rate magazines. But their continuing interest is not in their quality alone. It has been said that nothing is so old as yesterday's newspaper. Magazines probably don't fare much better; they fade from memory as soon as they are stashed in the closet. There are few alive today who remember the look and personality of the *Smart Set*, or of the original *Vanity Fair*. The reason for dwelling on these magazines is not simply that they were exceptional, or that they had an enthusiastic following, but that they had a considerable influence on the American culture of their day, and, what is more important, they opened up wholly new vistas and publishing opportunities for many young American writers and artists. The continuing interest in the smart magazines is that they stepped onto the enormous stage that was print journalism at the beginning of the twentieth century and drew an irresistible spotlight to themselves.

The magazine field was dominated by vigorous but shabby commercialism in those days, but the smart magazines almost magically lifted the sphere of magazine publishing to a hitherto unattained excellence. Too, these magazines opened up broad vistas and new possibilities for the large numbers of individuals who were rapidly becoming liberated from the restraints of Victorianism and from an older print journalism that was either squalid or drab. The smart magazines acted as a magnet for the talents of several generations of writers and artists, and this subsequently had a large impact on American life.

The stories of the magazines profiled in this book make interesting chapters in the history of American enterprise and resourcefulness. Commercial publishing is a fragile and quixotically changing business. Even the greatest and most celebrated magazines can be apparently healthy but still only one step away from oblivion. All of the leading smart magazines suffered strong adversities at various times during their histories, yet they all had an unforgettable force and charm that made a lasting impact on the imaginative arts in America. Looking back at their often hard-fought achievements and upon their individuality and style gives us more than a few delights and satisfactions.

· ONE ·

The Smart Magazine Legacy

· 1 ·

Fin de Siècle— An Opening for New Talents

When smart magazines began to appear in the United States during the 1890s and early 1900s, their appeal was to be to a reading public that had not existed, or at least not been discovered, in earlier times. Smart magazines were written and edited for the leisured classes (although not necessarily for the very rich)—for sophisticated urbanites, for the kind of person who was well traveled, well read, well acquainted; for people who wanted to be entertained, but on an exalted plane; people wishing to sidestep the bromides and sugar-coated confections being dished out to standardized middle-class culture by the mammoth mass-circulation magazines.

A few generations earlier, an audience for such magazines would not have existed. In the years following the Civil War America made a rapid and sometimes painful transition from a rural to an urban society. Leisured classes had existed before this time, but they had been small, isolated, and lacking in any sense of self-identity (or identified with self-limitation where theocratic traditions obtained). But in the diamond-studded decades after the Civil War sharp divisions of class had appeared in the social structure, with the upper classes no longer afraid to flaunt their wealth by the acquisition of stately homes, horses, yachts, gilded carriages, large staffs of servants, art collections, and so on. Some of the newly rich gave a good account of themselves, serving on the boards of newly founded opera companies, colleges or symphony orchestras. And their ranks would shortly be swelled many times over by daughters who had traveled abroad, even married impoverished European noblemen; by sons who had studied architecture in Paris or ransacked the palaces and galleries of Europe for art treasures. These were not the people who had been the creators of large banking or industrial fortunes or whose daily life was circumscribed by matters of railroad finance, or silver policy or labor unrest, but who instead enjoyed the affluence and leisure to remain at play. Above all they were people who could be choosy about their forms of entertainment. They could set their own tastes, and, being people of ample means and freedom of maneuverability, they could set the tastes of others. These were people in a position to influence the general culture.

Were the smart magazines then restricted in appeal to these new elites? Had they sought a small and limited public? Not at all. The smart magazines were always general magazines intended to reach a sizable audience. They were reasonably priced. Some of them attained lofty circulation figures. Their readership could accordingly never consist solely of members of the upper crust. To pay their way, such magazines would have to appeal to a substantial number of middle-class readers, perhaps to *any* readers aspiring to an enhanced lifestyle. There were simply not enough rich people to make a magazine profitable—even if all the rich people were to become subscribers, which was highly unlikely. Many members of the upper class, in fact, regarded a few of the early smart magazines with suspicion, believed them to be frivolous and lightweight. Many an old dowager or Wall Street financier would not be caught dead reading magazines that purported to tell about, and thereby popularize, the doings, habits and lifestyles of their own social circles—sometimes in a jocular or scandalous vein.

Accordingly, the smart magazines, insofar as they had an appeal for any sizable audience, had to make their pitch to the great aspiring middle classes, or, at least to the younger sons and daughters of the social elite, perhaps to some of their miscellaneous hangers-on—free love poets, out-at-pocket artists, highly paid courtesans, and many other semicultured individuals at loose in the metropolis.

Thus there was an easy and ready-made audience for the smart magazines when they first made their appearance. While they would never enjoy circulation figures that would match those of the *Saturday Evening Post* or *Ladies' Home Journal*, neither would they be "little" magazines. The appeal to an elite was always something of a mannerism or affectation; they were and needed to be "commercial." Furthermore, the smart magazines had a considerable success because they struck a neat balance between the older highbrow magazines such as *Harper's Monthly* and *Atlantic*, on the one hand, and the mass-circulation giants on the other. These were magazines for people who believed themselves witty and clever (a group that is never in short supply), for people who didn't want to be bombarded with sermons about the state of the nation, who didn't want to have their days spoiled by the obligations of "thoughtful essays," or dignified fiction, who didn't want their minds "improved." Their minds were already sufficiently improved, thank you! They wanted to be entertained and enlightened by others who shared their more expansive and uninhibited tastes.

What precisely the smart magazines were, where they came from, what constituted their various and diverse personalities will be our subject in succeeding chapters. But historically the appearance of smart magazines—and there were to be only a handful of really good ones—was dependent on more than an increase in the size and leisurely habits of the upper classes. The smart magazines arose at a time—the last decade of the nineteenth century and the first decade of the twentieth—in which the entire magazine industry was in a period of unprecedented growth and resurgency. This period may well be seen as a renaissance or high-water mark of the American magazine with many new giants entering the field, and many older ones becoming bigger and more affluent than they would have dreamed possible before. In 1900 radio broadcasting as a practical reality was a quarter century away, television a half century away; accordingly, newspapers and magazines provided a principal form of mass entertainment for most Americans. The magazine was a medium clearly invented to entertain, and now it was about to have its moment of glory.

By the 1890s magazines had become big business. It was an era of big business for America generally, but a series of developments at the end of the nineteenth century made this a particularly propitious time to start new magazines and breathe life into those oldies that had been limping along. The first big impetus to this magazine renaissance came in 1879 when Congress decided to stimulate the growth of periodicals by offering a low-cost mailing privilege to magazine publishers. Before this time magazines had taken little hold on the American imagination; indeed from Colonial times, and for the first hundred years of our national history, magazines had been scraggly sheets, usually living short unhappy lives. Before the American Revolution there had been only fifteen magazines in the United States, and most of them had been failures; by 1800 there had been seventy magazines established. By the post–Civil War period there were some seven hundred magazines, most of them highly unstable and ephemeral. But this was just a drop in the bucket compared to the flood of the next several decades. By 1885, in the wake of the favorable change in postal rates and revolutions in print technology, there were some three thousand magazines.

In the 1880s and 1890s there were a great many developments, some technical, some economic, others social, perhaps, which led to a splendid flowering of the magazine as a popular product of American culture. Printing and production methods had made great strides in this same period. Coming rapidly on the scene were new and faster printing presses and typesetting methods, mass production conveyor systems and assembly lines for wrapping, labeling and processing. The old and slow flatbed press known to generations of printers gave way to swifter rotary presses originally developed to make possible the fast runs needed to produce daily metropolitan newspapers. In 1886 R. Hoe & Co. built a rotary press for *Century* magazine, and four years later, for the same magazine, it built a rotary art press that produced high-quality halftones from curved plates.

And the invention of the halftone process in the mid-1880s was sufficient to revolutionize completely the technology of magazine production. Before this time, any magazine wanting to use illustrations would have to depend on expensive fine-line engravings on wood plates; all this work, naturally, done by individual artists. When halftones came in an illustrated magazine could buy a halftone for twenty dollars, or less. Formerly they might have had to pay a skilled artist and the cutmaker up to three hundred dollars for a one-page wood engraving. Shortly, too, color, in the form of chromolithography and rotogravure printing, would help to make magazines, once nothing but ribbons of black type, more appealing to the eye. At first only the covers of magazines got the color treatment, but in a few years color crept inside also.

With magazines now much cheaper to produce, and the final product far dressier and more appealing, it was only natural that the search would be on for formulas to sell inexpensive magazines to an ever-increasing and eager mass audience. Heretofore, magazines—good magazines in any case—sold in the twenty-five- to thirty-five-cent range, effectively putting them out of the reach of the typical middle-class householder. By the early 1890s all this would change, with a new generation of aggressive and resourceful editors ready to put good material before the American public at an affordable price.

One of the geniuses of what would soon be called the ten-cent magazine was S. S. McClure, an Irish immigrant who had enrolled in Knox College in Illinois in 1874 at the age of seventeen with only fifteen cents in his pocket. He subsequently recalled that during his whole college career he had never been able to afford the price of a magazine, and in this land of opportunity he made up his mind to do something about it. After leaving college he started a bicycle magazine in Boston, but what was always in the forefront of his mind was a lively high-quality monthly magazine at a reasonable price. Impressed that in England there were a number of inexpensive large-circulation popular magazines—like *Strand* and *Country Life*—he had also been heartened by the existence in the United States of the *Ladies' Home Journal*, which had managed by 1893 to roll up a circulation of 700,000 at ten cents a copy.

McClure's Magazine was begun in that same year of 1893 with an initial capital of only $7,300. This was a grim depression year that boded ill for any new business venture, but the upstart magazine was an almost instant success. After a scary few months, it began catching on, reaching a circulation of 175,000 by 1895 and 250,000 in 1896. *McClure's* was a big, hefty, generous-looking monthly, soon to carry over a hundred pages an issue. It was filled with vivid articles and stories, and plenty of pictures—in the early days about half of them halftones. McClure, who was his own publisher, and mostly his own editor as well, was not a man of rarefied taste, but he was also one of the first great idea men in the magazine business—his briefcase ever bulging with new projects, manuscripts and suggestions, which he would scatter among his staff like drops of rain tossed by a windmill. Luckily, McClure was an average man who was also not a numbskull; he knew by instinct the things that Americans wanted to read about and he dished them out with unerring common sense.

Around the time that *McClure's* was in its infancy, the magazine field was exploding everywhere, and there was immediate competition for the newly discovered masses of readers. John Brisben Walker bought the feeble *Cosmopolitan*, cutting the price drastically and skyrocketing circulation figures. In 1897 Cyrus H. K. Curtis bought the old and doddering *Saturday Evening Post* for a thousand dollars and began the process of turning it into one of the most lucrative American magazines, a process that accelerated rapidly after 1899 when he offered George Horace Lorimer the editorial chair.

There were, of course, bogus imitators of these giants. One was *Munsey's* monthly magazine, established the same year as *McClure's*. Its owner, Frank Munsey, a schlockmeister if ever one was born, hit upon the idea of producing a big, gaudy, illustrated magazine mostly filled with junk, the editorial content always vastly inferior to that of *McClure's* or *Cosmopolitan*. But so voracious was the public's appetite for magazines that *Munsey's*, too, was enormously successful, at least for a time.

Lowlife characters such as Munsey aside, the 1890s saw the rise to national prominence of a breed of editors who almost singlehandedly created the mass-circulation magazine as we know it today. They were men of forceful character, who etched the stamp of their personality on every issue of their magazines so that they created a format and a style for their publications that was seemingly fixed for eternity. Some of these editors had long tenures at the top—Edward K. Bok, the enormously successful editor of the *Ladies' Home Journal*, presided over his magazine for thirty years (1889 to 1919). Starting out as a bachelor editor of a woman's magazine who boasted that he knew what appealed to the feminine mind—a boast for which he took a lot of ribbing from pundits and newspaper poets—Bok apparently did have a faultless sense of what women wanted to see in a magazine and produced what was perhaps the most deftly formulated magazine ever to appear in America. (Bok had a cagey financial sense also apparently—the bachelor editor married the daughter of his boss Cyrus H. K. Curtis.) Lacking Bok's intelligence and taste, George Horace Lorimer also had a sharp intuition as to what was right for the *Saturday Evening Post*, a magazine that bore his stamp for close to forty years (1899 to 1937).

Neither McClure, Bok nor Lorimer was a man of letters; their readership was never an elite. But singlehandedly they produced a new kind of mass-circulation magazine for America. They were the giants that everyone would come to look up to. There was plenty of room for creating new magazines apart from the patterns set down by the giant monthlies, but in a very important way, the mass-circulation titans had made all things possible.

There was, however, one other major influence at work in the 1890s beyond that of the gifted editors and resourceful publishers. Indeed, if it had not been for this other ingredient in the magazine equation, the mass-circulation magazine in the modern sense would never have been possible. This ingredient, of course, was advertising. The magazine bonanza in the 1890 to 1910 period was due as much as anything to a complete rethinking of the nature of advertising and to a discovery of ways to make magazines pay off in millions, something that would not have been dreamed of before.

Several things had to happen, however, before magazines could be completely transformed by the medium of advertising. One was a change in advertising practices generally, a new state of mind about the nature of advertising. Magazines had been carrying advertisements for a long time, just as had newspapers, but the advertising section or page of a typical magazine was a dreary and uninviting place until well after the Civil War. Monotonous columns of small type, unrelieved by illustration, assaulted the reader's eye. Looking not unlike the classified section of today's newspapers, they were in fact worse, since the typefaces were smaller; there was no provision for display type. Furthermore, the advertising section wasn't even "classified," that is, organized into categories—the very notion of classification took a long time to emerge.

Neither magazine publishers nor newspaper publishers believed that an advertisement should be anything other than pure type and very unreadable type at that. In 1833 the Boston *Evening Transcript* reduced the size of its conventional agate type (5 ½ point) to the even smaller diamond type (4 ½ point), a size that many a farsighted person could not read even with spectacles. In the 1840s one of the country's most innovative newspaper publishers, James Gordon Bennett of the New York *Herald*, the man often credited with inventing the modern American newspaper, briefly permitted departure from the "agate rule" and introduced a little typographical variation. But even the venturesome Bennett eventually backed away from this experimentation and returned to the agate rule because it was "democratic." All advertisers would henceforth be treated alike—that is, terribly—no matter how much they could afford to pay.

One of the reasons advertising took so long to be discovered by a people used to upsetting traditional rules and proprieties was that for most of the nineteenth century advertising was assumed to be a local function. The sales ladder descended from the manufacturer, to the wholesaler or jobber, then to the retailer and finally to the consumer or customer. If a certain product or service was to be advertised, this function was carried out by the local seller—a department store, hotel, an express company, or whatever. Advertising was generally considered to be a process of local selling until about 1885; accordingly, most advertisements before that time appeared in newspapers. Magazines, except for a few local publications or trade papers, seldom contained advertisements.

In the late 1880s, however, all this began to change drastically. Manufacturers, many of them now large companies, were making products that withstood stiff competition from similar products of other companies, so there was a strong impetus to widely disseminate information about a product or brand name. Let's say you were a maker of soap (and what is interesting or fascinating about soap from that day to this?), or a chocolate bar, or mustache wax. How could you differentiate your product from some other product that in most respects was almost exactly identical? Advertising was quickly perceived as the answer to this puzzle. You find a way to call the public's attention to *your* product, its name and its peculiarities. Calling attention to something in magazines and newspapers obviously meant breaking loose of all the old restrictions; it meant breaking the agate rule; it meant slogans, pictures, jingles, catch phrases, or anything that jumped out of the page at the reader.

Magazines, national media as they supposedly were, or would very shortly be, became the prime beneficiaries of the advertiser's attention. By the late 1880s nearly all major publications were accepting larger display ads of one sort or another, so magazine publishers quickly became dependent on the manufacturer's willingness to pay their freight. During this period in which there was very heavy competition among bicycle manufacturers (a bicycle craze having struck the country in this era immediately before the appearance of the automobile), magazines usually carried one or more display ads with pictures of the latest bicycle models. Among the other companies taking avidly to the advertising technique in this period were the fountain pen manufacturers—Waterman's Ideal Fountain Pen was sold aggressively in magazine ads, forcing the competing Estabrook Company to devise its own ads.

These early display ads are primitive by today's standards, for strictly speaking there was as yet no such thing as the advertising specialist. There had been advertising agencies going back to the 1860s, but in the early days they had been nothing but sellers of space. For a long time manufacturers themselves had to create their own selling techniques, and many of them discovered or developed approaches that would later be taken over by creative "advertising directors." For example, the company that manufactured Lydia Pinkham's Vegetable Compound for Female Complaints (a later wit enjoyed calling this patent remedy "Lydia Pinkham's Pink Pills for Pale People") pioneered the "portrait ad" showing Mrs. Pinkham as a kindly, reassuring, motherly, understanding type. She was the first in a long line of inspirational female figures and trade names—Fannie Farmer, Betty

Crocker, and so on. Another fling at the portrait ad was that for the "W. L. Douglas $3 Shoe for Gentlemen," showing Mr. Douglas himself, a confident bewhiskered gentleman, who encouraged countless ads featuring other forceful-looking men who sold cough drops, saddle soap, rifles, and so on. In their pioneering days such ads were so startling to the average magazine reader that they gained national notoriety. In 1890 a magazine reader from San Francisco cut the picture of W. L. Douglas from an advertisement and pasted it on an envelope, then stamped and mailed his order without any further address. His letter was duly received and his order filled by the Douglas Company.

By the mid-1890s, advertising was big business in the magazine field. It was probably this new area of support that permitted the development of mass-circulation magazines, and brought about the revolution of the ten-cent magazines. Before the 1890s were over, all major magazine publishers realized that advertising was the name of the game. A decade before advertising had been the tail on the dog; now the tail was wagging the dog. Advertising revenues and not newsstand sale and subscription income were paying the magazine's way. A magazine like the *Saturday Evening Post* could hardly make up even a fraction of its production costs by subscription or individual sales, but it could rake in millions of dollars in advertising. One publisher of the late 1890s proclaimed: "If I can get a circulation of 400,000 I can afford to give my magazine away to anyone who will pay the postage." Needless to say, advertising revenues came pouring in to all the major magazines by 1900. By 1905, *McClure's* was printing an average of 165 pages of advertising a month at $400 a page. In 1904 the *Woman's Home Companion* estimated that its advertising business totaled $300,000 for the year!

This great surge in advertising revenues gave rise to a completely new industry consisting of advertising copywriters, market research specialists and many others. Attractive and well-produced advertisements gave mass magazines much of their glamor and appeal. The birth of the advertising dimension in the 1890s provided a pleasant surprise to several generations of American artists, and a shot of adrenalin to many careers that had been threatened when photographs began to take over magazine pages. The end of the nineteenth century and the beginning of the twentieth century saw not the decline but the rebirth of commercial illustration in America with such great talents as Charles Dana Gibson, Howard Pyle, James Montgomery Flagg, Edward W. Kemble, Frederic Remington, Joseph Pennell, Arthur B. Frost, Norman Rockwell and John Held, Jr., all contributing to magazines as illustrators or advertising artists, usually both. These artists saw to it that magazines became something more than ribbons of print, and in fact assured that at its best the American magazine could be a thing of beauty and taste.

The smart magazines when they first appeared during the early twentieth century were naturally also susceptible to the blandishments of advertising — not only those charms of pecuniary gain but of artistic excellence. Being magazines that were supposedly aimed at the "carriage trade," at people possessed of expensive tastes and habits, the smart magazines would be in a position to draw in classy advertising clients — luxury hotels, fashionable shops and restaurants, posh resorts, expensive jewelers, makers of panatella cigars, or expensive automobiles. When the *Smart Set* first greeted the world in 1900 it was well supported by advertisers of this sort. Theoretically, a magazine of this kind would have a very natural and easy-to-tap circle of advertisers. In turn, lush advertisements would help sell the magazine to subscribers.

Of course in 1900 the biggest advertisers were looking for a somewhat different vehicle for their wares. The large-circulation general magazines were the favored lot, and for a number of years giants such as the *Saturday Evening Post, Collier's, Cosmopolitan*, with their undifferentiated masses of readers held the greatest attraction for advertisers. But by the middle years of the twentieth century, some of these once great and seemingly immortal giants had been toppled, unable to reach out to the kind of target audience that had come to mean everything to advertisers.

When the smart magazines made their appearance at the turn of the century they were well placed where access to advertising revenues was concerned, but they received no easy windfall. For years the *Smart Set* limped along with low advertising budgets, poor paper stock and printing, generally inadequate support all around. On the other hand, when the idea of a sharply defined magazine audience came to the fore, the smart magazines became especially attractive to advertisers. Much of their subsequent success was the result of skillful orchestration of lavish advertising copy, sharp editorial content and rich design features. When *Esquire* appeared in the 1930s much of its appeal was due to the fact that its editorial content had been conceived organically; it was a single unified concept forged by individuals whose experience had been almost wholly in the field of advertising. The publishers were able to confer a singular and coherent style on the whole magazine before the first issue was on the stands. At the *New Yorker* such an orchestration of advertising and editorial content was not in evidence at the beginning, but it seems to have evolved naturally as the magazine found its own style and unique personality. With the passage of time the smart magazines came to be naturals for advertisers; their audiences were sufficiently appealing to well-heeled space buyers that extraordinary attention was lavished on their pages. Few magazines of the twentieth century, for example, were more justly noted for the quality of their advertisements than the *New Yorker* during its most prosperous years.

Still, the eventual commercial success of the smart magazines is hardly the main reason for their lasting importance in the history of American publishing and American culture. Smart magazines were not slick first and intelligent afterward; things worked out quite the other way. They started out as queer ducks swimming around in the backwater of a much bigger pond. They often seemed eccentric and even slightly unsavory in the beginning. They were the offspring of earlier magazines that occasionally had lurid or frivolous reputations. On the other hand, they almost immediately tapped into something new that allowed them to thrive and eventually to stand taller than the commercial giants.

The most noteworthy contribution of the smart magazines is that they were the first magazines to attempt unabashedly to reach a sophisticated metropolitan audience. The older quality magazines such as the *Atlantic* seemed tied to the tastes of the genteel New England literary culture; the new giants such as *Collier's*, *Munsey's*, the *Saturday Evening Post*, *the Ladies' Home Journal*, were written for what were proverbially called "down-home folks," people who, as H. L. Mencken liked to say, stashed their magazines behind the egg stove along with the Sears-Roebuck catalogue and advertisements for horse liniment and Bordeaux mixture. In the years between 1880 and World War I, the United States had quickly changed from a rural to an urban society. But on the level of the popular culture this change was strenuously resisted, and magazines like the *Saturday Evening Post* were fearful of tampering with a culture and a way of life that had strong agrarian roots, ties to the older (if largely imaginary) Jeffersonian ideal. Most of them wanted to exude an aroma of the older and more settled Americanism, and though they might have come from giant editorial offices and printing plants in New York or Philadelphia they did not mainly celebrate a metropolitan way of life. Until well into the twentieth century the leading women's magazines devoted most of their energies to telling women how to bake bread and offering them dress patterns for home sewing machines. The best-known general magazines of the land flourished in an environment of caution, quietism and restraint, lauding the advancement of traditional homespun values, of pluck and luck, sometimes of jelled success and enterprise.

The smart magazines did not have their roots in these older magazine traditions or in the still dominant small-town America. They immediately sought a metropolitan audience, an audience of individuals who had grown up in the city or its better suburbs, had attended finishing schools, or perhaps had traveled abroad—or people with aspirations to leave their small-town upbringing behind them. Discovering such an audience sometimes resulted in pretentions, arch posturing, but in the case of the smart magazines recalled in this book, it also resulted in a new sense of artistic and intellectual freedom and a kind of playfulness that had formerly been kept in check in the public prints. More important, the smart magazines, because they were different, because they were attempting to reach a new kind of reading public, developed completely new and innovative journalistic styles and mannerisms.

The smart magazines also introduced to magazine journalism a cosmopolitan or international flavor. Shortly after its founding the *Smart Set* began running a regular monthly story in French—bought up on the cheap, in fact, through a deal with a French publisher—but still a startling innovation. Whether these stories were widely read is not entirely clear, but this French connection also tended to bring the magazine contributions from other European writers, not only French, but sophisticated European emigrants recently arrived in America, and other established authors who had previously had no outlets in America.

When Frank Crowninshield began editing *Vanity Fair* in 1913 he immediately established the magazine as a voice for what was then being called the avant-garde. Crowninshield had studied art for two years at the University of Rome and spent much of his youth on the standard tour of museums, cathedrals and libraries then characteristic of the upper-class lifestyle. He was himself a moving force behind the famous Armory Show in New York and subsequently came to possess one of the finest art collections in New York. There were some subscribers who found too much that was European in *Vanity Fair*; there were some who complained of effeteness and snobbery; who believed that foreign tastes were being shoved down the throats of reluctant Americans. Crowninshield's publisher, Condé Nast, believed that *Vanity Fair* was too far ahead of its time, at least until the 1920s; but when the magazine finally became firmly established, advertising intended to reach the upwardly mobile classes flowed in. More important, in its prime, the magazine was enormously admired for its cultural leadership.

Because the smart magazines aggressively moved in a new metropolitan environment they acted as a powerful magnet for youthful talent in America. When H. L. Mencken took over the editorship of the *Smart Set* he said that one of his principal objectives was to give all of the young "literary bucks and wenches" a place to show off their work. His magazine became such a place, a forum for the unconventional, the iconoclastic, the insurgent. It was a place for the renegade spirit in all its forms. And all kinds of youngsters came rushing to the magazine hoping to establish themselves there. Yes, they couldn't make the kind of money that they could on the *Saturday Evening Post*, but writing for the *Smart Set* was fun, not just hack work. Here was a place that was looking for art, not just for craft.

A generation or so later the *New Yorker* similarly became a spawning ground for new American talent. Because he had the fearsome burden of producing a weekly magazine with a wholly new image, founding editor Harold Ross had to develop a stable of reliables and regulars almost out of thin air. He assembled his stable of writers and artists slowly and painfully over a number of years—they were individuals for the most part who grew up with the magazine and breathed at one with it. Originally Ross believed, like the original editors of the *Smart Set*, that boulevardiers and top-hatted members of New York society could be prevailed upon to contribute to the magazine. In the end he had to fall back on raw and still directionless talent, drawing on the vast pool of seasoned newspaper writers in New York, dropouts from advertising agencies, and those literary bucks and wenches that Mencken spoke about—whatever their station in life or place of birth.

It was these vast infusions of fresh young talent, sometimes the veritable creation of new and previously unrecognized opportunities, that made the smart magazines such a considerable force in American cultural history. The fact that some of them relished thumbing their noses at traditional values or at the ethos of an older America that was quickly passing away, but still in the saddle, was not really their essence. Their sometime appeal to "men-about-town," gowned women in salons, girls from finishing schools, was always incidental to their importance. Their major contribution was that they opened up the floodgates to new forms of writing and variant forms of creativity. The pretended appeal to "smart sets" was a managed necessity and a convenient mannerism. The makers of the smart magazines had cosmopolitan pretentions in common with the upper crust, but, more importantly, they had in common a desire to savor life in a playful and unrestrained environment. In this spirit they did in fact flush out the best that was being done, perhaps the best that could have been done in the magazine field of their day.

· 2 ·

Of Society Magazines and Urban Weeklies

The great burst of prosperity that transformed the magazine industry of the 1880s and 1890s witnessed not only an improvement in the quality of magazines but a rapid increase in their number and diversity. Erupting in merry profusion (and sometimes confusion) were trade magazines, religious magazines, sports magazines, women's magazines, humor magazines, magazines of public opinion. There were specialty journals for physicians, educators, mechanical engineers, livestock producers. There were magazines produced for every imaginable pastime or vocation—for bicyclists, home decorators, horse fanciers, baseball enthusiasts, flower growers, yachtsmen, dog lovers, and so on *ad finitum*. Long before 1900 the magazine field was as cluttered as it is today.

The smart magazines that thrived so magnificently during the first several decades of the twentieth century were not intended for people hoping to master the complexities of some hobby, for mothers wanting to be instructed in nursing their babies, or for stockbrokers looking for sage advice about the market. The smart magazines were *general* magazines intended for the entertainment of cultural elites. Possessing the sorts of audiences they did, the smart magazines were not really rooted in the older magazines at all, but in more lighthearted fare; in contrivances of humor, of gaiety, of urbanity, of high style and fashion. The rich, it seemed, were not usually interested in "uplift," in the birthpangs of reform and good works; as often as not they enjoyed the demimonde, even low life; they wanted to hear about the lives of actors, poets, of theatre people, pugilists, polo players. They loved gossip and scandal, even when at times they had to endure the agony of reading lurid and scandalous revelations about themselves. As had always been the case, the rich and affluent classes did not want to be bruised by the poor and struggling classes beneath them; they did not want to trouble themselves listening to talk of patent-remedy cures for the sorrows of the world; they simply wanted to be entertained, not by coarse, vulgar humor, by the diluted confections produced for simple minds, but by people they recognized as possessing force and charm and imagination.

Magazines for smart or sophisticated people did not begin to appear in America until after the Civil War, but they sprang from journalistic forms and practices that went back at least to the 1830s. In 1835 Scottish-born James Gordon Bennett founded the New York *Herald*, and almost immediately revolutionized the whole concept of "news." Bennett's *Herald* was what they called in those days a penny paper, a term that revealed not only its price but something of its personality. There were a number of penny papers in New York, all highly competitive and all offering forms of debased news for the multitudes—lurid police reporting, stories about prize fights, illicit sex relations, sensational criminal trials, political donnybrooks.

Bennett, too, hoped to produce a paper that was "spicy" and "saucy," but he cast a much wider net than any of the other penny papers of the day, squeezing more imaginative writing from his reporters, treating all the news with greater gusto but also more depth. One of the fresh subjects that captured the attention of the paper's readership was news of society—Society spelled with a capital S. Partially supplanting lurid stories of low life, of courtroom melodrama, was coverage of the doings of society matrons and playboys. Who was giving the most expensive or outrageous parties, who was traveling abroad for the year, which son was marrying which daughter of New York society?

In the beginning the socialites were shocked by this attention to their comings and goings. Later they found them amusing, and even began turning to the "society" pages for their own enjoyment. Such coverage of high society was expanded over the years, eventually becoming an essential part of all large metropolitan dailies. By the time society news reached its perihelion during the first three decades of the twentieth century, papers like the *Herald Tribune*, the *Sun*, the *Times*, had Sunday supplements devoted to the doings of the Four Hundred, later of cafe society, and so on. They were richly illustrated supplements printed in one-color rotogravure, a prized possession of many who would rapidly throw away the white-faced straight news.

Long before society news infiltrated the great urban dailies, another type of journal appeared to amuse and edify the upper crust, a weekly newspaper or magazine serving the social set of a particular geographical area. They were the so-called urban weeklies, and they flourished, quite naturally, in those great metropolitan areas that had already developed complex social stratification and a strong sense of social nuance. Very early, even before the Civil War, papers or magazines of this sort began to flourish in Boston, then the financial hub of the nation. Boston possessed a large leisure class based mostly on mercantile and shipping fortunes. Already well supplied from an early date with posh suburbs such as Wakefield, Beverly and Brookline, the Boston area quickly developed a powerful thirst for society papers. As early as 1846 the *Suffolk County Journal* in Roxbury began serving its community with a mix of items that was predominately social in nature. In the post-Civil War era this paper came to the city and was known as the *Boston Home Journal*, providing society news for the entire Boston area. Another major competitor entering the field during the 1870s was the *Saturday Evening Herald*, which announced itself as being "devoted to literature, art, music and society." Anyone looking at the paper could not help but see that the word "society" really belonged first, and that the excursions into the realms of the arts were somewhat pretentious and exaggerated.

Still, there was certain significance to those pretentions nevertheless. The urban weeklies went to a more educated and worldly circle than the large-circulation dailies, and their readership hungered for more than chitchat. Accordingly, in time, many of them did offer good literary and musical reviews as well as essays on travel, art, and all the good things of life. And away from staid Boston, many society papers became quite innovative and daring indeed. A few years later there were three lively society sheets in San Francisco—the *News Letter*, *Argonaut*, and *Wasp*, all of them from their inception making a serious effort to offer good writing and a certain amount of substance. San Francisco society was drawn toward art and literature from the beginning, and its tangy urban weeklies had writers such as Ambrose Bierce who used them to stir up critical storms and an interest in the arts.

Generally, all of the booster cities away from the East Coast took their culture seriously, and their urban weeklies were accordingly of rather high quality. Chicago had a fine urban weekly in the *Saturday Evening Herald*. This and the *Chap Book* (later merged with the *Dial*) became something of an early prototype of our twentieth-century smart magazines. During the 1870s and 1880s, Chicago had *World Magazine*, which offered drama and fiction as well as social news.

In New York things were a little different. The local aristocracy was slow to develop and never achieved the coherency and easy stratification of the Boston Brahmin cast. New York had its counterpart of the Boston society weeklies in the *Home Journal*, which also had its beginnings in the 1840s; it was stately in behavior and at the same time seriously devoted to the arts. But New York's society was so fragmented that the very notion of "society" was never infused by the same kind of gravity as it was elsewhere. Accordingly, the city began to develop magazines for its social leaders and other elites that were a little more frivolous and lighthearted, and eventually even daring and scandalous.

A good example of the quixotic development of New York society magazines was *Truth*, which made its apperance in 1881, calling itself "A Journal of Society, the Clubs, Sports, Drama, and the Fine Arts." Originally a ten-cent quarto of twenty-four pages, the magazine did not live up to its rather ambitious-sounding subtitle, at least not in the beginning. There were attempts to go beyond a grim chronicling of society events, and to cover the arts, the drama, to publish some sprightly writing, but for its first ten years at least the magazine staggered from pillar to post, not finding a workable formula. It became shabbier and its size was reduced by a third. By 1890 it looked as though the magazine was ready to breathe its last.

However, after financial reorganization in 1891, the magazine received a new editor, Blakeley Hall, a man who throughout the latter half of the gay nineties was to be associated with various "spicy" magazines that featured pictures of actresses and bathing girls. In a few years the bathing girls began to assume special importance in *Truth* also, but more significant changes were taking place as well. Beginning with the issue of December 12, 1891, the magazine appeared with a colored cover, looking somewhat like *Puck* and *Judge* and other satirical weeklies. The writing picked up, and shortly Hall had managed to assemble a pool of gifted writers who offered the magazine the literary verve that it sorely needed. Among these were Edgar Saltus,

Ella Wheeler Wilcox and Edgar Fawcett. The magazine also made an attempt to find people prominent in public affairs to contribute to its pages. Among its finds was Chauncey M. Depew, president of the New York Central Railroad, probably New York's most popular after-dinner speaker. In time, too, it was carrying in its pages more celebrated literary names such as Alfred Lord Tennyson and Henry James (who contributed a serial in the late 1890s).

Truth quickly became a very appetizing looking magazine with a colored chromolithographic center spread. The format was faintly tinged with eroticism—mostly pictures of pretty girls and actresses that would be considered wholly harmless and routine today but that were still considered somewhat raffish at the end of the Victorian era. The gigantic American News Company, which frequently acted as a censor in such matters, refused to distribute the magazine's issue of August 3, 1892, because it contained a double-paged spread demonstrating the comparison between ancient and modern naughtiness. Representing the world of ancient myth was a picture of a satyr spying on some nymphs disporting themselves in the water; representing the present day was a picture of a well-dressed young man taking Kodak snapshots of bathing girls.

The most salient truth about *Truth* and other magazines of this kind in New York is that they had discovered a route of escape from the bland and usually stale formula of the typical society weekly. Instead of being produced by people who were timid pawns of the social interests, they quickly came under the dominance of a group of editors who were more open to explosions of the imagination and to antic disruptions of the very kinds of stereotyped behavior they were supposed to be praising. Such editors were more than willing to extend a welcoming hand to those who could write and those who could grapple with the world in playful and zesty ways, who weren't afraid of thumbing their noses at their rich but usually elusive patrons. Society magazines, in short, began taking risks—risks that would eventually lead to some of the best magazines that would ever appear on American soil. Not all of the risks led to fruitful results, of course, and during the 1890s some of the magazines produced for smart society were far more naughty than they were smart. Some of them edged perilously toward the scandalous and the libelous before they pointed the way to better things.

The most popular and legendary society weekly in New York during the 1890s was undoubtedly *Town Topics*, which had an unexciting beginning but went on to become a magazine whose very name set nerves ajangling and tempers flaring during the years of its notorious reign. The name suggests that it might be a prototypical *New Yorker*, and in a certain broad sense it was. In its heyday it attracted some of the best writing to be found in any New York magazine, and it was clearly edited and produced for the urban elite. On the other hand, cheek by jowl with its literary achievements was an unbridled appetite for salacious chatter and slander, which were products of a venomous and even dishonest turn of mind.

Like so many other society magazines, *Town Topics* was reared in dullness. It took its parentage from an earlier society and fashion magazine in Cincinnati called *Andrews' Bazar*. The original appeal was mostly to women, and the magazine's founder, W. R. Andrews, won early success by presenting pages of women's fashions and patterns for women's dresses. With his magazine selling thirty thousand copies a month from its Cincinnati base, Andrews was tempted to leap upward to the national magazine scene in New York. In 1879 he established a magazine called *Andrews' American Queen: A National Society Journal*. Issued twice a month, the magazine tried to cover social news of the entire nation as well as the expected news of trends in feminine fashion. Each issue contained long lists of guests, of parties and social gatherings and descriptions of costumes from all over the country, but with special reference to fifty major cities. It was deadly stuff.

The magazine struggled along without too much recognition, but it brightened slightly after adding fiction and a humor department. Still more was needed for success, however, and, in 1883 Andrews sold the magazine to a New Yorker named E. D. Mann, who almost immediately changed the name to *Town Topics*. Mann intended to give up the futile attempt to report on national society, and began to focus more sharply on the society of New York. He also hoped to bring more wit, more cleverness, more art, to the magazine's dreary pages. After only a few months at the task, Mann sold controlling interest to his older brother, William D'Alton Mann, who right away set the magazine on the peculiar course for which it remains notorious to this day.

William D'Alton Mann, Colonel William D'Alton Mann as he was known (his colonelcy won, by the way, in an honest manner during the Civil War, and not by the indulgence of some sybaritic Southern governor), had made his money in business and law and earned notoriety as a designer and builder of a splendiferous railway sleeping car known as the Mann Boudoir Car—patents for which were later sold to the Pullman Company. By the 1880s, Colonel Mann had been accepted as a kind of fixture in New York society, distinguished by his Old Testament whiskers, the rakish angle of his silk top hat, his jaunty manner and his expensive Havana cigars. Beneath this cultivated exterior and air of affable propriety beat the heart of a black-mailer. Colonel Mann loved being of high society, he loved the rich; even more he loved taking the rich to the cleaners. And possession of a gossip magazine allowed him to achieve his jollies as a voyeur of social peccadillos while tapping the bank accounts of the super rich or anyone he disliked, or even some of his closest friends.

It was an opportune time in history for such exploits. At the end of the Victorian age there was a publicly adhered to code of behavior for the genteel classes—insistence upon virginity, the sanctity of marriage, the propriety of domestic relations, belief that any breath of scandal could ruin a wellborn woman or an aspiring man of business. As everyone knows now—and presumably knew then as well—reality and the assumed propriety were not always identical. Gossip, if allowed to circulate in an unbridled manner, could spell disaster for any less-than-discreet socialite. All such individuals were completely at the mercy of any rascal who published a magazine of society gossip. And Colonel Mann was such a rascal.

The Colonel's way of operating was devious but tasteful. He cultivated an army of informants from among those who served or interacted with the wealthy—butlers, grooms, valets, personal maids, social secretaries, coach-men, cooks. Nearly all such were paid trivial sums for whatever they could produce in the way of eavesdroppings, purloined letters and below-stairs gossip. Disgruntled servants were naturally a big source of information, but many household workers were delighted to pay a visit to the Colonel's ornate office, where they were greeted as important personages. It was reliably reported that the Colonel kept a cache of silver dollars in his office to hand over to young parlormaids and saucy soubrettes and that he frequently managed to extract a kiss as part of the deal.

The Colonel was ingenious at discovering new informants everywhere along the social ladder. A genial and highly intelligent man, little escaped his attention. Since he himself was a member of the upper crust in good standing, even with his reputation somewhat tarnished in becoming a gold-plated gossipmonger, he had the charm and the skill to get the rich to spill the beans on themselves, to tattle on their families and friends, sometimes with the expectation that their revelations would serve as insurance against the Colonel's disfavor. But the Colonel was not opposed to spending lavishly on any reliable sources of information. For example, he suborned the offices of the chief night telegraph operator of the Western Union at Newport, this at a time when the long lines of the telephone company were still in the infant stage. This personage reliably turned over to *Town Topics* whatever spicy missives and mash notes were sent out over the company's wires using the inexpensive night rates for such longer notes of endearment.

The Colonel's actual methods of blackmailing his society friends were always benevolent, subtle, even kindly. It is said that he frequently took lunch at some favored society watering hole such as Delmonico's where proofs of the next issue of his magazine would be delivered to him from the printers, ink not yet dry. When he saw in attendance some gay young blade or elderly rogue whose indiscretions had been set up in type he might call the culprit over for a drink and gently show him the copy that was ready to roll. If he found that his companion was horrified by the revelations or wanted them expunged forthwith, the kindly old Colonel obliged without questions asked. He wanted, he soothingly told his victim, no hurt feelings, so of course he would be happy to see that the item in question ended up on the composing room floor. It was just that some time later the Colonel might ask the same individual for a little loan, say of five thousand dollars—a loan that almost inevitably would never be repaid.

Well, this was the bad side of Colonel William D'Alton Mann, the side that has perpetually consigned him to the rogue's gallery of colorful American characters. But there was another side to the man on which a more happy and enduring fame rests. In *Town Topics* he was to create, even if only by default, a pretty good magazine. And in 1900 he would found another magazine, a sister publication, the *Smart Set*, which was to have a revolutionary impact on the quality and style of magazines in America. The Colonel's achievement was a peculiar one, and stemmed not from his own skills as editor and publisher but from his ability to preside over his magazines as a kind of benevolent father figure. He never bothered to question the authority and editorial judgment of his working editors, allowing the staff of strange fish he had assembled to put together the kind of magazine that tickled its own fancy. There had never been anything like this before in the magazine field—editors had been puppets controlled by management or by the business office. Colonel Mann was a playful man and he wanted his editors, writers and artists to have a good time too. Accordingly, the *Smart Set* and *Town Topics* reveled in their independence and individuality. They eventually drew to themselves a great many writers of high talent and creativity who might otherwise have been lost in the inhibited and stultifying world of commercial publishing.

If *Town Topics* was considered a low and scurrilous sheet by many in high society, if most bluebloods refused to display the magazine in their drawing rooms or disclaimed that they followed its pages, everybody who was anybody in New York knew about the magazine and delighted in looking at it, *sub rosa*. Even years after the Colonel abandoned the magazine and it lost all its zip in other hands, most New Yorkers had vividly etched in their minds the appearance of the magazine of the 1890s—it was a handsome, black and white quarto with its cover showing two pretty ladies whispering some obvious secret. The magazine's literary quality did not manifest itself in the first few years of Colonel Mann's reign, but by the late 1880s the magazine offered an editorial credo that was not only apt but prophetic of the aims and intentions of most subsequent smart magazines. Boasted the editors, this is

> the newsiest, brightest, wittiest, wisest, most original and most entertaining paper ever published. A complete and perfect journal for cultivated men and women, being a topical and outspoken critic and chronicle of the events, doings, interests, and tastes of the fashionable world. It is always up to date, and carries with it the atmosphere of the metropolis.

And so it was, too, in spite of the obvious hyperbole. For those who got beyond the titillating tidbits of scandal (most of which were relegated to a department called "Saunterings"), *Town Topics* was refreshing, lively and often intelligent. The magazine offered some fine review sections, and it covered books, theatre, the art galleries, opera, the concert halls. It had a first-rate literary editor in Percival Pollard, who would perform the same function later on the *Smart Set*. The sagacious James Gibbons Huneker contributed a splendid annual review of the musical scene for many years.

There was fiction, too, and some of the best light verse appearing at the time. The short stories were invariably light, sophisticated, well polished. The Colonel was not a very good payer when compared with some of the editors of mass-circulation magazines in New York, but this had the tendency to encourage new talent, to result in an infusion of young blood and a cross-pollination of ideas. On the magazine, the full-time staff was a remarkable collection of charming ne'er-do-wells, dipsomaniacs and intellectual tramps, many of whom would have willingly written for the magazine without taking a cent. The magazine had a way of magnetizing the very sort of person who ought to be writing for it. Among the regulars was a merry Englishman named Charlie Roper who had a knack for graceful society verse that added an undisputed dimension of wit and elegance to the magazine. Roper apparently could not find his muse until he was as stiff as a socialite's shirt front;

accordingly, Colonel Mann, instead of paying him, established credit for
him at the bars of several nearby hotels.

While *Town Topics* was clearly not a magazine of the first rank by the
standards of that day or this, it was an uncommonly venturesome and lively
publication and pointed the way to other smart magazines that were born in
the years just ahead. And in its years of greatest popularity—the 1890s—
there appeared a number of other kinds of magazines, some of them more
specialized, which catered to sophisticated urban tastes, to refined lifestyles,
to charm and wit. One kind of magazine that undoubtedly bore a certain
resemblance to urban smart magazines and society weeklies in these days was
the woman's magazine of fashion. A number of these were enjoying good
health before 1900, and the better ones attempted to be more than slickly
produced showcases for haute couture. There were, of course, many femi-
nine-interest magazines at this same time, and there were fashion magazines
that also presented household hints, patterns for shirtwaist dresses and practical advice for the typical middle-class woman. These were giants, of
course—the *Ladies' Home Journal*, the Butterick magazines, *Good House-
keeping*, *Ladies' World*. But the women's fashion magazines of decidedly
snobbish appeal were those that also paid attention to culture—the arts,
theatre, literature, and the rest.

Probably the best-known magazine for women of high fashion was, in
1900, as it is today, *Vogue*, founded in 1892. The *Vogue* of the 1890s was
a handsome publication, lavishly produced by the standards of the day, but
otherwise quite different from today's plastic and stereotyped flagship of the
fashion industry. The early *Vogue* displayed a diversity of interests, although
its central selling point, then as now, was its very impressive plates illustrating the latest in high fashion. But in stating its early editorial credo under its
editor Mrs. Josephene Redding, it announced its intention to be "a dignified,
authentic journal of society, fashion, and the ceremonial side of life." There
was no doubt from the beginning that the magazine would retain its dignity,
since of the 250 stockholders of the publishing company that controlled the
magazine, nearly all were women whose names appeared on the "Social
Register"—Mrs. Cornelius Vanderbilt, Mrs. Stuyvesant Fish, Mrs. D.
Percy Morgan. There would be no mischief makers, no antic playboys, no
indiscreet blackmailers behind the scenes of *Vogue*.

Still, in its conception, the magazine, in spite of its stiff-backed sense of
propriety, had a zesty personality in those early days. It was a quarto weekly
and thus in strict competition with other magazines of society (it remained a
semimonthly until after it was bought by Condé Nast in 1909). There were,

in addition to the fashion sections, columns on coming-out parties, dinners, dances, betrothals and marriages—pictures of brides, dances, members of the gentry at table, soirees. But there were also reports from the theatres, concert halls, art exhibitions and the like. There were a good number of travel pieces, accounts of high living in Europe, and so on. With only a little effort in those days the magazine might have been gently prodded in the direction of a true smart magazine.

A slightly more playful, and therefore promising woman's magazine in the 1890s was *Harper's Bazar*, founded by the house of Harper shortly after the Civil War, and originally conceived as a women's version of the firm's lively *Harper's Weekly*. The curious name *Bazar* came from *Der Bazar* of Berlin, a fashion magazine from which the American *Harper's Bazar* received duplicate electrotypes of most of its fashions. *Harper's Bazar* (the spelling of the name was changed to *Bazaar* in the 1920s) never mimicked the snotty air of *Vogue* and seemed to address itself to chic but nonetheless more adventuresome women, probably younger and more middle class than the readers of *Vogue*. This magazine contained good light fiction (among the contributors were William Dean Howells and Mary E. Wilkins), some verse, essays of an instructional or amusing flavor, and above all a touch of humor. For a long time one of the most popular features of the magazine was its "Facetiae" page, conducted by John Kendrick Bangs who headed the humorous department at *Harper's Monthly*. The magazine was an immediate success—far more successful than *Vogue* in the days before Condé Nast took it over. Most importantly, it appealed to women, young women mostly, with a lively curiosity and a keen sense of humor and play. Since women were the principal custodians of culture in the gilded age, in this era of getting and spending, the feminine influence would always be marked on all of the smart magazines, not just these women's-interest publications.

Rather curiously, no similar magazines for men appeared at this time. There were, to be sure, special magazines for sportsmen, for horse fanciers, and there was a profusion of lowbrow magazines for men of the *Police Gazette* variety, but popular male taste of the Victorian era was sufficiently prosaic that no magazine devoting itself to male notions of cleverness and fashion appeared. Such a confection would have to wait for the venturesome Arnold Gingrich and his *Apparel Arts* and *Esquire* in the dark years of the 1930s.

There were, though, certain kinds of magazines that appealed to the male sense of fun, however crude and untutored these tastes may now seem in retrospect. There was the decidedly lowbrow fare, of course, magazines of ribaldry that men would bring home under their coats containing pictures of actresses, burlesque queens, girls in tights or bathing costumes or even occasionally in the nude. Some of these magazines, though, were beginning to grow up and appeal to more sophisticated tastes. Some of them would shortly be looking for good writing, better art work, slicker production methods, and perhaps, with a little luck, the best of them would be able to attract advertising revenues and even gain enough respectability that they could be displayed on the parlor table.

Consider the case of the ten-cent "white-light" monthly called *Broadway Magazine*, which took off from the starting gate in 1898. A crude, cheaply produced affair whose announced intention was to cover the Broadway beat, its real intention was to sell off-color stories and pictures to the libidinous male. Using an avowedly "shock-'em-and-sell-'em" approach, the two founders, Broadway roustabouts, dished out a regular diet of risqué stories, tempt-the-censor pictures of bloomer girls, girls in tights, "living picture" studies, décolletage, classic nudes, and so on. "Red Soubrette" told "saucy truths in a saucy way." Pretty awful stuff by and large, but circulation zoomed immediately to 100,000. Not that the magazine was commercially successful; few quality advertisers would draw nigh this naughty creature of the night.

Broadway Magazine was sold several times before 1906, at which time management brought in as editor Theodore Dreiser, a lanky ex-newspaperman who had most recently been toiling as an editor for the big pulp publisher Street and Smith. A lugubrious, scowling fellow who had already written one of the great American novels in *Sister Carrie*, although few knew it at the time, Dreiser was an unlikely candidate for the job of transforming *Broadway* into something respectable. Seemingly lacking in humor, certainly lacking in sophistication and wit, Dreiser was nonetheless an uncommonly intelligent man who immediately set about making over and upgrading the image of *Broadway*, and turning it into a respectable smart magazine. No more peculiar choice for the editorship could be imagined; yet Dreiser knew what he wanted; he knew witty stuff when he saw it, although unable to write it himself. By this time, of course, he had before him several highly successful smart magazines, all of which were doing pretty well. The *Smart Set* had been established in 1900, and *Ainslee's* and other mass-circulation magazines were aping it. This was what readers wanted, and, above all, as Dreiser knew, this was what advertisers wanted also. Within a year, *Broadway Magazine* was out of the mud and standing tall. It retained some of its old sauciness, but abandoned its adolescent excesses. Dresier rounded up a lot of good fiction, added serious departments, and was moving the magazine quickly into the realm of respectability.

Unfortunately, Dreiser didn't stay, but was lured away a year later by the Butterick Corporation, where he became editor-in-chief of their three enormously successful women's magazines. When Dreiser left, the magazine fell into the editorial hands of its latest publisher, Benjamin Bowles Hampton, a man who had made a small fortune in the advertising business and who had his own ideas for the magazine. Changing the name to *Hampton's Broadway Magazine*, Hampton turned the magazine away from Dreiser's formula in the direction of muckraking—another faddish development in the magazine field in the 1900 to 1910 period. The magazine never really found itself along these lines and it died in 1912, largely unmourned.

Theodore Dreiser, in spite of his oafish manners, his often awkward prose style, his own tenuous connection with the smart circles of society, had correctly perceived exactly what should have been done with *Broadway Magazine*. The time of the smart magazine had arrived. People were looking for magazines that were carefree and fun, that mocked the old proprieties and had something new and better to put in their place. The various forebears of the smart magazines had often been tawdry and undistinguished, sometimes phony and dishonest, but they had already let in some light. They had paved the way for a kind of magazine that could walk lightly but devote itself to fresh young talent, to high style and, deep down, to an actual seriousness of purpose.

· 3 ·

FROM THE HUMOROUS VEIN

When magazines for urban sophisticates began making their appearance, most of their readers would surely have perceived that they bore a close resemblance to several other kinds of magazines with which they were already familiar. There were the society magazines, of course, but even more importantly there was the humor magazine, not a lordly thing in the 1890s perhaps, but holding promise of vast potential. Smart magazines, from the very beginning, had an obvious affinity to the humor magazine. They were, at the very least, light of touch, nimble of foot, edited with a sense of good youthful fun; all seemed to hold the faith that the world was basically untroubled, and that cares of politics, or economics or foreign uproars were little more than rumbles that could be stilled by a little creative play and natural exuberance.

It is not surprising, therefore, that in their heyday the smart magazines cornered the market on American humor, or at least the humor of the more sophisticated and intelligent variety. And it is also not surprising that the years between 1910 and 1940, the years that marked the high tide of the smart magazines, saw the appearance of most of our best humorists — James Thurber, Robert Benchley, Dorothy Parker. H. L. Mencken, Ring Lardner, Donald Ogden Stewart, E. B. White, S. J. Perelman, Ogden Nash, Clarence Day, and many others whose talents, alas, are sorely missing today. All of these individuals wrote for one or more of the major smart magazines; a few wrote for all of them.

Humor magazines themselves had been slow to develop on the American scene. Very early in our history foreigners had been willing to admit that Americans were not defective in a sense of humor, and from the days of the early republic European writers and intellectuals looked for this trait to shine forth in the nation's magazines, in the public prints generally. But during the first century of American history this expectation was never realized. Washington Irving was lionized in England to be sure, but many Europeans took note that his sense of mirth was not of the indigenous American variety.

There was a growing strain of American humor in the nineteenth century. There was the humor of the frontier, of the West. On the frontier people could be forgiven for displaying a sense of humor in public so there was an effusion of dialect writers, tellers of tall tales, of crackerbarrel philosophers. Americans welcomed these humorists for generations, although humorists were generally excoriated by the intellectual elite, especially the good noble heads of New England — men like Emerson, Hawthorne, Thoreau, all of whom were bathed in a harsh light of puritanism, and surely convinced that literature must serve some commanding moral impulse.

What the great minds of America thought of Mark Twain when he first burst upon the national scene is still a matter for debate. But for years the greatest of all our humorists had tough sledding among the custodians of culture. He sparked no recognition among pedants and schoolmarms, among polite literary societies, or among assemblages of genteel women poets and poetasters. The plain people were instantly drawn to Twain as were the eminences of *old* England, who immediately and rightly, found in him the authentic American voice and flavor. But for years Twain sat below the salt in American polite society. He was, they said, the product of newspapers in his early days, and in the first half of the nineteenth century newspaper humor was widely esteemed as a low essence. That which appeared in newspapers as humor was considered no more elevated than the joke books or cheap comic papers that were sold by railroad news butchers, and peddlers of hard candy. Still, Twain's great comedic gifts quickened something in the American spirit and made clear that there was an unsatisfied thirst for comic material.

Until some years later after the Civil War, no major magazine in America took humor as its center of focus. There were a number of attempts to ape the British *Punch*, but they looked silly in the act. Nearly all were ephemeral, coming into existence one month and disappearing the next. All were cheap, poorly printed. A contributor to the *British Quarterly Review* wrote as late as 1871 that the much acclaimed American quality of wit had never found expression in print: "The Americans," he said, "have not a single comic periodical like our *Punch*. . . . In the course of a dozen years many attempts have been made to establish such a print, but without success. . . . All the comic papers that flourished for a few years were only remarkable for the immense amount of bad wit that they contained, for a wilderness of worthlessness, for an endless process of tickling and laughter. . . . There is hardly anything the Americans need more than a good comic paper."

A mere six years later a good comic paper did appear in America, and it led to the gestation of a number of others before the nineteenth century was out. This first respectable and enduring humor magazine was named *Puck*, and it was not a pale imitation of the British *Punch* at all. There were now other ethnic influences loose in the land, and America's first really successful comic weekly was the work of a Viennese immigrant artist named Joseph Keppler. Keppler had already tried to start two German-language comic papers in St. Louis, one of them also called *Puck*. Both had failed. Later he established a German-language *Puck* in New York, this with somewhat more success. After a year, in March 1877, an English-language edition of the same magazine was put out, and in time this eclipsed and then killed the German version.

One of the reasons for the success of the American *Puck* was that it devoted itself to satire, which many could see as more high-minded than the jokes of backwoodsmen and jitney storytellers. And the prime object of satire in America was politics and political corruption—matters that could be considered uplifting even when treated in a comic vein. Politicians have always been fair game in the United States. Even when the American required dignity and decorum in every other department of life, the Yankee was a fellow who universally agreed with all his neighbors that in politics the rules are off, that anybody in public office is richly deserving of mud pies of any shape and constituency. The founders of *Puck* had discovered an area where

Americans accepted humor as appropriate and respectable for the print media.

The first number of the English-language *Puck*, which appeared in March 1877, was a large quarto of sixteen pages, and sold for ten cents. Keppler drew two large cartoons for the magazine, to which were added some good swift satirical writing, a poem by Brete Harte, theatre reviews, the first installment of "Fitznoodle" by B. B. Valentine, some short pieces and a little advertising. Keppler took as his partner in this venture a German named Schwartzman who became the business manager. They installed as an editor a young playwright named Sydney Rosenfeld. After a year, Rosenfeld was succeeded by Henry Cuyler Bunner, who kept at the helm of the magazine for almost two decades.

And *Puck* thrived almost immediately. Within five years it reached a circulation of eighty thousand—surely a mass-circulation magazine for that day and age. During the 1880s and 1890s *Puck* became a much loved and enjoyed American institution. It became known for its colorful cartoons and its excellent writing. In the early years much of the latter was the product of H. C. Bunner himself. Bunner was apparently a man of tremendous energy, sometimes as much as half of an issue coming from his own facile pen. He seemed to be equally adept at all sorts of comical writing—rhymes, humorous ballads, satirical sketches, short stories, pasquinades, comedies, lampoons. He wrote most of the dialogues that went under the drawings; he wrote verses to go under cartoons. He poured out an endless stream of puns, epigrams, nonsense, fillers, jabs—every form of comicality known to that day and this.

Keppler, too, was a man of formidable energy and fecundity of imagination. Every week for the first several years of *Puck*'s existence he drew three large cartoons for each issue, including those for both covers and a large spread in the center. Like Bunner, he poured out work of all sorts—drawings for text illustration or advertisements, decorations, small cartoons—all work of the bold, daring and pungent Germanic school of cartooning. Printing processes were improving very rapidly during the 1870s, and by the time the magazine was only two years old the major cartoons were being reproduced in color by chromolithography. No other contemporary magazine had this feature, and the vibrancy and the daring appearance of the magazine helped drive circulation skyward. There were few Americans of the day who did not recognize the cover of *Puck*, containing a sassy, impudent picture of Puck himself, staff in hand, surmounting a banner that announced the motto of the magazine, "What fools these mortals be." (In German folk culture "Puck" is a somewhat malicious child.)

The main objects of *Puck*'s satire were the political villains of the day. The magazine found such villains everywhere, but most especially in Tammany and other hotbeds of urban political corruption. It came out fighting in nearly every national political campaign, and was credited with the defeat of James G. Blaine in his run for the presidency in 1884. Not specifically partisan in politics, *Puck* nonetheless leaned toward the Democratic Party in national campaigns, but was generally conservative in its views. The magazine supported the "Gold" Democrat Cleveland, was harsh on the emerging labor movement, but was also tough on the moguls of business and on grubby political hacks of any stripe.

Religion was another regular victim of *Puck*'s attacks. The paper attacked Henry Ward Beecher, and other high-living and flamboyant clergymen. It came down hard on the Catholic church, Mormonism, all oddities of religion, although always proclaiming that Puck himself was "neither Catholic, Protestant, Hebrew nor Mohammedan." Puck took after all church abuses—high rents on church pews, bigotry, the dalliances of preachers, hypocrisy, the evils of camp meetings and religious fairs.

Outside of these two provocative areas of politics and religion, the humor of *Puck* was usually gentle and mellow. Indeed, Bunner himself was not highly disposed toward hard, biting satire; that function more perfectly suited the atrabilious Keppler and a number of other cartoonists of the magazine. The magazine's stories, sketches and other pieces were often rather tame and not unkindly, so that this first really prestigious American comic paper actually held out a welcoming hand to all sorts and moods of American humor and opened its pages to the talents of a wide spectrum of wits. Much of the magazine was eventually devoted to genteel but still sprightly and effervescent writing.

Puck survived into the early twentieth century, although by 1900 it had collected some very brisk competitors. Bunner and Keppler died in the 1890s, and their several successors were not up to the task of adapting the magazine to a new age; the magazine languished, made several rebounds, finally went to a slimmer and cheaper format, was bought by William Randolph Hearst in 1917, then given over to light persiflage on the foibles and fads of high society. World War I stringencies and paper shortages were too much for it and it died in September 1918, two months before war's end.

The years just before the Hearst takeover were good ones, however, with George Jean Nathan writing sharp comment on the New York stage,

Dana Barnet doing the news in rhyme and the learned James Gibbons Huneker conducting a memorable column on "The Seven Arts." There continued to be many prominent artists and cartoonists, including Frederick Opper, Henry Mayer, Tony Sarg, W. E. Hill, John Held, Jr., Raphael Kirchner and W. J. Enright. Until a few years before its demise the magazine was carrying on with great flair and bravura, although in many respects it had been cruelly overtaken by its competitors.

Puck proved that America was receptive to a solid humor magazine, and it paved the way not only for several other quality magazines like *Judge* and *Life*; more importantly, it was a training ground for several generations of American humorists and cartoonists. It would not be an exaggeration to say that the unadulterated powers of *Puck* filtered downward to the newspaper comic papers, to the Katzenjammer twins and to the yellow kid, but also upward to the more rarefied heights of the *New Yorker* and *Esquire* in their heyday. It was a magazine that attacked the world with gusto and style, and in this it had no predecessors.

The years after the Civil War seemed to open up many possibilities for humor in American magazines. Accordingly, ever so slowly, the prestige general magazines began to intrude humor here and there, usually in confined spaces, but nearly always to the delight of their readers. Some of the humor sections or columns were feeble efforts, such as the "Editor's Drawer," in *Harper's Monthly*, conducted by Rev. Irenaeus Prime (*sic*). A little more pungent was "Etchings" in *Scribner's* (later to be "Bric-a-Brac," and "In a Lighter Vein"). The best of such columns was doubtless Mark Twain's "Memorandum" in *Galaxy*.

The youth of the nation were also taking to humor in the 1870s and 1880s. The *Harvard Lampoon* was founded in 1876 (a year before *Puck*!), and a number of other college humor sheets followed shortly and had the effect of fostering the comic muse—often quite genuine and sometimes overextended—in many generations of American youth. General college literary magazines such as the *Yale Lit*, the *Nassau Literary Magazine* and *Acta Columbiana* were receptive to contributions from campus humorists, and in a few years there were a goodly number of sophisticated humorists, many of whom would be drawn to the magazine scene in New York during the first few decades of the twentieth century.

The two greatest American humor magazines appeared on the scene in the 1880s. They were *Judge* and *Life*, founded in 1881 and 1883 respectively. The two were not very different from one another in style and appeal; both reached their pinnacle in the first few decades of the twentieth century, and both floundered in the late twenties, with many new magazines detracting from their lustre. Perhaps they had finally become burdened by formulas that had been used too long. Both were sad victims of the magazine shakeout in the 1930s. In 1936 *Life* sold its subscription lists to *Judge* and its title to Time Inc., which passionately wanted to use the name for its great and enormously successful photojournalism extravaganza. The old *Life*, loved and enjoyed by millions of Americans, passed from the scene almost unnoticed in the dark years of the depression. *Judge* staggered on for three more years as a pale shadow of its former self, then it too died on the eve of World War II. Historically they remain what they had been in their prime: two of the most splendid and sparkling American magazines. There was nothing like them before, and there has been nothing quite like them since.

Judge was born first, and at the time of its appearance in 1881 it was nothing more nor less than a crude facsimile of *Puck*. And well it might have been since the founders were disaffected members of the art staff of that naughty satiric giant who had made up their minds to rebel. Leading the group of dissidents, nearly all of them young, was James Albert Wales, a gifted cartoonist who had done many of *Puck*'s color spreads. When the magazine first appeared on October 29, 1881, it was called *The Judge* (the title *Judge* was adopted in 1886), the cover showing a berobed and bewigged figure who looked down at the world scornfully from his lofty bench. The old judge was merely a variant symbolic figure replacing the youthful Puck; the magazine itself was a sixteen-page quarto that looked for all the world like a copycat version of *Puck*, with its bold chromolithograph cover.

In spite of its youthful talent and goodwill, the magazine in the beginning was just too much like *Puck* to make the grade. It staggered around aimlessly not able to find its own identity, always teetering on the edge of bankruptcy. But *Puck*'s triumphant success in lambasting Blaine in the 1884 election had opened up the eyes of some wealthy Republicans who perceived the wisdom of having a comic weekly at their own beck and call. Accordingly, a hard-driving and well-fixed young man named W. J. Arkell reorganized the Judge Company, probably with a little aid from the G.O.P. Brought in as editor was Isaac M. Gregory, formerly editor of the *Elmira Gazette and Free Press* in upstate New York—a true blue Republican paper. Apparently Gregory was a venturesome sort, open to all kinds of humorous effusions, and the paper never limited itself to the political arena.

Under the revised title *Judge*, the enlivened weekly took after everything in sight. Yes, it had its favorite political nincompoops and villains to flay— Tammany and Grover Cleveland being the victims of choice during the 1880s and 1890s. But outside the political arena, *Judge* became a more freewheeling agent than the heavily Germanic *Puck*, and this doubtless accounted for its meteoric rise to success in the late 1880s. Everything was fair game—marriage, bachelorhood, high society, policemen, hoboes, children—with the sober old judge becoming something of a lighthearted critic of all wrinkles in human experience. Still, there was a lot of head bumping, and plenty of noses to be bloodied in all quarters. Only in the political arena was *Judge* venomous, and here it could be unbelievably so by today's canons of taste.

The content of *Judge* in the 1880s and 1890s would doubtless surprise many readers in the latter half of the twentieth century; no magazine of recent memory is remotely like this bumptious youngster. In a typical weekly issue, that for September 5, 1896, the magazine was in full stride as a political roustabout and mud wrestler. The campaign between William McKinley and William Jennings Bryan is about to begin. The cover, in full color, shows Bryan dressed as a country bumpkin sitting by the side of a stream fishing for "suckers." The magazine, a sixteen-page quarto, consists of this colored cover, six pages of jokes and cartoons (mostly pen and ink, although an occasional photograph to break the uniformity), then two pages of a color spread in the middle (again, Bryan is flagrantly attacked, but in high style and good humor, appearing as an Indian fakir with a turban), this followed by another page of jokes, cartoons and miscellany, then five pages of ads, and a back cover (in color) with eight smaller cartoons, mostly political in nature.

The politicizing was flagrantly vitriolic and it would get worse before the election. The cartoons are nonetheless enormously clever and executed with tremendous bravura and polish. On the cover of one subsequent election-season issue Bryan appears as a scraggly organ grinder's monkey, begging for the silver interests. A week later, he is using his "cross of gold" to batter the Bible. The following week, under the legend, "The Only Good Act of the Cleveland Administration," Bryan is shown as a vagrant being pummeled to the ground by Cleveland dressed as a cop. Another week, Bryan takes to the cover as a naked baby with an adult sized head (a view from the rear quite fortunately), trying to smash butterflies against the wall. The legend reads: "Little Billy Bryan chasing butterflies." When conceptualized, all of these cartoons seem garish in tone, yet they are executed in such a brilliant manner, that it was probably not possible even for prudish Victorians to take exception to them.

The inside of the magazine, except for the other color spreads, was much tamer in nature. The black and white cartoons appear about five or more to a page, and are interlarded with jokes, humorous sketches, some doggerel and miscellany. The cartoons are usually tied to a joke, the captions invariably a bit longer than those associated with magazine cartoons today, which reduce their legends to a few words or none at all. A typical cartoon shows a husband and wife, or boy and girl, with the legend, He: She: Or, Judge (to a woman who has tried to get out of jury duty by claiming that she doesn't believe in capital punishment): "But, madame, so few cases involve capital punishment. This case, for example, only deals with a husband who took his wife's household money and gambled it on horses." She: "I'll serve. And maybe I was wrong about capital punishment."

Most of the cartoons are single and self-contained; occasionally they take one or more panels to tell a story. One series shows a small boy nailing his father's carpet slippers to the floor. But he is caught in the act, and in the next panel the father is using the slippers to give the rascal a good spanking, nail side down. The legend reads: "A youth's trick turned upon himself." (In the nineteenth century boys were invariably "bad" or "naughty" — today they are "disturbed.")

Judge changed a bit over the years. Politics boosted circulation enormously after the 1896 presidential campaign, but with the beginning of the twentieth century, the magazine started to diversify. The strong political slant continued until 1910, at which time the magazine underwent a big reorganization. But even before that the magazine's horizons had been broadened. The humor became smarter, more sophisticated. There were pictures in many styles, and a new generation of artists including Art Young, Penrhyn Stanlaws, R. F. Outcault and James Montgomery Flagg, adding vigorous new talent and diversity to the magazine.

James Melvin Lee became editor of the magazine in 1909, and he lived through the sale of the magazine and the shift away from politics. He left in 1912 to become dean of the School of Journalism at New York University, but by the time he left, *Judge's* circulation had reached 100,000, far outstripping the older *Puck* and the younger *Life*. In the years between 1910 and World War I, *Judge* was at the height of its popularity and had assembled the best talent it would ever have, except for another short renaissance in the early twenties. Magazine critic John Tebbel called it the best humor magazine ever published in America, which well it may have been.

If *Judge* was in its stride during the early twenties it was probably because it was no longer purely a humor magazine. In 1922 the magazine merged with *Leslie's Weekly*, and became more departmentalized. With very little push it might well have shucked its somewhat sophomoric past. Under the reign of Douglas H. Cooke and Norman Anthony after 1922, the magazine contained regular editorials by William Allen White. There was a book review section by Walter Pritchard Eaton. Heywood Broun edited the sports department. Ruth Hale (Mrs. Heywood Broun) wrote movie reviews. George Jean Nathan wrote on theatre. There were radio and automobile sections, crossword puzzles. What is more important, a wholly new generation of wits had grown up, many of them drawn to the magazine's long-established reputation—people who would influence magazine journalism for years to come as writers, cartoonists, editors, humorists. On the staff of *Judge* during these years was Harold Ross, soon to become the founding editor of the *New Yorker*. On hand too, were some of the great talents of the *New Yorker*'s golden age. There was Ring Lardner, already a star, and there was a youthful S. J. Perelman, just graduated from Brown University where he had been editor of the *Little Brown Jug*. Perelman was hired as a cartoonist by *Judge* with much of his verbal dexterity already in evidence. (One of his cartoons has the legend, "I have Bright's disease, and he has mine.") The pool of talent was excellent and in 1923 the circulation of the magazine (now selling for fifteen cents) rose to 250,000, the highest that had ever been achieved by a humor magazine.

By the 1920s, with *Puck* now in solemn repose, *Judge*'s main competitor in the humor field was *Life*, and *Life*, too, was showing signs of changing and growing up. During the 1920s it would in fact enjoy an even greater pool of talent and of regular contributors than *Judge*. And a great deal of *Life*'s popularity and prestige was due to the fact that from its inception it had considered itself a rather "elevated" humor magazine and one that had cultivated very important new ground.

Life was only two years younger than *Judge*, having first faced the world on January 4, 1883. The magazine was the brainchild of John Ames Mitchell, a Harvard graduate who had studied architecture and then painting in New York and had gained some magazine illustration experience in New York. Tiring of receiving assignments from others, he asked himself why not start his own humor weekly as an outlet where he could draw what he liked. Hardheaded businessmen warned him away, and no printer was willing to advance money for printing the first issue. Everyone pointed out that there were already two well-established humor weeklies, and that all of their recent competitors had failed. But Mitchell, with a small inheritance of ten thousand dollars in the bank (none too small in 1883) was determined to go ahead.

Mitchell managed to find two other Harvard men who became partners in the enterprise. The first was Edward Sanford Martin, who had served a term as editor of the *Lampoon*. Also sharing enthusiasm for the idea was Andrew Miller, who took the job as business manager of the magazine while Martin became the literary editor. Mitchell took a half interest, the other two a quarter each.

As the dark winter months of 1883 passed, and one early issue after another went into print, the three youngsters began to understand why cooler and wiser heads had advised against the enterprise. A fair number of the inaugural issue had sold, but then copies of the second, third, fourth, began coming back. By the fifth week, the young entrepreneurs were shocked to find 6,200 returns—they had only printed 6,000. Leafing through the returns for that issue they found returned copies of previous issues. It seemed to be clear that *Life* was not going to come to life.

Strangely, though, just when it seemed as if the fledgling was about to breathe its last, a slight upturning in its fortunes caused the owners to hold out a little longer. In May not all of the magazines came back; in June things were quite a bit better. With this little encouragement the partners believed that they could weather the summer slump suffered by all magazines. Miraculously there was no summer slump; the magazine's circulation continued to rise. By the fall the firm was breaking even, and by its second year *Life* was selling twenty thousand copies a week.

What brought this about? Why was *Life* not elbowed aside by *Judge* and *Puck*, as all of the other comic upstarts of the 1880s had been? Clearly it *was* different, and very shortly it became better. It was different because from the very beginning it tried to be more than a joke magazine. It was not locked into a rigid formula—*Judge* and *Puck* had a quality of sameness and repetitiveness about them. From its inception *Life* began experimenting with a wide variety of pictures, verse, sketches, reviews. *Life* began running book and theatre review sections years before *Judge*; *Puck* bothered with such things only at the end of its days. John Ames Mitchell knew what he wanted for his magazine—bright young fellows from the best college humor magazines—the *Harvard Lampoon*, *Acta Columbiana*, and others. And the young fresh intellects arrived in goodly numbers in the first few years of the magazine's existence. Noting this trend in 1882, *Puck* devoted several of its issues to making sport of the "silly" college humor magazines, a futile gesture that only served to underscore the fact that *Life* was coming alive with new and better talent.

And some of these youngsters were very good indeed, far better on the whole than the hack political satirists on *Judge* and *Puck* in the 1880s.

Among *Life*'s early acquisitions was John Kendrick Bangs, who came to the magazine from *Acta Columbiana* in 1884. Bangs was an excellent comic writer, capable of handling all departments of the magazine. He wrote editorials, prose and verse, conducted a widely read and quoted "By the Way" page, sometimes contributing so much to the magazine that he had to hide behind pen names such as "Carlyle Smith." Even before Bangs's arrival, which marked a clear-cut turning point in the magazine's fortunes, a large roster of bright youth had been recruited. Mitchell had brought in some of his Harvard classmates during the early years—Alfred J. Cohen, who wrote dramatic criticism, and W. J. Henderson, who wrote on sports. John Bangs brought in Frank Dempster Sherman and H. L. Satterlee from Columbia. Henry A. Beers from Yale contributed a funny undergraduate's diary and condensed some novels for the magazine; Robert Bridges, Princeton '79, began doing book reviews for the magazine during its first year.

In one definite area, *Life* gained almost immediate ascendancy over its rivals. It had better pictures. Surely its cartoons could not surpass those of the masters who worked for *Judge* and *Puck*, but *Life* was really interested in more than cartoons. Mitchell, with his wider understanding of art and broader cultural base, wanted to make *Life* a first-class picture magazine. In time it became probably the best such in America in its day, so that there was no little aptness to the sale of the magazine's name in 1936 to Time Inc. for its foray into photojournalism. In the 1880s and 1890s the pictures in *Puck* and *Judge* were formulaic and standardized. Mitchell wanted to break out of that mold, and he did so with enormous flair, although never departing from the guiding principle that pictures should be bright and entertaining. Ten years after the magazine's founding, Mitchell expressed the principles that had guided him in selection of illustrated material. He wrote:

> It was necessary that drawings representing scenes in high life should be of a style and quality unlike anything then published this side of the Atlantic. . . . For *Life*'s uses, such drawings, while being true to nature and clever artistically, must show a lightness of touch, an ease, brilliancy, and force of expression which are not demanded in other work. Moreover, a sense of humor, a playfulness, and a gentle exaggeration are indispensable to the perfect work.

It would be hard to imagine a more perfectly worded manifesto for the smart magazines of the twentieth century, and at its best *Life* was a progenitor of those magazines.

In addition to its light touch, the pictures in *Life* were noted for the diversity in style and subject matter. At a time when *Puck* and *Judge* were tied to story cartoons in pen and ink, *Life* was experimenting with halftones, discovering pretty girls, offering sketches and cartoons of a less brash and ascerbic variety. Mitchell, of course, in the early years, was the most noted cartoonist as well as editor, but he was shortly joined by a number of other artists with their own style and charm. Harry W. McVickar had a decided knack for society figures and scenes, as did W. H. Hyde. Edward W. Kemble was noted for his facetious drawings of darkies (and contemporaneously as the illustrator of Mark Twain's *Huckleberry Finn*); C. Gray-Parker delightfully captured the horses and equipages of the upper crust.

Probably the most famous artist to be associated with *Life* was Charles Dana Gibson, whose great gift to posterity was the "Gibson girl," an image of American femininity to all the world in the years between 1890 and 1905. Gibson first appeared in the magazine in 1887 at the age of twenty-one when he received a four dollar payment for one of his drawings. For a few years thereafter Gibson was not a regular contributor, his talent still in search of a style. For a time he tried to imitate the drawing elegance of Du Maurier in the English *Punch*; he played around with the styles of some of *Life*'s own artists, including Edward Kemble. But soon his pen lines became varied, his whites rich and supple; and behold, he had discovered his own brave style. By 1890 Gibson was appearing in nearly every issue of the magazine with full-page drawings of wizened patriarchs in evening dress, handsome young men, and above all, the Gibson girl, who managed to move with a stately grace even though weighted down by her sleek, heavy coiffure and her lustrous satin train.

Somehow, as if by magic, the Gibson girl became the personification of American womanhood. She was tall (often taller by a head than her male counterparts), exuded an air of refinement and civility, impregnable in her independence and self-reliance. She seemed extraordinarily healthy, slim, well exercised, resilient. She could be playful, too, but her playfulness appeared stately, decorous. This was a self-assured age, and the Gibson girl was never in doubt about herself or the security of her world.

There were Gibson men too, youthful counterparts of the Gibson girl. And they had their own style—they were entirely clean shaven, and thus in rebellion against their bewhiskered elders. There were stereotypical Gibson matrons, dowagers and old men also, and altogether the visual renderings of Charles Dana Gibson created a whole era in American social history, or, at the very least, in American womanhood. Women everywhere in the 1890s wanted to look like the Gibson girl. Clearly she was mostly an inhabitant of better suburbs, a well-turned-out product of the middle- and upper-class values, but she quickly became an ideal, a prototype, the precise object of desire that every young woman hoped to project. Gibson had proved once again the truth of the notion that life imitates art, not vice versa.

The appearance of such a highborn creature as the Gibson girl in the pages of *Life* suggested that the magazine was more elevated in style and substance than any of its earlier competitors. *Puck* could be coarse and brutal, but still zestful; *Judge* could be thin at times; but *Life* had high style and character. Until the end of its days it continued to be a humor magazine, and it had its share of burlesques and low-boy jokes, but its essential lightness was of a contemplative and serious sort.

Underneath, too, *Life* always seemed to be driven by strong social concerns. It did not play around with politics as did its principal competitors—the nasty political fracas of the presidential year would have been beneath its dignity. It urged the reelection of Cleveland in 1888, but mainly because Cleveland, a middle-aged bachelor, had married the very attractive twenty-two-year-old Frances Folsum. "We need Mrs. Cleveland in the White House," said *Life*, "to teach conduct and manners to American society." Needless to say, Mrs. Cleveland looked suspiciously like a Gibson girl.

Life did have its strong likes and dislikes. Generally the tone of the magazine was conservative; it sent sharp shafts of wit after high tariffs, labor organizers, anarchists. But it also regularly took out after rigid Sabbatarians, Anthony Comstock and other censors of literature, Christian Science, vivisection, cruelty to animals. Although a muted apologist for the upper classes, it nonetheless made merciless fun of upstarts, parvenues, dudes, cafe society, mindless plutocrats, the "trusts," conspicuous consumption. *Life's* philosophy was that wealth and prosperity conferred obligations, obligations of decency, concern for one's fellow man and for the downtrodden—views not universally appreciated in the age of the robber barons. Since the high life also conferred the responsibility to react to the world with dignity and propriety, *Life* itself was always a magazine of smartness and stylish wit; it never even remotely approached the vulgar, the impulsive or the stupid.

Altogether, *Life*, at its very best, was one of the great American magazines. It probably enjoyed its highest popularity and esteem just before and just after World War I. Mitchell, unfortunately, died in 1918 and the magazine passed into other hands. In the late twenties there was brisk competition from the *New Yorker*, which in the beginning was not a great deal different from *Life* in style, although it had discovered a fertile new focus for a smart magazine, one that would stand the test of time.

The depression years were grim ones for humor magazines of the older sort, with *Life* and *Judge* going into a tailspin from which they would never recover. Moving into the humor field were brawling vulgarians such as *Ballyhoo* and *Hooey*, which dealt in the lowest of materials—sex, bathroom humor, parodies of advertising. Taste, like a lot of other things, was not in demand during the dark years of the depression nor has it been in high demand since. Humor magazines from that day to ours have been inspired in their dumbness, insipidity and bad taste.

In its prime *Life* was a highly prized possession in the living rooms and drawing rooms of comfortable and intelligent Americans. Its writing was charming and stylish, its art work and its pages of advertising were delights to the eye. It appealed solidly, and without self-doubts, to a secure and confident elite. It thrived at a time when there was much to be complained about, surely a great deal to be made fun of, but it could all be done in high style, because there was little fear that the world itself was under threat, that civilization was under the gun. Indeed *Life* appealed to a world that believed that civilization itself was the product of play and youthful discovery. If *Life* was ever frivolous, and it seldom was, it more than made up for the defect by its good spirits and vitality, by its belief that the expenditure of the comic spirit was one of the healthiest manifestations of civilized life.

· TWO ·

THE
SMART
MAGAZINES

· 4 ·

THE
SMART SET

n 1900 rascally old Colonel William D'Alton Mann, flush from picking the pockets of millionaires by means of his unscrupulous New York tattle sheet *Town Topics*, decided to establish a new magazine for members of the very social elite he had been pestering throughout the gay nineties. He had been having a jolly good time writing gossipy things *about* the rich and about members of cafe society; why not put out a magazine *for* them? The new magazine in question, a monthly, made its appearance on the newsstands March 10, 1900. It was entitled the *Smart Set*, and bore the intriguing subtitle, "A Magazine of Cleverness." It sold for twenty-five cents a copy—a steep price in times when run-of-the-mill magazines often sold for a dime or less.

The magazine was an almost instantaneous success. Colonel Mann knew his audience, and he knew that his own larcenous brand of salesmanship would be supported by the new generation of advertisers who in only the last few years had brought a revolution to the entire American magazine industry. So, yes, the magazine was a commercial success from day one. The first issue had a press run of 100,000 (or so the Colonel said), and by 1908 over 160,000 copies were rolling off the presses.

Curiously, though, we do not remember the *Smart Set* today because of its immediate popularity and affluence. The *Smart Set* may well have faded into the annals of publishing curiosa like *Town Topics* itself. We remember it fondly because in time it became one of the best and most influential magazines on the American scene—this, curiously, long after it had fallen from the old Colonel's Midas-like grip and lurched forward with its own distinctive style and manner. The *Smart Set* began as a commercially successful magazine, and when it fell on hard times it became a great one.

The *Smart Set* would become a solid American institution, a springboard for a new generation of American writers. As such it may have become something that the Colonel would neither have predicted nor appreciated. Nonetheless, the later triumphs of the magazine were largely due to the Colonel's loose administrative style, and to an open, playful and experimental editorial policy present from the beginning. The Colonel's concept of the magazine was to produce a literary and artistic monthly for the consumption of the rich, the idle and the clever. "The purpose of the *Smart Set*," he wrote, "will simply be to entertain 'smart' people," that is, people capable of sparkling conversation, light badinage, people presumably possessed of uninhibited manners and morals. Here would be no mere lurid social chatter and innuendo—a province already exploited fully by the magazine's sister weekly, *Town Topics*; rather the attempt would be made to produce a handsome and "arty" publication that people would be delighted to display on *top* of the drawing room table, not hidden away behind the potted palms.

Doubtless the Colonel's notion of the magazine was rather nebulous and indistinct. He really didn't know what kind of material he was going to be paying for, although this proved to be something of a blessing in the years ahead. And one major goal could not be realized. The Colonel cherished the idea that his new magazine would not only be *for* the members of the "Four Hundred," but *by* them. He harbored the belief that somehow many society belles, debutantes, yachtsmen, dowagers, fox hunters might be prevailed upon to entertain their friends and peers with glamorous tales of life at the top; perhaps of dalliances at Newport, excursions to Europe, collations at Saratoga or Bar Harbor. The idea was to get the rich to write, to talk about what interested them, as they did in Fifth Avenue hotel dining rooms or at Delmonicos. This hope, fortunately for the magazine's readership, was never realized, perhaps could never be realized. Starting out a quarter of a century later, with somewhat the same objective, country boy Harold Ross found a similar problem with the *New Yorker*. If the idle rich are really idle, and already sufficiently supplied with gold coin, no amount of coaxing by the old tattler Colonel Mann could prompt them to tell their secrets. And even if the desire had been there, one wonders if the "Four Hundred" could have mustered the talent.

If Colonel Mann was a bit hazy about how such a magazine could get off the ground, he sagely selected an editor who did. The editor was young Arthur Grissom, a *Town Topics* staffer who had gotten into the magazine game through newspaper work. Beginning as a reporter for the *Kansas City Star*, then working his way East where he became a free-lance writer for magazines like *Puck*, *Judge* and *Life*, he had a wide acquaintance with the literary scene. Grissom was hardly a wealthy man himself, but he had returned to Kansas City at the end of the nineties where he had edited a lively urban weekly known as the *Independent*. While there he had run off with a banker's daughter, which had gotten him into all sorts of trouble, eventually forcing his return to New York. But Grissom was a sensitive and thoughtful editor with at least some experience on the fast track; he was also a published poet well-acquainted with the literati, so that Mann's confidence in him was amply justified.

Grissom was aware from the very beginning that it would be an impossibility to put out a magazine month after month filled with the writings of the rich. He felt that he could get out a magazine that would appeal to the rich but not one written by them. Accordingly, to fill up his pages, he began casting his net far and wide, drawing in some of his old friends from the New York magazine scene. Which isn't to say that Grissom made no attempt to attract writers with aristocratic-sounding names; the roster of authors in the early years was liberally sprinkled with the names of countesses and princesses (some bogus no doubt) or perhaps *noms de plume* of people vaguely suggestive of the social register. There was always an unusually large number of three-named authors, seemingly then a sign of social stature, but one cannot help but suspect the spuriousness of such nominal monstrosities as Van Tassel Sutpen and Cecil Carlisle Pangman. There were a few bona fide aristocratic names on the contents page from time to time, but these were usually overshadowed by such highly disputable worthies as The Infanta Eulilie and Countess Loveau de Chevanne.

Phony or real, high-bred names never monopolized the magazine. Grissom (and Colonel Mann for that matter) knew that they must have good writers if the magazine was to fly. The very first issue of the magazine contained a lead novelette called "The Idle Born" by two social lions who had established small reputations as writers, H. C. Chatfield-Taylor and Reginald De Koven. (In his prepublication publicity the Colonel had offered some very handsome prizes to contributors, ranging from ten dollars for witticisms or epigrams, fifty dollars for poetry, accelerating to a hundred dollars and up for short stories, and a thousand dollars and up for novelettes.) Chatfield-Taylor and De Koven had pulled down a thousand dollar prize to get everything moving with a bang. There were a few other gilded names in that first issue, but there were also contributions from (among others) Gelett Burgess, Bliss Carmen and Ella Wheeler Wilcox.

Although not slick by today's standards, the first and succeeding issues were artfully and expensively produced. There were 160 pages of text and 20 pages of advertising under a bluish-gray cover designed by Kay Wormath, with large sinuous vermilion lettering for the *Smart Set*, with "A Magazine of Cleverness" running down one side. Pictured are a dancing couple in evening dress, seemingly jerked about on strings by a masked Pan, a playful Cupid at their feet. The jaunty cover itself was enough to justify the comment of the *New York Tribune* that here was a magazine intended "to entertain rather than instruct or edify."

For the first two years of its existence, the *Smart Set* had offices in the St. James Building at Broadway and 26th Street—a few spartan cubicles allowing little elbow room. Even Arthur Grissom had to share an office with one of his assistant editors. Colonel Mann was a paternalistic but not an authoritarian publisher, and seldom visited the *Smart Set* offices, which was certainly a boon in the early years. The Colonel did benevolently invite his editorial "family" to extravagant parties at his brownstone mansion on West 72nd Street. Rarely were matters of grave editorial concern discussed. The Colonel was deliciously absent of intellectual pretentions, and this gave his editors free reign. For a number of years the Colonel's divorced daughter (who called herself *Miss* Emma Mann-Vynne) was supposed to be his link with the magazine; she came in occasionally to read manuscripts, but her appearances were actually few and far between, and the editors always managed to sidestep whatever implied authority she might have sought to exercise.

During the first few years of its career the *Smart Set* kept to a rather consistent format. Each number began with a novelette, followed by ten or a dozen stories usually interrupted somewhere along the line with a fact piece or two dealing with literature, the stage, travel, high living. Sprinkled throughout on half pages or odd pages were epigrams, jokes, satires and a required quota of verse contributions. The interior of the magazine in the early years was hardly snazzy even by the standards of the day—pages of straight type with few design features and not very imaginative visual treatment.

Yet the magazine's light touch, its refusal to take the world seriously, gave it a certain robust appeal in an era when even the popular magazines were stiff and pompous. The style and format were not strictly novel; some of the inspiration seems to have been taken from Chicago's *Chap Book*, which for a few years in the nineties charmed people with its naiveté and insouciance resembling a good and clever college magazine. The *Chap Book*, in its brief five-year life span, drew upon the talents of Eugene Field, Henry James, Hamlin Garland, H. G. Wells and W. B. Yeats.

Perhaps of still more importance, the *Smart Set* mocked the indolent mood of the vaguely notorious British *Yellow Book*, another meteoric product of the 1890s. The *Yellow Book*, under the art direction of Aubrey Beardsley, with its fin de siècle decadence, its elaborate scrollings and deviant eroticism, had a visual bravura that the *Smart Set* never attained; yet the *Smart Set* hoped to move in the same direction. Under an outward surface of vanity, social snobbery, superciliousness, epigrammatic forced cleverness, there was much room for the creation of new talent, and between its lurid covers were works by Oscar Wilde, Arnold Bennett, Henry James, Richard Le Gallienne, Edmund Gosse and Ernest Dowson.

The *Smart Set*, naturally, relished and cultivated the "international dimension," through an appeal to global sophistication. Very early in its history the magazine began to publish occasional stories, poems, and one-act plays in French. Grissom had astutely finagled a contract with a literary agency in Paris, the Société des Gens de Letters, which agreed to furnish poems, short stories and one-act plays for the preposterously low fee of twenty-five dollars a year. Most of the material the magazine got was from obscure penny-a-liners. But there were some out-of-copyright sources, and occasionally some well-known French authors would surface—Gautier, Anatole France, and others. The contract lasted for twenty years (from 1901 to 1921), and even if only a small portion of the magazine's readers actually struggled with the French offering of the month, it indisputably added a touch of sophistication or smartness to the magazine, and surely at the very least appealed to members of the American affluent classes, many of whose members had enjoyed the requisite boarding school education and taken the ritualistic tours of the Continent.

Grissom's attempt to find regular and dependable sources of material at cheap rates was not always successful. The Colonel was a believer in keeping to the customary low magazine rate of one cent a word for prose and twenty-five cents a line for poetry. This probably would have been typical in most magazines at the time, although the mass-circulation giants could afford to do much better for their regular stable of writers. Occasionally the Colonel relented, and allowed a slightly more generous rate for some well-established writer or someone whose name provided snob appeal. But generally even the well-known writers had to be content with the base rate. One poet who received a five dollar check for his contribution wrote to the editors: "Now I know why you call yourselves the smart set," to which Grissom responded with a memorable dictum: "Poets are born not paid."

In these preinflationary times, five dollars was hardly a paltry sum, and a novice poet could treat his best girl to a dinner (for two) in a first-rate restaurant for that amount. The twenty-five dollars one might receive for a fiction piece could pay a month's rent in a New York apartment.

On the other hand, with the Colonel's purse strings held tight, many established magazine regulars would not submit spontaneously to the *Smart Set*. For this reason, even as its circulation soared, the magazine needed to remain receptive to young unsolicited writers. Everything was read that came in, and any contribution of real quality had a good chance of being accepted. Almost from the start the *Smart Set* became a haven for a new generation of American literary figures who were looking to crack into the formidable New York literary establishment. Among the early contributors were a number of youngsters who themselves would be prominent writers and editors in the years ahead.

Among those delighted to appear in the *Smart Set* in spite of its penurious ways were Henry Seidel Canby, Dorothy Canfield Fisher and William Rose Benét. Up at Columbia, studying German romantic poetry, Ludwig Lewisohn could find no outlets in what he considered an American wasteland. Nearly all of the magazines he read were full of "dishonest, sapless twaddle, guided by an impossible moral perfectionism . . . and strung on a string of pseudo-romantic love." The *Smart Set* he saw as a tolerable alternative, and as an outlet for higher and liberated twaddle.

Very shortly, too, the *Smart Set* had latched onto a few writers who seemed to fit the ironical style and mood of the magazine to perfection. One of these was William Sydney Porter—O. Henry—heretofore an obscure roustabout newspaperman who had written a daily column of humorous anecdotes for a Houston, Texas, newspaper. Born in North Carolina, Porter had drifted west, working in a drug store and a bank, while also holding a number of part-time newspaper jobs. While employed in Austin as a bank teller in the mid-nineties he put out his own small-scale humor magazine called the *Rolling Stone*. Later, however, he was accused, probably falsely, of embezzling money from his bank job and he fled to Honduras. Upon returning to Texas to be with his wife on her deathbed, he was imprisoned for three years, during which time he began developing his remarkable gifts as a writer of short stories. These stories, with their ingenious plots, their sharp-edged humor, their deft depiction of life's little ironies, were mostly drawn from O. Henry's personal experiences in Honduras, Texas and elsewhere, and they took on a very special lustre after he moved to New York in 1902, traipsing the city's Tenderloin and Bowery in the gaslight era, which subsequently became the ideal setting for his work.

O. Henry sent his first story from Pittsburgh, written in hand (even then the vast majority of manuscripts received by magazines were typed, but hand-written contributions were not rejected summarily). The story fell to young Charles Hanson Towne, then an assistant editor and just beginning a long and illustrious career as a magazine editor in New York. Towne was immediately struck by the boldness and legibility of the hand. "It was like copperplate," perfection itself, he thought. And he was immediately struck by the force and incisiveness of O. Henry's prose, although he could not have foreseen that he was looking at the work of a man who in only a few years would be recognized as one of America's great short-story writers. But the story was immediately accepted, with Towne writing on a little blue slip for the cashier: "Pay Sydney Porter (O. Henry) for story entitled 'By Courier,' Seventeen dollars ($17)."

If the small payment was disappointing to O. Henry he didn't show it, and in no time at all he had sent in a second story, this one sixty thousand words entitled, "The Lotus in the Bottle." O. Henry asked if he might have immediate payment so that he could come to New York City, expressing a willingness to let the story go for fifty dollars quick cash. Grissom did send the immediate payment, but at the full rate of sixty dollars, along with his warm wishes and an invitation to the author to call at the *Smart Set* offices. So immediately caught up in the maelstrom of life in New York was O. Henry, so infatuated was he with this city that was to become the inspiration for some of his best tales, that he forgot to stop in. Still there would be other stories for the *Smart Set* in the years ahead.

But so quickly would O. Henry's fame accelerate and so productive was he as a writer that his stories were almost immediately gobbled up by *Ain-*

slee's and *Munsey's* and better paying mass-market magazines. O. Henry would churn out stories sometimes at the rate of one a week for the remaining years of his life (he died prematurely in 1910), and he quickly reached the point where any large debt of gratitude to the pinchpenny *Smart Set* would only have been a perpetuation of foolishness. But he could not have been unaware that he and the *Smart Set* had at one time been perfect for one another.

Another early author soon to find fame, if not riches, was James Branch Cabell, whose first published story, "As Played Before His Highness," appeared in the *Smart Set* in 1902. Unlike O. Henry, Cabell never forgot this debt of gratitude to the magazine that gave him his start. Perhaps this was because even more than those of O. Henry the writings of this son of the Old Dominion, this flower of southern gentility, fitted in with the aims and ideals of this magazine edited for airy sophisticates. Cabell's worlds, his various realms, of aristocratic courts, of medieval legend, of indistinct historical Never-Never Lands, his overly refined conceits, his shimmering and dazzling prose style, were admirably suited to the *Smart Set*. There was a kind of archness, a mild and rarefied tendency to scoff at the gaucheries of the culture and society of twentieth-century America, the hustle and bustle of a futile modernism — all this putting Cabell on the *Smart Set's* wavelength from the very beginning.

Cabell, to be sure, was never a "popular" author, at least not popular in the sense used in the mass media. True, he had his enthusiastic supporters, including Theodore Roosevelt and Mark Twain, but basically there was nothing in him that could have appealed to the multitudes. Later, in the twenties, when his novel *Jurgen* received "the protection of the censor," and was hawked in the bookstores at forty dollars a copy, Cabell became a cult figure. But he was a writer superbly unsuited to any kind of mass audience; his appeal was to those who liked the in-jokes of history, who relished the lightest fantasies of romanticism whipped up into meerschaum. He was a courtier in a country that had no court, an antiquarian for a people who could not abide anything that was not new and tingling. Still, there were an elite few who were ready to be amused, and the editors of the *Smart Set* pined to reach them, those who were tired of the worlds of getting and spending, of reform, of dreary realistic novels: these were the people who were drawn to the puffs of fancy, the wild uncontrollable illogic of James Branch Cabell. He could never reach *hoi polloi*, but he could amuse and entertain those driven by wit and fancy.

By the second year of its existence, the *Smart Set* had settled into a very

well ordered routine of ministering to a definite and select audience, probably
not one of social butterflies but of those graced by imagination. Its circulation
was rising monthly, and it was clearly paying its way. Accordingly, the
magazine moved out of cramped quarters in the St. James Building, relocat-
ing uptown in the Knox Building on Fifth Avenue—all New York was moving uptown at the time, and the precincts of the softer side of commerce were
clearly more suitable for the offices of a magazine purportedly edited for the
carriage trade. And the quarters in the Knox Building were not only ample
but plush. Downtown, editor Grissom was forced to share an office with one
of his assistant editors. Here everyone had his own partitioned office, and
the suite itself looked, said one contributor, more like a club than a magazine
office.

Carl Dolmetsch in his charming sketch of the magazine's history described the Knox Building offices: "The suite itself was sumptuously appointed, even by the standards of 1902." There was a long deeply carpeted
corridor off which were the editor's offices. At one end of the corridor there
was

> a burgundy and gilt reception room furnished with horsehide sofas, massive
> mahogany tables and potted palms. . . . At the corridor's other end the colonel
> had his "Editorial Chambers," as he grandiloquently styled a spacious room
> done in polished mahogany and red plush and gilded fringe and tassels. The
> crowning touch of this room (almost literally) was a cigar-lighter in the shape of
> a gold Cupid suspended just above the colonel's oversized desk by a chain of
> gold hearts.

But the Colonel seldom visited his grand editorial chamber, leaving day-
to-day decision making to Grissom and his associates. The limitations (other
than financial) put on the staff were few, offering a glorious sense of freedom
to those charged with decision making. And Arthur Grissom turned out to
be a first-rate editor. Curiously for all of his experience as a wit and poet he
seemed by manner and demeanor an unlikely head man for a smart magazine. In time it would become something of an American legend, or at least
a half truth, that editors of smart magazines would be old sourdoughs, dip-
somaniacal newspaper reporters, unfrocked college professors. If so, Grissom was no more typical, or untypical, than the lot. A man of quiet, leisurely
manner, no one would divine in him the zest and drive to preside over the
stable of wits and iconoclasts that had rapidly been assembled by the *Smart
Set*.

Charles Hanson Towne, who came in as assistant editor in the first year, and who later took the editorial chair himself, found Grissom an agonizingly slow and reflective editor. Having moved to the *Smart Set* from *Cosmopolitan*, where he had worked under a frenzied and hard-driving editor, Towne could not at first believe that this vibrant young periodical could have at its helm a man as calmly deliberative as Arthur Grissom. Having slaved under a dynamo at *Cosmopolitan*, and being something of a dynamo himself, he thought he had come upon a slow-ticking grandfather's clock. "He never hurried. One could not make him hurry. I verily believe that it someone had cried 'Fire!' he would have ambled form his desk—after he had finished calmly reading the manuscript that was in his hand."

Yet Towne developed a decided admiration for his slow-moving boss, soon realizing that the man almost never made a wrong decision. Still, decisions came haltingly, sometimes agonizingly. But when they did come they were nearly always faultless. On one occasion, Towne, a man of quick and incisive resolve, did manage to push Grissom to sudden action. It was on the occasion of the arrival of that wonderful first story from O. Henry. Towne took the manuscript to Grissom—with tears in his eyes as he later testified—insisting that the boss accept it on the spot.

"If you don't accept this, I resign!" Towne said, standing over Grissom's desk while the chief read all seventeen hundred words.

" 'Again you're right.' he said, looking up as he finished the last page. 'Make out a voucher, please, at our regular rate.' " Seventeen dollars.

Unfortunately, Arthur Grissom did not live to see the fruits of his painstaking labors. He died suddenly in October 1901 of typhoid fever, his magazine hardly out of its infancy. Clearly, though, he had by then established policies that would put the magazine in good stead in the years ahead. With very feeble resources he had in only a year and a half produced a magazine that seemed to have a bright and forward-looking future and whose early achievements had not gone unnoticed among the editorial offices of New York. His editorial credo, expressed to Towne on his deathbed, really said all that he would have wanted to say: "Take only the best—only the best."

Before Towne took the helm there was a brief interregnum with Marvin Dana in the editor's chair. Dana, a scholarly man with numerous academic degrees to his credit, was a superficially facile writer who had turned out two novels and a long string of stories and poems that had appeared in American and European magazines, most of them written after he had given up a prestigious post at the Boston Public Library, where he was an editor of a series called the Ridpath Library of Universal Literature. Dana made only scant changes in the format or quality of the magazine and in 1904 was lured away by a well-known New York newspaper. The editorship of the *Smart Set* then passed to Towne, who after several really good years used the job as a stepping stone to a long gilt-edged career in commercial publishing. A native New Yorker, Towne had established his own magazine of cleverness at the age of eleven called the *Unique Monthly*. While still a stripling he worked for the *Brooklyn Eagle* and contributed light verse to magazines like *Ainslee's* and *Munsey's*.

Towne moved up rapidly from free-lancer to editor, first under John Brisben Walker at *Cosmopolitan*, then under Grissom. In 1904, when he took over the *Smart Set*, he was twenty-seven years of age, but already had the soul of a witty, kindly, quick-thinking and highly polished magazine editor. Since his early youth, Towne had been a passionate devotee of the Broadway stage, and during his tenure on the magazine he made considerable improvements to the back section, to drama, books, the arts. Years later, after he had been a highly successful editor of *Harper's Bazar* for Hearst (after 1929, *Bazar* was spelled *Bazaar*), Towne took up acting, becoming the Episcopal clergyman in the long-running stage hit *Life with Father*, a role that seemed to fit his qualities of amiable precision and measured jollity. Towne's career at the *Smart Set* was short-lived, and not entirely satisfying for reasons mostly beyond his control. He left in 1907 when Theodore Dreiser hired him to be the fiction editor of the *Delineator* and other Butterick magazines. The quality of the magazine did not diminish during Towne's tenure; circulation continued to rise, but Towne was saddled with perilously low rates of payment to contributors, and these forced many authors well disposed toward the magazine to take their material elsewhere. The magazine continued to be substandard in printing and production qualities; design features were uninspiring. Still, there were many, particularly younger writers who loved the *Smart Set* for what it symbolized, and continued to offer their wares at a pittance. Whatever the magazine's defects, everybody agreed that it was a lively and enchanting sheet. There were also a number who continued to look on the magazine as somehow lurid, persisting in the belief that it was tarred with the same brush as the colonel's naughty *Town Topics*. But American mores were rapidly changing as the Victorian era rapidly faded into history, and most of the young, the bright and the restless could readily have assented to Carl Van Doren's keenly felt observation that the *Smart Set* "was to older magazines what a circus is to a library."

The inviting and intriguing qualities of the magazine were such that they shortly brought signs of trouble. As early as 1902 there were imitators. The first and most important was *Ainslee's* magazine. Since the mid-1890s, *Ainslee's*, a product of the great pulp giant Street and Smith, had been limping along as an undistinguished everyman's monthly in an atmosphere of heavy competition. Apparently the editors at *Ainslee's*, Richard Duffy and Gilman Hall, had been eyeing the *Smart Set* for a long time, and suddenly decided that there was no reason why one magazine should be having all the fun. Accordingly, in October 1902, a new *Ainslee's* was born that could not be mistaken as anything but a copycat version of the *Smart Set*. The typeface, format, size, display headings were all imitations, and the reborn competitor had the effrontery to adopt the subtitle: "The Magazine of Clever Fiction." This first issue and many subsequent issues were sprinkled with contributions from *Smart Set* regulars (including, believe it or not, a poem by Charlie Towne). Before long some old standbys of the *Smart Set* were selling their stuff at more inspiriting rates to this well-financed interloper. An even greater threat was the magazine's price: fifteen cents. This may not, in and of itself, have been a devastating blow to the *Smart Set*'s economies, but in very short order the circulation of *Ainslee's* was double that of the *Smart Set*, which probably had the effect of chilling Towne and his staff at the *Smart Set* with fear that their potential for further growth was henceforth blocked, which in fact it was. The circulation did not decline dramatically in the wake of this development, but it leveled off slowly.

Trouble was brewing in another quarter, however, and this would be far more destructive than any internecine competition among magazines. The *Smart Set* continued to be produced by the Ess Ess Publishing Company; it continued to be a sanitized twin of Colonel William D'Alton Mann's unsavory *Town Topics*. To the eternal benefit of the *Smart Set* the Colonel had maintained his policy of not meddling in the editorial affairs of his literate monthly, even when times got tough, but he continued to be embroiled in various shadowy doings in the demimonde. With two successful magazines under his belt, the Colonel embarked on some additional ventures of his own that would eventually have dire consequences for the *Smart Set*, at least in the short run. He first established a personalized advice service, giving tips by subscription on topics of strong concern to *Smart Set* readers—fashions, resorts, European vacations, restaurants, hotels, and so on. But the idea was a money loser. Then, flushed with pride by Arthur Grissom's success in negotiating a deal for French material at bargain-basement prices, the Colonel established another monthly magazine entitled *Transatlantic Tales*, the idea of which was to reprint stories from European magazines in English translation, paying only a few farthings for the originals, even filching them whenever possible. The magazine had the very respectable James G. Huneker at the helm, but it never caught on and the Colonel found himself embroiled in nasty copyright infringement suits.

Next the Colonel embarked on another venture that turned out to be a source of real trouble. He proposed to issue a book-length annual to be entitled *Fads and Fancies of Representative Americans at the Beginning of the Twentieth Century*. This book, which made its appearance in 1906, was perhaps the most outrageously executed puff sheet of all time, presenting sketches of the lives, pursuits and possessions of great American plutocrats as well as some assorted hangers-on. Intended to be sold at $1,500 a copy, higher than the annual wage of a typical American in 1906, the book was bound in gilded morocco with end papers of heavy watered silk, with top and sides of 18-karat gold leaf. The printing consisted of red and gold lettering in addition to the usual black letterpress.

The scheme was to offer a decidedly snobbish portrait of the lives of the rich—pictures of their town houses, motor cars, stables and greenhouses, art collections, wine cellars, blooded cattle, packs of hounds, private railway cars. There was ample room for puffed-up biographies of the grandees and their families; there was room for anecdotal material of a titillating nature, about their hobbies, predilections, travels and intimate lives. The Colonel obviously hoped to put the squeeze on the various "biographees" to foot the bill for production costs, but he also planned to reserve copies for the rare book rooms of a few major libraries. The Library of Congress and the New York Public Library were both offered copies. The New York Public Library let it be known that it would have nothing to do with such a shameless expression of human vanity and refused to accept its copy. (Nonetheless, a much-treasured copy of the book does repose there today, kept under careful guard in the Rare Book Room.)

Almost immediately the Colonel got himself into hot water because of this extravagant volume. The age of the muckrakers had suddenly fallen hard upon the land, and men of responsibility wanted nothing to do with a book that glorified the rich. President Theodore Roosevelt, now advancing against the trusts, and allied with those who were damning "malefactors of great wealth," strenuously denied that he had authorized inclusion of himself in the book, or that he had paid to be included. (And surely he hadn't paid—the Colonel would naturally be delighted to include a nonpaying president of the United States and a number of other well-known worthies.)

The truth was, however, the book was yet another of the Colonel's schemes for blackmailing and milking the rich, however genially carried out.

The Astors, the Vanderbilts, the Schwabs, the Morgans and so on were dipping deeply into their pockets to pay for gilt-edged copies. Still, many of them did not take too kindly to being dunned in this fashion, and eventually a few raised a ruckus in the press. One complainer was a young New York broker named Edwin Post (later the husband of etiquette authority Emily Post), who had acted as a decoy for *Collier's Weekly*, long a detractor of *Town Topics*, and now, under the editorship of Norman Hapgood, a pronounced muckraking publication that was hunting for peccadillos of just this sort. In the weeks and months ahead Hapgood hammered away at the Colonel, digging up all the dirt he could, asserting in one particularly venomous and heavy-handed editorial that the Colonel was known all over New York as "something worse than an ordinary forger, horse-thief, or second-story man."

Eventually *Collier's Weekly* goaded the Colonel into seeking the protection of the courts, and a libel case seemingly vindicated the Colonel on the charges that he was a common blackmailer. But in a very extensive newspaper smear that held the New York headlines for weeks, the Colonel was essentially tried in the press and found wanting. *Collier's* and Hapgood had never attempted to blacken the *Smart Set*, but the Colonel's name was so firmly bound up with that publication as well as with *Town Topics*, that the magazine was damaged by all the unseemly publicity surrounding the trial.

The results for the *Smart Set* were chilling. Not complete disaster, perhaps, but running the edge. The circulation in 1906 dropped by nearly 25,000. More importantly, advertising revenues dropped alarmingly. Some of the important regular advertisers began to shy away, including, sadly, those with the most slick appeal. Many of these were replaced by others paying the same rates but offering decidedly less éclat than the purveyors of champagne, jewels, Parisian frocks, chandeliers or hand-built motor cars. The magazine almost immediately lost the base of its old snob appeal. Some authors of long standing dropped away and more and more the editors had to rely on beginners and unknowns. The magazine's image became somewhat restrictive and stifling, progressively less fresh and innovative month by month.

Charlie Towne struggled desperately against oblivion. He tried to recruit new staff and new authors but the pickings were slim. He did succeed in introducing more variety to the magazine over time, knowing now with certainty that he could no longer depend on any material by bluebloods, which turned out to be a saving grace in the long run. And there were other happy improvements. In 1907 the *Smart Set* raided its closest competitor, *Ainslee's*, hiring Channing Pollock to do a monthly theatre column. With its reversal of fortunes, the *Smart Set*, once the imitated, now began aping some of the imaginative changes made by Duffy and Hall at *Ainslee's*. Towne knew that he was not always in a position to follow Arthur Grissom's dying charge to run only the best. Accordingly, in the spring of 1908, after seveaerl years of declining circulation, and with no relief in sight, he departed for greener pastures at the Butterick magazines. The *Smart Set* was without a rudder.

With Towne gone, the Colonel had few prospects for finding a comparable editor to rebuild the magazine. But he didn't give up the ship. He determined to plunge forward in ever-darkening waters, taking the editorial helm himself, at least nominally. To handle the day-to-day chores he hired two well-intentioned neophytes, who, in and of themselves, were poorly positioned to make drastic changes in the magazine. Coming on board as managing editor was twenty-two-year old Fred C. Splint, and as assistant editor a young Baltimore newspaperman named Norman Boyer. As history has shown, neither of these young men would make a lasting impression on the destinies of the *Smart Set*, but in a twinkling, so to speak, mounting the stage were two other men who would. These two were also just youngsters at the time, unknowns. But in a few years they would be very well known throughout the land—and this mostly through the vehicle of the *Smart Set*.

It all came about because of the desire of the magazine to modernize and vivify the back sections of the magazine—all in imitation of *Ainslee's*. The Colonel either decided himself or agreed with Splint that the magazine would need a literary editor to write book reviews. It would also shortly need a new dramatic editor since Channing Pollock had expressed a desire to leave. So, shortly filling the dramatic slot was a young man who would live to become the dean of New York drama critics, George Jean Nathan. Coming in as literary editor? Who would it be? Norman Boyer thought of a brash young newspaper writer from his hometown of Baltimore—Henry L. Mencken. Splint wrote to Mencken to ask if he would be interested, and, if so, would he come to New York? Mencken wrote back to say that he was definitely interested and would come right up. An early meeting was arranged in Boyer's office in which two of the most scintillating figures in American letters met for the first time, leading eventually to one of the most fruitful editorial collaborations in the history of American magazines. Together for posterity were George Jean Nathan and Henry L. Mencken.

These two bright youngsters who answered the call of the *Smart Set* in the spring of 1908 had never met one another and knew nothing of one another. In six more years, after a great deal more water had gone over the dam, they would become joint editors of the magazine and would lead it to its greatest days of glory. For the time being they would have to be content to come in at the back of the magazine and add to it a hitherto unknown verve and regularity.

It was, they later recalled, May 8, 1908, when Henry L. Mencken and George Jean Nathan sat in Norman Boyer's office at the *Smart Set*, listening impatiently as their duties and functions were explained. Channing Pollock was not yet ready to give up the drama slot, so Nathan would not begin work for some time; Mencken would start writing book reviews immediately. In any case, neither of them needed much guidance on their duties and were amply supplied with ideas of their own. Henry L. Mencken (a short time later he would become known to the world as H. L. Mencken) was twenty-seven years old; Nathan two years younger. Mencken, already tending toward rotundity, had the appearance of a rather brash but quickwitted college sophomore, an oversized imp ready to set off a firecracker or spring a crude practical joke. Nathan, an overly fastidious, even effete looking young man, seemed to be cut from a completely different cloth, but the two studied one another in Boyer's office and immediately perceived that under the skin they were two fellow iconoclasts, two literary Katzenjammer kids ready to make some mischief in the world.

Mencken had come up from the hurly-burly of city journalism. He had been a reporter and editor on the old *Baltimore Morning Herald* and the *Sunpapers*. His early newspaper days had been spent covering the requisite number of fires, mayhems and church socials. He did not, however, rise from the city streets, at least not precisely. His father had been a prosperous cigar manufacturer, and Mencken was reared in a stately Baltimore row house and encapsulated in comfort and convenience. He graduated first in his class at the Baltimore Polytechnic High School, and could have advanced directly to one of the nation's better colleges. But suspicious of academies of learning (a trait he would maintain all his life), he picked up a job on the second-rate *Herald*, and learned the trade thoroughly under a great city editor named Max Ways. Before he was out of his teens he had learned to write with charm and considerable force, demonstrating a prodigious efficiency and productivity in grinding out as many as five thousand words of copy a day.

Before long Mencken was turning out materials of every sort for his Baltimore employers—editorials, theatre reviews, feature pieces—all written with high style and gusto. But even twelve-hour days on the newspapers of

Baltimore did not dampen his energies, and by the age of twenty-five he had published his first book, a study of the plays and ideas of George Bernard Shaw. And the year he began his association with the *Smart Set*, he published a book entitled *The Philosophy of Friedrich Neitzsche* — the first English-language book on that then very mystifying German philosopher — all ample proof that Mencken had not let his lack of a college education impede his intellectual development. There was about Mencken a Germanic thoroughness and an almost startling erudition, which nonetheless were always kept concealed under his light and buoyant exterior. He came to think of himself as a "critic of ideas," perhaps better yet as a critic of American culture, but he was always first and foremost a writer. In later years Robert Frost would call him the greatest American essayist, a distinction that may be not at all far-fetched.

Mencken continued to live in Baltimore throughout his life. He preferred his slow-moving city of faintly Southern gentility to the tumult of New York where he would come to have most of his professional commitments and obligations. For all of his working life he kept up an association with the *Sunpapers* of Baltimore. He believed himself to be above all a working newspaperman retaining a hard intimacy with the grit of ordinary life. But his interests as a man of thought ran all over the map.

George Jean Nathan was quite unlike Mencken in physical appearance and quite unlike him in tastes. A tall, handsome man, always sartorially correct, he had about him something of an air of a spoiled aristocrat who never in his life had had to lift his finger in pursuit of anything. Like Mencken he had come from the "provinces," having been born in Fort Wayne, Indiana, but he was college educated (at Cornell), had spent ample time in Italy studying fine arts, and considered himself a connoisseur of all the best that had been said and done in the world. He had spent several years on New York papers, eventually moving into drama criticism, but he never shared Mencken's delight in roustabout journalism. He had little desire to rub shoulders with the man on the street, never read the political news; cared nothing at all about sports, the popular arts or any of the lowly manifestations of American culture. His sole passions were art and beauty; he was drenched in the predilection d'artiste.

Nevertheless, Mencken and Nathan suited each other like hand and glove. Both were iconoclasts, both seemed to scowl at everybody with a sense of Olympian detachment, both looked upon the world as a kind of cosmic circus there for their own enjoyment. Nathan later remembered the meeting in Boyer's office when he met Mencken for the first time, and claimed that Mencken thrust out his hand and introduced himself, saying: "I'm H. L. Mencken from Baltimore and I'm the biggest damn fool in Christendom and I don't want to hear any boastful reply that you claim the honor."

On that day in the spring of 1908 when the two met, both sat fidgeting and smirking while Norman Boyer gravely explained the current plans, objectives and present difficulties of the *Smart Set*. When a long and tedious hour of this was over, Mencken and Nathan, who both despised meetings and conferences and believed that no good ever came out of them, retired to a nearby watering hole and had a few good laughs over the meeting. "Boyer is a horse's ass," proclaimed Mencken as the two drank Florestan cocktails and listened to schmaltzy Viennese music. Both immediately agreed that working for the *Smart Set* would probably be fun, although they understood that there wouldn't be much money in it. They could use their separate columns to urge their prejudices and intellectual fancies on an unwary world, and maybe, just maybe, in time, they could make something good out of this rapidly fading monthly. Both seem to have been drawn to the *Smart Set* for pretty much the same reason: they could live within the jaunty and somewhat irreverent style that already existed, and otherwise realized that the magazine was a tabula rasa on which they could write and create whatever mischief struck their respective fancies.

Mencken appeared in the magazine first, his inaugural book review column (the first of 181) running in the November 1908 issue. Nathan's theatre reviews didn't begin until a year later, but his first actual appearance in the magazine, a humorous essay entitled "Why We Fall in Love With Actresses," was published in the October 1909 issue. Both young authors began a bit lamely as critics, as if they were trying out their wings, but in a few months both began to soar, and it wasn't long before they began to attract national attention.

Unfortunately, in the beginning, neither Mencken nor Nathan was strong enough to carry the magazine singlehandedly, and during the first few years of their association with it, the magazine continued to slide. The old Colonel's books were drenched in red ink; he was now nearing seventy and probably tired of the magazine business. For some time, by 1909 at least, he had been looking for a buyer for the magazine, but the nasty scandals of a few years earlier had kept them away. Meanwhile, Splint and Boyer were having a hard time filling up the magazine, occasionally needing to resort to agents and their expensive fees as a way of bringing in articles.

The magazine muddled through and had no relief from its financial woes for the next two years, but things began to look up rapidly in the spring of 1911 when the Colonel finally did manage to find a buyer for the magazine. The buyer was John Adams Thayer, a highly successful advertising man with long magazine experience. Hardly a patrician type in spite of his three names, Thayer had been born into a working-class family in Boston and begun work at an early age as a printer for the Riverside Press. Later, moving into the field of magazine advertising, he worked for the *Ladies' Home Journal*, *Munsey's*, and the *Delineator*, eventually obtaining his own magazine, *Everybody's*. He made this an enormous success with another hard-driving editor, Erman J. Ridgeway.

Almost immediately there were big changes, especially in the advertising departments. With the Colonel's unsavory reputation now a memory, Thayer doubled and then tripled the number of monthly advertising pages. Following the old business precept that you can't make money unless you spend money, he revived the long-defunct English edition of the magazine; he had the magazine redesigned in a modern style by the highly skilled commercial artist James Montgomery Flagg. Then he turned to the more difficult problem of finding a first-rate editor to point the magazine in a new direction. Thayer thought of Mencken as a possible editor, but wary of his new boss, and perhaps believing that Thayer really wanted to set policy himself, Mencken refused. And doubtless Mencken was right about this since after the departure of Fred Splint (who had only taken the job as a prelude to a career in medicine), the ineffectual Norman Boyer held the job briefly as a straw boss while Thayer decided where to go next.

While unwilling yet to accept the top job himself, Mencken apparently took every opportunity to prod Thayer to abandon the magazine's current formula, which he believed to be nothing but a pale imitation of *Ainslee's*. The road to salvation, said Mencken, was to make the magazine a true representative of the avant-garde, to seek out the best that was new and daring in American writing and the arts, Thayer temporized, however, and following Boyer's term, the editor's chair was briefly filled by Mark Lee Luther, a writer of mystery stories. In spite of its increased advertising revenues and new design, the magazine was only limping along and had not found a new style and image.

By 1913, however, Thayer was apparently willing to listen to Mencken, and an editor of vigorous personality and forceful ideas was given a chance to make drastic changes in the *Smart Set*'s formula. The new editor was Willard Huntington Wright, who had worked for a year as an associate editor and was strongly supported by Mencken, who apparently thought highly of him. Wright was yet another youngster, but of a personality that dominated everyone who came into his orbit. A Virginian by birth, and twenty-five years old when he took over the *Smart Set*, he had come by way of Harvard (where he dropped out without a degree because "they had nothing more to teach me") and the *Los Angeles Times* where he had been literary editor at nineteen. Wright, who sported a mustache like the Kaiser's, resembled a fierce young Hun or Magyar, and accepted his position only after extracting a promise that he could have an absolutely free hand in the editorial policies of the magazine. He received the promise, and gained his year. It was to be a great year, but also one of bone-jarring trauma.

Wright wasted no time completely making over the *Smart Set*, replacing what he thought to be false cleverness with modern intelligence. The original *Smart Set*, he believed, while running counter to the simplemindedness or the stodginess of the age, nonetheless wasted its efforts trying to serve up confections for the rich and the idle, thereby deluding itself with pseudoculture and smart-aleck sophistication. In an early issue of the magazine, he stated his editorial credo with gusto and bravura: The time had come, he said, for a magazine to provide enlightenment and first-rate intelligence and not triviality. "Men and women have grown tired of effeminacy and the falsities of current fiction, essays and poetry. A widespread critical awakening has come, and with it a demand for better literary material. The demand for pious uplift, for stultification, and fictional avoidance of the facts of life has diminished. The reader of today demands truth."

In his search for truth Wright sent out the word that he wanted to open his pages to a whole new generation of writers and poets ready to overturn all of the conventional applecarts, give the back of their hand to the smug Victorian middle-class platitudes. He wanted writers who would offer tough realistic pictures of modern life or romantic material that didn't studiously avoid reference to sex and human perversities. He aggressively sought out such contributors from around the globe.

And fresh new material came pouring into the office from authors who were on the verge of becoming some of the most celebrated authors of the twentieth century. From Great Britain came contributions from D. H. Lawrence, George Moore, May Sinclair, Robert Bridges, Joseph Conrad and William Butler Yeats. Wright, who seemed to have an especially strong passion for Continental literature, greatly expanded the roster of European writers. The agreements with the French Société des Gens de Lettres were renewed, bringing in its quota of nearly free material, but Wright acquired works by German writers like Schnitzler and Wedekind, as well as other

European writers such as Strindberg, D'Annunzio, "Maartens," and Artz-
ybashev. Like Mencken, Wright had strong pro-German leanings and ten-
dencies, and his greatest wish would have been to make over the *Smart Set*
in the image of the pungent German satirical weekly *Simplicissimus*, which
had had its origins in the beer cellars and avant-garde cabarets of 1890s
Munich.

But this was the era of the avant-garde in America also—the famous
Armory Show shocked New Yorkers two years before that Wright took over
the helm of the *Smart Set*, and the previous year had seen the publication in
Chicago of *Poetry*, the progenitor of a whole series of "little" magazines that
would open outlets that never existed before to all sorts of experimental writers and artists. And hoping to establish just such an innovative magazine
himself, Wright opened the floodgates to all manner of American writers,
some of whom had been scorned or neglected. Rushing into the magazine's
pages during Wright's brief tenure as editor were Theodore Dreiser, Floyd
Dell, Albert Payson Terhune, Robinson Jeffers, Sara Teasdale, Joyce Kil-
mer, Witter Bynner, Harriet Monroe, Louis Untermeyer, and many others.
It was an exhilarating year, and writers and critics at home and abroad were
convinced that the *Smart Set* was rapidly on its way to becoming the premier
intellectual magazine in the United States.

Alas, this noble venture was not allowed to continue. Alarmed by the
loss of his traditional readers, shocked by fiction that was "sordid"or dis-
tressing and poetry that was unintelligible, Thayer fired Wright at the end
of his agreed-upon year and once again installed Mark Luther as editor,
promising in an editorial to offer once more a magazine that would primarily
"amuse and entertain," but with class. Wright left as suddenly as he had
come, moving on to a rather strange and checkered career as a writer and
editor. (In the early 1920s he was in eclipse, but when a serious illness stifled
his creative work in the mid-1920s, he began turning out very popular mystery stories under the pseudonym S. S. Van Dine.)

Mencken and Nathan, of course, were terribly distressed at the loss of
this distinguished, forward-looking editor in whom they had placed so much
confidence. They expressed no public disapproval of the latest upheaval, but
Mencken wrote to his friend Theodore Dreiser that the *Smart Set* was falling
back to its dismal paternity, that it had become "as righteous as a decrepit
and converted madame."

The fruits of Wright's labors were not permanently lost, however, for
John Adams Thayer's own term of ownership was about to come to a hasty
and dramatic conclusion. The previous year had been a disappointing one

financially, but 1914 would be even more unlucky, in part because of a nationwide financial slump. In the summer of that year, with war clouds on the horizon in Europe and his indebtedness from the *Smart Set* weighing heavily on his shoulders, Thayer sold the magazine to his biggest creditor Eugene B. Crowe, the magazine's paper supplier. Crowe brought in a partner with magazine experience, a snappy Princetonian named Eltinge Warner, who had made a smashing success out of the once moribund *Field and Stream* magazine. Something of a sportsman himself and hardly a man of letters, Warner knew that he would have to find an editor to save the magazine, but the matter was not immediately settled. What finally did happen came about under peculiar and fortuitous circumstances.

During the fateful summer of 1914, with Sarajevo and the outbreak of hostilities commanding all the world's headlines, George Jean Nathan had taken a short trip to Europe. He was returning on the S. S. *Imperator*, when he had a chance encounter that would affect for all time the destiny of the *Smart Set*. By strange coincidence, on board the same ship was Eltinge Warner, also returning from a short holiday. The two had not met, and Warner was unaware of the talents and characteristics of his drama critic. On the next to the last day before arriving in New York the two walked on deck, having donned their top coats against a brisk wind. The coats were nearly identical, and a brief discussion between the two revealed that both coats were from the same London tailor who had promised exclusivity. The two men adjourned to the bar to toast their deceitful tailor and discovered that they got along marvelously. Accordingly, when Eltinge Warner got back to New York, with the problem of finding an editor for his new magazine a pressing consideration, he decided to look up his shipboard drinking companion Nathan in his suite at the Hotel Royalton—the suite that was Nathan's residence until his death in 1958. Would Nathan consider being editor of the *Smart Set*? Yes, he would, provided Mencken were brought on as co-editor. When the deal was finally struck, Mencken and Nathan also came in as part-owners, each taking a one-sixth interest in the company in lieu of salary—this until the massive backlog of debts was paid off. Mencken and Nathan were immediately upbeat about this arrangement, even though, as things turned out, they would see no income for many months. They were especially delighted because they felt that Warner would be a good-natured and supportive boss, but, most importantly, because he had firmly promised autonomy to his editors, that is, a separation of business and editorial functions.

All of this harmony in the beginning could not conceal the truth to all of the partners that the magazine was in a very perilous condition in 1914. Circulation had fallen to a mere forty thousand; Thayer's old debts (some of them going back to the time of Col. Mann) were staggering. With war fears rampant in the land, new advertisers were reluctant to take a gamble on a shaky magazine enterprise. Mencken, Nathan and Warner pitched in, however, the first goal being to drastically slash operating expenditures. At Warner's suggestion the first major austerity move was to give up the magazine's plush "editorial chambers" on Fifth Avenue where the Colonel's once lavish furniture had now become threadbare and seedy. The whole editorial operation was moved into a little two-room suite adjoining Warner's *Field and Stream* offices at 458 Fourth Avenue. There were no assistant editors, now, only a secretary-receptionist. Mencken and Nathan were to be the whole operation. Actually not a great deal of room was needed for these two live-wire editors: Nathan usually came in only two or three days a week (when he was not on one of his many jaunts abroad), and Mencken usually came up from Baltimore only one week a month. Accordingly, with limited time at their disposal, and with both editors despising meetings and group decision making, submissions were disposed of with alarming rapidity—perhaps faster than on any other magazine before or since.

And there were other economies. For the time being, the number of pages of each issue was cut back from 160 to 144. Cheaper paper was used in printing, a factor that would doubtless work against the magazine a decade or so later when it would be absolutely essential for a smart magazine to also be "slick." In going through the warehouse stock of back issues, Warner came up with the clever idea of taking some of the returned stock and binding up two separate issues under a fresh cover and creating a new magazine called *Clever Stories*, selling these for ten cents, mostly on trains and out-of-town newsstands. This venture was successful enough that a short time later Mencken and Nathan were inspired to start another auxilliary magazine, perhaps inspired by Col. Mann's lowly old *Snappy Stories*. Taking advantage of a current infatuation for all things French in 1915, including the ever-persistent American belief that French stories are invariably "naughty," the pair began another sideline venture called *Parisienne*, the title being what Mencken called "boob bait." This poor relation was able to take advantage of the *Smart Set*'s French connections, but occasionally it was also used to siphon off some of the *Smart Set*'s inferior manuscripts, which otherwise would have been hastily rejected. *Parisienne* was so successful that eventually it outstripped the *Smart Set* in sales. Truth to tell, there was never really much that was "naughty" about the magazine, although occasionally it came afoul of the law. Generally the articles were lightly satirical and some of the stories were faintly suggestive or tinged with eroticism—all to a degree that would be regarded as harmless today. The magazine was strictly Mencken's and Nathan's sideline enterprise, and they edited it *sub rosa*, scarcely admitting the activity to their close friends. Mencken took a sophomoric delight in the magazine, calling it "junk," but in a few years he and Nathan tired of the business side of the thing and sold the magazine at a very handsome profit to Warner and Crowe.

Shortly thereafter, buoyed by this success, Mencken and Nathan established another cheap vest-pocket confection called *Black Mask*, a mystery magazine. This, too, became an instant success, although Mencken and Nathan tired of it swiftly. Eventually, this magazine was also sold to Warner and Crowe. The latter, Eugene Crowe, a wealthy printing magnate, was an elderly man nearing the end of his life but he had taken a great fancy to his ebullient young editors; accordingly he gave them an especially generous price, which relieved both Mencken and Nathan "from want permanently." During the dark years of the depression, when his productivity was at a low ebb, Mencken had reason to be grateful for, even as he chuckled over, the "louse magazines" that he and Nathan had put together in their spare time during World War I.

Meanwhile, though, the *Smart Set* itself was becoming once again a good magazine. In a few years, in spite of its drastic economies, in spite of the fact that the circulation never matched that of the early days, the *Smart Set* would achieve a lofty eminence in American cultural history. In spite of the fact that Nathan and Mencken were nursing their own careers and could give the *Smart Set* only a portion of their energies, they were a superlative editorial team, dedicated to encouraging young writers and offering their readers the best material they could obtain. They were worthy and able successors to the mantle of Willard Huntington Wright, trying to follow assiduously the paths he had laid down, without falling into those dangerous excesses that doubtless would have pushed the magazine out of the commercial category and into the parched no man's land of the "little magazine," or, at best, into a somewhat antic imitation of *Atlantic*.

Of course Mencken and Nathan wanted to keep up Wright's search for good unconventional writing, and they continued Wright's practice of encouraging new writers from Europe. Making use of their contacts abroad and corresponding with authors who took their fancy, they managed, even during their fallow years, to rope in such figures as Lord Dunsany, Conrad, Anatole France, Max Beerbohm, George Moore and James Joyce. (Joyce was "discovered" by another favored contributor to the *Smart Set*, Ezra Pound, who sent in a number of Joyce's "Dubliner" stories, two of which appeared in the May 1915 number.)

Burdened by the *Smart Set*'s pinchpenny schedule of rates, there was a limit to the number of first-rate contributors Mencken and Nathan could bring in. Still, over the years they did manage to lay hands on some extremely valuable literary properties. In the early twenties, for example, they captured Somerset Maugham's story "Miss Thompson," perhaps the British author's most memorable story and later the basis of two legendary films. Maugham was already rich and famous and would ordinarily have surrendered nothing at the *Smart Set*'s dismal rates. But one day Maugham's American agent dumped the manuscript in Nathan's lap over lunch at the Royalton Hotel, explaining that because of its unsettling moral message none of the big New York editors would take a chance on it. The *Smart Set* immediately bought the story, paying twenty-five dollars, but Nathan agreed to let the word go around that an exception had been made for Maugham and that two hundred dollars had been paid in this instance. Every issue of the magazine in which the story appeared was sold out almost immediately.

Needless to say, Mencken and Nathan did all that they could to encourage the magazine's old standbys. They would continue to run contributions, all inadequately rewarded, by Dreiser, Willa Cather, James Branch Cabell and Stephen Vincent Benét. Some of these complained vociferously about their shabby treatment from the treasurer's office, and the editors often had a difficult time smoothing things over. Dreiser, for example, had lost his job as the editor-in-chief of the Butterick magazines over a sexual indiscretion, and was going it alone in Greenwich Village without very much in the cookpot. He complained loudly about the payments, and also about the magazine's frivolity. On the other hand, he had every reason to be grateful that his old friend Mencken would pay anything at all for some of his free verse and early plays, most of which were unsalable at any price.

Quite clearly, the "new" *Smart Set*, like that of the very early years, was determined to discover young and vigorous writing by unknown American authors. Shortly after taking the helm, Mencken and Nathan let it be known in the editorial fraternity and to the magazine's readers that the *Smart Set* was once again hoping to spark all the "literary bucks and wenches" in the land. And, true to their word, in the very first issue under their direction, they published a short story, "Barbara on the Beach," by twenty-two year-old Vassar student Edna St. Vincent Millay, as yet completely unknown either for her lyrical verse or her bohemian lifestyle.

What gave the magazine a renewed vigor and appeal, apparently, was not mainly an influx of young writers, but the force and personality of the two new editors. They completely dominated the magazine with their style, with their enthusiasms and prejudices. Both appeared monthly in the back of the magazine, Nathan's drama section always coming next to last and Mencken's review of books at the very last. It was said in Baltimore that many readers of the *Sun* turned to Mencken's "Free Lance" column before they read anything else in the paper, even the headlines. So it was, too, with the *Smart Set*. Readers would regularly turn to the back so that they could see what applecarts Mencken would upset this month, what icons would be smashed, what Victorian stuffed shirts would be punctured. His sparkling literary style was high-class entertainment by itself.

Nathan's prose style was more restrained, but similarly polished. In a sense, Nathan was the perfect editor for a magazine that aimed at city sophisticates and at the literate and educated upper classes. His regular writing was as jaunty and playful as Mencken's, but it also had a measured quality, a kind of aloofness, a powdered elegance that could fit quite nicely into the atmosphere of salons. Mencken's style had something of the flavor of a street fighter, Nathan's, although equally pungent, could also have a kind of patrician restraint and even sometimes philosophical world weariness more European than American in nature. Here, and perhaps typical of Nathan's regular contributions to the *Smart Set*, are some "Undeveloped Notes," which appeared in the magazine's number for September 1922:

Criticism is the art of appraising others at one's own value.

Great drama is the souvenir of the adventure of a master along the pieces of his own soul.

Art states what we know in terms of what we hope.

In the baggage of three immigrants, German, Russian and Polish, who were recently detained at Ellis Island, there was found respectively (1) a copy of Hauptmann's latest play, (2) a novel by Gogol, and (3) Paderewski's "Legende No. 2" for pianoforte. The taste of the last three Presidents of the United States has been respectively (1) for golf, (2) for Keith vaudeville, and (3) for Griffith moving pictures.

The useless always has an irresistible appeal for me; that is why I devote myself to dramatic criticism, perhaps the most useless thing in the world. I have an unconquerable fondness for the purposeless luxuries of life, the things that are not practical, the little circuses of the soul and heart and taste and fancy that make for the merriment and pleasure of the race if not for its improvement and salvation. Years ago, in my nonage, I said to myself: "What is the pleasantest and most useless thing to which you may devote your life?" After considerable deliberation I concluded and replied to myself, "Dramatic criticism"; and I have since followed, and profitably, my own advice. For centuries men have written criticism of the drama in an effort to improve it, and with it the public taste. What has been the result? The "Frogs" of Aristophanes, written 405 years before Christ, has never been bettered in any way for dramatic satire; the "Iphigenia" of Euripides, written 425 years before Christ, in any way for profoundly moving drama; or the "Oedipus Rex" of Sophocles, written 440 years before Christ, in any way for stirring melodrama. The imperishable romantic drama of Shakespeare fingers its nose at all the dramatic criticism written before its time, or since. And in the matter of improved public taste the most widely successful play in the civilized world in this Year of our Lord 1922 is a crook mystery play by Avery Hopwood and Mary Roberts Rinehart called "The Bat."

Criticism should be written not for the dramatist, the actor, the producer or the public, but largely for itself alone. Generically an art out of an art, it achieves authenticity as an artistic entity in the degree that it weans itself from its sire and stands upon its own legs. In this way and in this degree was Horace a greater artist-critic than Aristarchus, Cervantes a greater than Molina, Sir Philip Sidney a greater than Ben Johnson, Dryden a greater than Addison, Goethe a greater than Lessing, Voltaire a greater than Diderot or Beaumarchais, Zola a greater than Hugo, Dumas *fils* or Sarcey, Coleridge a greater than Hazlitt — and is Walkley a greater than William Archer.

There is a type of critic that vaguely believes there is something about a pretty woman that prevents her from being as capable an actress as a homely one.

The old critics live in the past. The young critics live in the present. The theatre lives in the future.

There is probably not a single educated, civilized and tasteful man in all America who, though richly appreciating the mediocrity of "Uncle Tom's Cabin," hasn't gone to the theatre at one time or another in his life to see it acted. Than this, I can think of no better and no more convincing illustration of the spell of the theatre.

Art is not the meal of life; it is the appetizer. Only poseurs regard it as the former. Life without art would be indeed dull and tasteless, but life with art only would be sickening in its surfeit. There are other things in life than art, and some of them are equally beautiful, equally inspiring, and vastly more contributive to the health and happiness of the human soul.

A dramatic actress should be shot as soon as she begins to get fat.

Satire is unpopular and unsuccessful in the theatre not because the public cannot comprehend it, but precisely because the public can comprehend it. What the public cannot comprehend very often proves a success in the theatre. Witness, recently, Andreyev's "He Who Gets Slapped," which not only the general public but the professional critics themselves, including myself, could not understand. Satire is unpopular simply because it is founded upon popularity. If it isn't unpopular, it isn't satire. Its very life depends upon its unpopular nose-fingering of everything that is popular. Popularity and attendant success are merely targets for its custard pies, each one of which contains a slice of brick.

Art never follows a flag.

Even to the finest dramatic tragedy there is an air of demagoguery that irks me. The tragic dramatist has about him always more or less a trace of the moralist and exhorter.

Drama is literature. But literature is not necessarily drama. This is why good literary critics often prove themselves bad dramatic critics.

Strong hearts are moved most often by the tremours of weak ones. We are touched not by dramatists who have dominated their emotions, but by those whose emotions have dominated them.

The drama may be realistic in almost every department save that of love, which is commonly held to be the field of its most realistic endeavour. If the average love-making scene out of life were to be placed on the stage word for word, gurgle for gurgle, and gesture for gesture, the audience would, after a few preliminary sardonic yawns, go soundly to sleep.

The two editors dominated the magazine through their selection of all the entries, but, more important, they contributed regularly to all parts of the magazine, never limiting themselves to the back pages. Indeed in astringent times (and this was nearly always at the *Smart Set*), they wrote a great deal of the magazine themselves—sometimes as much as half of an issue, as Mencken explained to one of his later biographers.

Often they wrote so much in fact that they had to use pen names for some of their contributions. Mencken alone must have employed at least a dozen aliases over the years. Among his *noms de plume* in the *Smart Set* were: Herbert Winslow Archer, Pierre d'Aubigny, William Fink, James P. Ratcliff, Ph.D.—Mencken could never resist the temptation of joshing those who held academic or honorary degrees—and George Weems Peregoy. One of his favorites was the Duchess of Boileau (surely this would have been a delight to old Col. William D'Alton Mann). Since Mencken's prose style was so forceful and distinctive it is unlikely that regular intelligent readers were fooled by these aliases.

The best-remembered alias in the *Smart Set*, and a regular "contributor" for many years, was Owen Hatteras, a name used by both Mencken and Nathan. The Hatteras persona went back to the time of Willard Huntington Wright, who had approved the hoax as a way of allowing Mencken and Nathan to contribute anonymously to a column entitled "Pertinent & Impertinent," which contained some of their most trenchant and barbed criticisms of American life and culture. This alias, apparently, was selected by Nathan, who thought that the name of the windswept North Carolina cape would be suitable for an author who was a blustery and mercurial character. During World War I Hatteras became Major Owen Hatteras, and his alleged patriotism was perhaps Mencken's and Nathan's only contribution to the war effort.

Unfortunately, in the nature of the collaboration between the strong-minded editors and a few other authors who wrote occasionally under the name, Owen Hatteras never became a distinct and memorable character himself like Finley Peter Dunne's Mr. Dooley. Nonetheless he received a good deal of fan mail and invitations to lecture or to dine, and keeping up the hoax to the last, either Mencken or Nathan would send his regrets, the most usual excuse being an acute case of dyspepsia. And not confining his talents to the *Smart Set*, in 1916 Hatteras wrote a dual mock biography of Mencken and Nathan, *Pistols for Two*. This book gave him literary immortality of sorts because it earned the patriotic Major a card in the catalogue of the Library of Congress (the librarians helpfully establishing his date of birth as 1862).

By 1916 or 1917 both Mencken and Nathan were famous literary figures, known throughout the land. Not that the *Smart Set* was now a smashing success—it continued to limp along just barely making a profit. But the magazine was known and cherished by the elite and by a wholly new generation of American writers who were delighted to find themselves petted and fawned over by the two best-known literary lions in the land. A great deal of the notoriety of this engaging duo can probably be ascribed to their broader literary wanderings, and not merely to their editorship of the *Smart Set*. The two were writing books of their own that would attract widespread readership, but they were, more importantly, protectors and encouragers of all their young literary friends and acquaintances. Never ones merely to reject or accept stories or articles in a cold or mechanical manner, they wrote extensive critiques, offered helpful suggestions, rejected things in humorous, kindly and witty ways. They wrote their authors, took them to lunch, even made love to lady poets when necessary. On one occasion Mencken took the subway out to the Sheepshead Bay section of Brooklyn where he endeavored to inculcate higher literary values in a young Polish immigrant girl whose father ran a seafood restaurant and gambling casino. The young lady, who had submitted some stories under the pen name "Lilith Benda," really only wanted the chance to work her wiles on one of the two dashing bachelor editors. (On returning to New York, Mencken fired off an uproarious memo to Nathan suggesting that it might be necessary henceforth to better husband their editorial talents. The literary wenches were great fun, but there were now too many of them and they were about to break the bank.)

Most important, Mencken and Nathan stood up for what they believed in. In his book review pages Mencken praised the young American authors who took his fancy with loud whoops of praise. He was never afraid to bloody the noses and box the ears of the literary establishment—of pedants, prophets, sellers of conventional literary wares, bluenoses and puritans of any stripe (puritanism in Mencken's vocabulary was any standardized or mummified habit of mind, any attempt to protect the enlightened minority from what was new and unsettling). In 1916 Mencken began a battle royal with the New York Society for the Suppression of Vice and its chief, John Sumner, who had taken legal action against Dreiser's latest novel *The "Genius."* Mencken hadn't particularly liked *The "Genius,"* felt it wasn't up to Dreiser's best work, but he went to bat for it anyway. Believing that Dreiser was one of the great American novelists, Mencken continued to accept stories, plays and (gasp!) poems from Dreiser, even when Dreiser was exercising talents he did not possess and would never possess.

Similarly, Mencken brought to national prominence a long-time *Smart Set* contributor, James Branch Cabell, whose works had always been enjoyed by a few but never captured a large national audience. In July 1918 the *Smart Set* published a story entitled, "Some Ladies and Jurgen," which Mencken suggested be expanded into a novel. When the novel *Jurgen* appeared in the early twenties and was lucky enough to be banned in Boston, Mencken raised the kind of an uproar guaranteed to make Cabell a literary celebrity, a distinction that had previously eluded him. Of course Mencken and Nathan could not have built their reputations as the brash twins of modern letters without also collecting a number of enemies along the way. Mencken, particularly, received more than his share of hostility and went into a kind of temporary eclipse during World War I for his seeming pro-

German outlook. Too, Mencken had irritated many influential people, including Stuart Pratt Sherman, an English professor at the University of Illinois, who had written an article entitled "The Barbaric Naturalism of Theodore Dreiser." Throughout the 1920s, Mencken continued to rail against Sherman and some of his very influential academic allies, especially Paul Elmer More at Princeton and Irving Babbitt at Harvard. And there were not a few others who believed that the literary Katzenjammer kids at the *Smart Set* were little more than very clever, but superficial, sophomores.

Some occasionally went after the *Smart Set* and its bosses more jocularly, but still with impact, suggesting that they represented too great a concentration of power in one place. That two such young men should be arbitrators of the national taste rankled in the breasts of many. In a charming parody of Eugene Field's "Wynken, Blynken and Nod," Berton Braley spoofed Mencken's and Nathan's claims of omnipotence:

There were three that sailed away one night
Far from the madding throng;
And two of the three were always right
And everyone else was wrong.
But they took another along these two,
To bear them company,
For he was the only One ever knew
Why the other two should Be.
And so they sailed away, these three—
            Mencken
            Nathan
            And God.

And the two they talked of the aims of Art
Which they alone understood;
And they quite agreed from the very start
That nothing was any good
Except some novels that Dreiser wrote
And some plays from Germany.
When God objected—they rocked the boat
And dropped him into the sea,
"For you have no critical facultee,"
            Said Mencken
            And Nathan
            To God.

The two came cheerfully sailing home
Over the surging tide
And trod once more their native loam
Wholly self-satisfied.
And the little group that calls them great
Welcomed them fawningly.
Though why the rest of us tolerate
This precious pair must be
Something nobody else can see
    But Mencken
    Nathan
    And God.

This was a minority report, of course, and as the decade of the 1920s dawned, the influence of the *Smart Set* and its two editors was stronger than ever. Now the nation itself was ripe for high jinks, for boisterous fun and good times. America was ready, it seemed, for the very sorts of things Mencken and Nathan had been dishing out for years. It was also an age of dark reflection and cynicism under the surface, and by a curious irony in a mere three years Mencken and Nathan would turn their backs on their charming and ever-amusing magazine that seemed so perfectly suited to this confident and uproarious decade. They would turn their talents to a new magazine wholly of their own invention, leaving the *Smart Set* to trail off into the annals of history.

But when the decade of the 1920s began, Mencken and Nathan were still in high fettle. Circulation still lagged and income continued to be disappointing, but the two editors were relishing the rewards and perquisites of their literary power and celebrity. They had learned the art of putting together a monthly magazine with efficiency and dispatch, devoting not more than a few days a month to their chores, yet making decisions that were thorough, well considered, highly professional.

All the usual editorial routines had been settled years before, neither of the chiefs having to come to the office to handle run-of-the-mill chores. Most of these were taken care of by the magazine's only full-time employee, Miss Sara Golde, a frighteningly efficient subway-riding secretary from Brooklyn who protected the editor's inner sanctum, shooed away phony poets and gave the brush-off to pesky literary agents.

After 1918 the *Smart Set* offices had been at 25 W. 45th Street, and consisted of one inner and one outer office. The outer office was a splendid microcosm of the magazine's mood and substance; at least it was an accurate rendering of the fey tastes of H. L. Mencken and George Jean Nathan. In the outer office Miss Golde held forth with a forbidding dignity seemingly out of character with the ambience of the place, but in case there was any doubt that visitors were in the home of the *Smart Set*, the walls were covered with copies of past covers of the magazines with clever designs by James Montgomer Flagg and John Held, Jr. Visitors sat on a polished golden-oak church pew, and on a nearby table were copies of numerous publications coming from Eltinge Warner's magazine mill. Mencken loved to lay out trade journals of undertaker's and plumber's suppliers for the enjoyment or annoyance of his visitors.

Ready to hand were a series of leaflets entitled "Suggestions to Our Visitors," containing "house rules" for authors visiting the office. Among the choice items were: "Visitors are kindly requested to refrain from expectorating out of the windows. . . ." "A woman Secretary is in attendance at all interviews between the Editors, or either of them, and lady authors. Hence it will be unnecessary for such visitors to provide themselves with either duennas or police whistles. . . ." "The objects of art on display in the editorial galleries are not for sale."

The inner office of the magazine was, if anything, still more waggish. The desks of the editors were surrounded by pictures of toothsome creatures, a French temperance placard, a streaming banner proclaiming "God Bless Our President," "personally autographed" pictures of Nietzsche, Beethoven and Bismark. The room also contained such objets d'art as a table made from a cemetary slab, a tea cozy woven from hundreds of cigar bands, a hideous claw-foot gilt chair over which was thrown a tapestry showing a baby being rescued by a Newfoundland dog. Mencken kept two oversized brass cuspidors and Nathan assaulted the eye with a vase of blue cornflowers. If the decor exhibited a kind of forced cleverness, it was also an adequate expression of the editors' desire to hector the sensibilities of American middle-class culture.

The growing fame of Mencken and Nathan during their last years on the *Smart Set* brought an increasing number of first-rate contributors to the magazine, this in spite of the company's dismal pay scale. The editors were especially gifted at uncovering good short stories, and a great many excellent stories appeared in the years between 1918 and 1923. Sherwood Anderson's "I Want to Know Why" appeared in the November 1919 number. Willa Cather's "Coming, Eden Bower!" appeared in August 1920. Ruth

Suckow (a personal Mencken discovery) contributed "A Homecoming" in November 1921, and "The Best of the Lot" a year later. Stephen Vincent Benét's "Summer Thunder" appeared in September 1920.

Probably the most important new talent discovered in this period was F. Scott Fitzgerald. Fitzgerald, just back from the army, with few prospects and desperately courting the beautiful Southern belle Zelda Sayre, found himself churning out streetcar ads during the day while writing stories in the evenings in a miserable apartment up on Claremont Avenue. He had collected enough rejection slips to stuff a mattress when, in June 1919, he sent off a story, "Babes in the Woods," to the *Smart Set*. Within a week he received a check for thirty dollars, and his first contribution to a major magazine duly appeared in September. Fitzgerald did not forget his gratitude to the *Smart Set*—his "The Diamond as Big as the Ritz" appeared in September 1919—even though his career quickly took off on its meteoric track almost immediately after his first *Smart Set* appearance.

Neither Mencken nor Nathan considered himself a great admirer of poetry, and both were decidedly suspicious of the "extravagances of the free verse movement"; the magazine nonetheless ran a lot of very good poetry during their tenure. Among the poets published during this period were: Sara Teasdale, Robinson Jeffers, Louis Untermeyer, Ezra Pound, Elinor Wylie, Edna St. Vincent Millay, Maxwell Bodenheim, Zoë Akins and Lizette Woodworth Reese.

And naturally, under Nathan's influence, modern dramatists made regular contributions to the magazine. Nathan became an early and life-long supporter of Eugene O'Neill, who shortly after stepping out of George Pierce Baker's drama workshop at Harvard and identifying himself with the Provincetown Players, began submitting his plays for publication. Nathan immediately accepted *The Long Voyage Home* for the October 1917 issue, and this was soon followed by several other O'Neill one-act plays. Drama, of course, was a regular feature of the *Smart Set* (it would be hard to imagine such a thing in a general magazine today), and a great many playwrights made their appearance under Mencken and Nathan including Lord Dunsany, Djuna Barnes and George M. Cohan.

To be sure, month in and month out what kept the *Smart Set* alive, what gave it its sparkle were the regular critical articles of the two editors. These readable, charming, opinionated, often pugnacious pieces not only provided the magazine's vitality, they somehow provided the mucilage that held everything together and drew in readers from around the country.

By 1923, however, the editors, after nearly ten years at the helm, were getting tired of the *Smart Set*. Mencken, particularly, had often expressed dissatisfaction with the magazine's cheap paper, its low production qualities and even its frivolous image. Circulation sank below 25,000, hardly a respectable figure for a commercial magazine. Mencken and Nathan also weren't getting along with Eltinge Warner over editorial policy. There were some especially harsh words over a piece that Mencken wanted to run about the death of President Harding that Warner considered in bad taste. Mainly, though, the magazine's key problem was that it hadn't kept up with the times. In an age of affluence magazines were supposed to look glamorous, and the *Smart Set* still looked like a glorified pulp magazine for all of its cleverness and inner sophistication.

Accordingly, Mencken and Nathan quietly laid plans to start their own magazine—the *American Mercury* it was to be called—a magazine of greater substance and, they hoped, wider appeal. Before making their move they had, with the help of the aggressive young publisher Alfred A. Knopf, attempted to buy the *Smart Set* from Warner, but without success. Shortly thereafter plans moved forward for Mencken and Nathan to withdraw, sell their interests to Warner, and begin preparations for the *Mercury*. The December 1923 issue of the *Smart Set* was their last. Honest to themselves, Mencken and Nathan conceded that something in them had died when they abandoned the *Smart Set*. They carried over to the *Mercury* much of what they believed to be the best from the *Smart Set*, and a great deal of the new magazine mirrored the old, in mood and style if not format and outward appearance. Too, in his valedictory Mencken admitted that the pulpy old *Smart Set* had been good to him over the years, and had been a splendid outlet for his own literary productivity. "I have composed and printed no less than 182 book articles—in all, more than 900,000 words of criticism," he confessed. "An appalling dose certainly. How many books have I reviewed, noticed, praised, mocked, dismissed with lofty sneers? I don't know precisely, but probably fully 2,000." No such sterling promise of immortality would ever come his way again.

The departure of Mencken and Nathan tolled the death knell of the *Smart Set* as a magazine of civilized worth. Its last years were a disgrace to the historical image of the magazine, although not immediately to the balance sheets. With Mencken and Nathan gone, Eltinge Warner decided to take policy command, determining to thrust the magazine immediately into the bowels of commercialism. A young newspaperman named Morris Gilbert was brought in as editor and he was instructed to make the magazine over into what Mencken surely would have called boob-thumping inanity. The price was slashed to twenty-five cents, the cover was redesigned and given over to come-hither pictures of flappers. The insides were hollowed out and replaced with sensational fiction, mostly of the sex and "true story" variety. Circulation did rise, and quickly, and so did advertising revenues, but the heart and soul had been torn from the magazine.

In a few months the magazine was sufficiently healthy that Warner was able to grandly negotiate its sale to the Hearst Corporation, after which, under a succession of editors, it wallowed even further in the depths of lurid commercialism. At least this new and completely different *Smart Set* was a money-maker, something it had never been before. Containing a noxious mixture of the folksy (verse by Edgar Guest, inspirational pieces by Rev. Frank Crane) and the lurid (stories and articles such as, "Is One Wife Enough?" "Gypsy Love," and "Buying Beauty at $22. a Week"), the circulation rose eventually as high as 350,000, a figure never even remotely approached by the *Smart Set* of old. Advertising was cheap and tawdry— but plentiful. The magazine was neither slick nor smart. Ruefully observing the magazine's slide into oblivion, H. L. Mencken summed up its newly discovered commercial success with his usual deft precision: "Nobody ever went broke underestimating the taste of the American people."

There was one last chapter—only a coda really—to the magazine's sad decline. In 1928 Hearst sold the magazine to James R. Quirk, who merged it with another once-great magazine, *McClure's*, which had also sunk into a state of dilapidated commercialism. The decision was to make this new product into a magazine for young women, containing inspirational pieces, practical information and wholesome stories for well-bred young ladies. But the depression was now hard upon the land, and there was a general shakeout in the magazine industry. It was just too late for yet another obscene manhandling of the magazine's formula. The *Smart Set* died with the issue of July 1930; its name has never been revived.

If the *Smart Set* is mostly forgotten today, the past issues of its prime years remain a monument to a buoyant and self-confident era in American history, a time when art and literature could be seen as good fun intended to provide edification and enjoyment to the general public. If the *Smart Set*'s name did not survive, if its persona was not taken up by any succeeding magazine, much of the verve and splendor of its best years infected several generations of American writers and a small cadre of editors and publishers who would create other magazines dedicated to smartness, to an eliteness that was also playful and uninhibited. Without the leadership provided by magazines such as the *Smart Set*, and by the simpler frivolities of *Life* and

Judge, Americans of our own time may well have been deprived of the triumphs of the *New Yorker*, and other magazines that prove that we are not only a hard-nosed practical folk, but also a folk who know how to play around with the world and to do so in high style.

· 5 ·

Frank Crowninshield's
Vanity Fair

The *Smart Set* had provided plenty of good fun for
Mencken and Nathan, and it had been an invigorating
and happy outlet for the talents of innumerable young
writers. It had been a vehicle for many who were fighting social inertia and the last vestiges of Victorianism in
America. It had served the cause of sophisticated liter-
acy for two decades. It had bucked the mainstream. It had been
the leading iconoclastic publication of its day. But the *Smart Set*
had always been a marginal publication financially, and even before 1920 it had been fighting an uphill battle in the marketplace
if not in the affection of its readers. By the early 1920s, Mencken
and Nathan had no choice but to let it go, since the magazine's
principal financial backers were unwilling to banish its old-fashioned format, its cheap paper, its poor printing. Even before the
twenties it was apparent that smart magazines, to survive, must

have the high-quality finish and gloss of the best mass-circulation magazines, and, if anything, surpass those popular magazines in appearance, aesthetic appeal, and editorial polish.

And even as Mencken and Nathan were taking over the *Smart Set* as joint editors in 1914, a very appealing competitor was appearing on the scene. It was *Vanity Fair*, owned by Condé Nast, publisher and recent innovator of the enormously successful *Vogue*, and edited by a remarkably witty, dapper and clever man-about-town named Frank Crowninshield. *Vanity Fair* would become, within a very few years of its birth, a splendid magazine in every sense of the word. Cleveland Amory, who put together an attractive anthology of the magazine a quarter century after its demise, declared *Vanity Fair* to have been the best of all American magazines, an evaluation that may seem unnecessarily extravagant, but certainly very far from preposterous. If it was not the best, *Vanity Fair*, in its days of grace, had few equals and probably no betters.

Vanity Fair was from the very start something that the *Smart Set* had never been: it was slick as well as smart. Expensively produced, on high-quality paper stock, it was as appealing to the eye as it was to the tastes of its intended readers. On the other hand it was never slick through to its heart; it was never a mere frivolity intended for the idle classes; it always had substance and it always had guts. Within the past decade, Condé Nast Publications, Inc., has brought back *Vanity Fair*, rich and gaudily redesigned, but little was there of the original magazine, which had died in 1936. The new *Vanity Fair* is just another fancy-looking magazine. The revived format looks good, it has visual appeal, it uses all the newly discovered tricks of advertising and print technology: its only fault is that it is just one of many slick-paper magazines that anybody can lay hands on in the supermarket. The old *Vanity Fair*, at its best, was something real and alive, something with an actual soul.

What was it about the old *Vanity Fair*, the real *Vanity Fair*, that gave it its distinction? Well, its charm was somehow genuine and indisputable. Maybe that charm was related to the time of the magazine's reign, a time of supreme self-confidence and even euphoria among the American people, a time when things were what they were supposed to be, a time when high-varnish trains like the "Twentieth Century Limited" ran on time—to the minute. *Vanity Fair* is reminiscent of real forged-steel penknives, of pencil erasers that actually erase, of sturdy children's toys that don't fall apart on Christmas morn. It is reminiscent of precision-made automobiles, like the Pierce Arrow—the manufacturer of which naturally took advertisements in

*Col. William D'Alton Mann,
founder of the* Smart Set, *moved
from a shadowy Victorian
demimonde to respectable
magazine publisher.*

Early Smart Set *editor Charles
Hanson Towne, a man of unerring
taste, went on to a long career in
New York publishing.*

The Magazine of Fifth Avenue

The Smart Set

A Magazine of Cleverness

George Jean Nathan and H. L. Mencken, the two bad boys of American letters, hoped to open up the Smart Set *to "the nation's literary bucks and wenches."*

OPPOSITE. *There was a naughtiness and a piquancy to the early* Smart Set, *but top-rate editing and writing made it a quality magazine.*

The cosmopolitan air and impeccable taste of Frank Crowninshield made Vanity Fair *a great magazine.*

BELOW. *The ads of the smart magazines always appealed to the carriage trade—even when carriages became horseless.*

OPPOSITE. Vanity Fair's *in-house artists imparted to the magazine much of its fey, highly stylized quality.*

DANIELS

Town Brougham

The new DANIELS motor—8-cylinder, V type and unique in design—has now been tried out for two years and is just as individual in design as is the body of the car. The angle of the cylinders—being less than 90°—assures smoothness, speed and heavy pulling power.

At the Salon Hotel Commodore, New York Nov. 27th to Dec. 3rd 1921

Specialists in Coachwork   *Makers of Daniels Eight*

DANIELS MOTOR COMPANY, READING, PA.

Vanity Fair's *mixture of popular art and the avant garde eased America out of Victorianism and into the twentieth century.*

Edmund Wilson's best talents could not have developed in his Vanity Fair *days, but he was a major force on the* New Yorker *in the forties.*

Another important writer who cut his teeth on Vanity Fair *was Robert E. Sherwood. He went on to edit the old comic* Life.

Clare Boothe Brokaw before her marriage to Henry Luce. She attempted to breathe new life into Vanity Fair *during the depression—but without success.*

The famous roundtable of the
Algonquin Hotel in a drawing by
Al Hirschfeld. There was probably
no greater assemblage of wits in
the American record.

Dorothy Parker's ascerbic wit was a
mixed blessing, her volatility a
nightmare, but none of the smart
magazines would have wanted to be
without her.

OPPOSITE. *Harold Ross, the
former hobo newspaperman who
always knew what he wanted at the
New Yorker — after he saw it.*

Rea Irvin, Harold Ross's elusive art director on the early New Yorker, was responsible for many of the magazine's enduring design features. Two of Irvin's early masthead designs are shown here.

the pages of *Vanity Fair*—an automobile that was made to go when it came out of the shop and did not need to be recalled. *Vanity Fair* never needed to be recalled and it never needed to be oversold—it delivered precisely what its image promised.

Like many American magazines, *Vanity Fair* had already undergone several transformations by the time Frank Crowninshield became its guiding light in 1914. In the 1880s and 1890s a magazine of the same name but of decidedly different personality had made an unsavory reputation for itself as a kind of Broadway roustabout. It was something like the old *Police Gazette*, a kind of peekaboo magazine that, as Crowninshield himself observed, "had never seen the inside of a club or a lady's house." The magazine had subsequently drifted from pillar to post. But the name was clearly an apt one for a magazine purporting to deal with matters of concern to high society. All literate readers in 1914 were likely to have read Thackeray's novel of high society; the especially well read would doubtless have recalled that the title had its origins in John Bunyan's allegory *Pilgrim's Progress*, where "Vanity Fair" was grimly conceived as a fabrication of the devil, a fair in which were sold houses, lands, trades, places, honors, preferments, titles, countries, kingdoms, lusts, pleasures, and delights of all sorts. The devil having been banished in anti-Puritan America, why not have a magazine for all the refined and epicurean pleasures and pastimes of the day? Such a magazine would be the new *Vanity Fair*.

The rebirth of *Vanity Fair* came about under a rather strange set of circumstances. Condé Nast, having made a smashing success of *Vogue* after owning it for only four years, decided to buy up another women's fashion magazine named *Dress*, which he saw as possible competition for *Vogue*. After he bought the magazine from the publishing house of Doubleday, Page & Co., he had two problems on his hands: how to make the magazine different from his own premier fashion magazine, and how to find a better title for the new publication—*Dress* seemed, somehow, awfully silly or simpleminded. Accordingly, for three thousand dollars he bought the name *Vanity Fair* from the company that produced the long-stumbling peekaboo magazine and projected a new publication to be entitled *Dress and Vanity Fair*. The first issue of the magazine under Nast's aegis appeared in September 1913. In this issue and several that followed the magazine contained articles on fashion, music, theatre, and some international news that seemed too specialized for *Vogue*.

Clearly, though, the magazine hadn't found itself, hadn't come into focus. What should be done about it? Nast had a talk with his friend Frank

Crowninshield, a man with a long history of ventures in New York publishing, and asked Crowninshield's opinion of how to get headed in the right direction with this new enterprise. More than eager to be of help, Crowninshield pointed out the magazine's various flaws and then offered his prescription for a remedy. "There is no magazine that is read by people you meet at lunches and dinners. Your magazine should cover the things people talk about at parties—the arts, sports, theatre, humor, and so forth."

Nast, a venturesome and far-seeing businessman, needed little convincing. He readily agreed that this was the way to go. What's more it didn't take him long to realize that in Frank Crowninshield he had found just the man to edit his new magazine. Crowninshield accepted the post with two stipulations: that the word "Dress" be dropped from the title, and that women's fashions be removed from the contents. Both of the stipulations were agreeable to Nast, and Crowninshield began his long term as editor early in 1914. An editorial in the March issue that year gave some idea of his guiding principles:

> *Vanity Fair* has but two major articles in its editorial creed: first, to believe in the progress and promise of American life, and second, to chronicle that progress cheerfully, truthfully, and entertainingly . . . Let us instance one respect in which American life has recently undergone a great change. We allude to its increased devotion to pleasure, to happiness, to dancing, to sport, to the delights of the country, and to all forms of cheerfulness. Now *Vanity Fair* means to be as cheerful as anybody. It will print much humor, it will look at the stage, at the arts, at the world of letters, at sport, and at the highly vitalized, electric, and diversified life of our day from the frankly cheerful angle of the optimist, or, which is much the same thing, from the mock-cheerful angle of the satirist . . . . For women we intend to do something in a noble and missionary spirit, something which, so far as we can observe, has never been done for them by an American magazine. We mean to make frequent appeals to their intellects.

If these words, if the repeated reference to "cheerfulness," suggest that Crowninshield's magazine was to be a thinly veneered essence of Pollyanism for the carriage trade, the actual reality was something altogether different. The magazine was cheerful, and always light of touch, but under Crowninshield's hand the pages were also immediately infused with a seriousness of purpose and a devotion to quality that belied the magazine's allegedly frivolous exterior. *Vanity Fair* also became a sharp reflection of its editor's tastes and interests, and in Frank Crowninshield the magazine had found a man of broad and free-ranging erudition, a man withal cultivated, urbane, witty and charming. It has sometimes been jocularly observed that our best smart magazines have been edited by wildly implausible individuals—one thinks of the boisterous Mencken at the *Smart Set*, or of Harold Ross, the "hobo newspaperman" of the *New Yorker*, Frank Crowninshield was in manner and mien and substance the picture of a smart magazine editor, just as one might have come from the stereotypical imagination of central casting.

Frank Crowninshield was born in Paris in 1872, and spent more than half of his first twenty years living abroad. His father, Frederic Crowninshield, was a Boston-born water colorist and mural painter, who, like so many artists of his generation, felt the need of discovering his inspiration amongst the art galleries, museums, and cathedrals of the old world. He lived on a small inheritance that went back through several generations of New England shipbuilders and merchants tracing themselves to Johannes Kaspar Richter von Kronenscheldt, who had left Leipzig, Germany, in the late seventeenth century after killing a man in a duel. The Crowninshields of Salem and Boston had recently shaken themselves of all garish Yankee traits of getting and spending and had joined the leisured gentry drawn to the worlds of the arts, letters, and the softer side of civilization. They were not disgustingly rich, but gracefully so, and Frank Crowninshield spent nearly all of his adult life as a wage earner, not as a coupon clipper.

At the age of eighteen, after two years studying art at the University of Rome, Frank decided to look for work in New York and thought he might like to try publishing. Bearing a letter from William Dean Howells, a friend of his father's, he paid a visit to Major George Haven Putnam, head of the house of Putnam. When asked what he would like to do he replied that he would like to evaluate manuscripts, meet authors, and generally involve himself in all matters of publication. Major Putnam graciously pointed out that no such position was available because he was presently filling it himself. A week later, however, he wrote Crowninshield a letter offering him a job in the Putnam bookstore at eight dollars a week. Crowninshield took the job, receiving a raise to ten dollars a week after one year. Throughout his life Crowninshield retained a soft spot in his heart for books and the book trade, becoming himself a book collector with an interest in rare books, leather bindings, and hand-marbled endpapers.

Crowninshield stayed with Putnam's for four years, winding up as the Major's personal assistant and general factotum. In 1895 he began his long career in magazine publishing, joining Dodd, Mead and Company as publisher of the *Bookman*. In the years that followed he was an editor of *Met-*

ropolitan Magazine, and of *Munsey's*. In 1912 he became art editor of the *Century Illustrated Monthly Magazine*, a position for which he was eminently qualified. The year before he had acted as an unpaid and unofficial publicity agent for the famous Armory Show, and continued thereafter to be a close observer of the art scene in New York, an avid connoisseur and collector. Before his death in 1947 he had assembled one of the most valuable collections of modern art then in existence, including especially choice samplings of Matisse lithographs and etchings, modern French illustrated books (Picasso, Matisse, Rouault, Derain and others), Bellows prizefight lithographs, African masks and sculptures, all of which if left intact would be worth millions of dollars on today's art market.

Of equal importance to Crowninshield in his position as editor of *Vanity Fair* was his standing in New York society. While not himself born to the super-rich, he was on terms of easy affability with people from all walks of life. A gregarious man, he could have dinner with Mrs. Vanderbilt or Mrs. Astor, but it would offend no one if he also took a show girl or an office secretary to lunch or dinner. If the complaint be made that he was a social climber—and few would have made that complaint—it was clear that he was far from being a snob. He was a democrat, a man who found himself equally well at home with acrobats, keepers of flea circuses, shoe shine boys, shop girls, stage door managers, and the cop on the beat.

Crowninshield was what the British would call in one of their remarkable coinages a "clubbable" man. He seemed to have belonged to more clubs than anyone in New York and somehow managed to visit all of them regularly. The Cavendish and the Stockbridge Golf were his elite clubs, but there were numerous others, including some he had a hand in founding himself such as the Atlantic Beach, West Side Tennis, and Coffee House Clubs. He was especially fond of the last since its appeal was to arty types, to publishers, members of the literati, and just plain good conversationalists. Crowninshield was particularly proud to say of the Coffee House Club, which was his special baby, that it had no rules, no bylaws, no officers, no rigamarole—nothing but the common interests and conviviality of its members.

Claire Boothe, who worked for Crowninshield many years later as managing editor of *Vanity Fair* before marrying Henry Luce and moving on to her career in national politics, probably summed up Crowninshield best when she remarked: "Crownie is the last and probably the greatest of a species, which is rapidly disappearing all over the world, known as the gentleman." And, yes, the gentlemanly type had mostly receded on the American shore where more rough-hewn democratic manners were the order of the day; nevertheless Crowninshield's innate kindliness, his smooth manners and polished exterior appealed enormously to everyone who knew him. He was the kind of man who could and would offend no one, the kind of man who if he had to fire a duncey secretary could do so leaving the girl feeling that she was better off than before losing her job

No one appreciated Crowninshield's qualities more than his publisher, Condé Nast. A man from the Midwest who had made a fortune in advertising and established a highly successful dress pattern business before getting into the magazine field. Nast always lacked Crowninshield's polish and social sensibilities. To be sure Nast had his own social resources. He had married a member of the "Four Hundred," he was a millionaire, and he was a highly capable business executive and judge of people—but he freely admitted to himself that he had "the soul of a bookkeeper." He could never match Crowninshield's charisma or his enormous circle of friends and acquaintances. Indeed there is good reason to believe that Nast hired Crowninshield for *Vanity Fair* with spontaneous delight because he saw in the man his own route of entry to the clubs and drawing rooms of the city. The two men became fast friends, and for a while in the early 1920s almost inseperable companions.

As a magazine, *Vanity Fair* did not get off to a running start; it built up its audience and its peculiar style slowly and reached the peak of its popularity only in the 1920s. But it was an attractive and distinctive publication from the beginning. In the early days the magazine had perhaps too strong an aroma of the avant garde to attract the kind of reader that would likely be its most consistent subscriber. Looking back over the early years, Condé Nast recalled Crowninshield's vast enthusiasm for modern art as having been something of an impediment:

> F.C.'s interest in the modern French art movement, at first, did us a certain amount of harm. We were ten years too early (1915) in talking about Van Gogh, Gauguin, Matisse, Picasso, etc.
> At first (1915 to 1925), people took the ground that we were (presumably) insane, and even as late as 1929 and 1930, our readers were still confused by the paintings we reproduced. Our advertising department, too, was greatly concerned because our advertisers . . . thought the paintings distorted, and, as they said, decadent. In time, however, as the movement grew, we derived a very considerable benefit from having published such pictures.

Crowninshield himself was well aware of the problem, and as a strong partisan for modern art admitted that revolutions in art are always more conspicuous than revolutions in literature. He believed that he had been just as assiduous in encouraging the latest trends in literature as he was the latest trends in the visual arts, but the former often passed unnoticed. Whatever the case, Crowninshield never budged one inch on his convictions, never surrendered to the doubts of his advertising department or even his publisher. Accordingly, the pages of *Vanity Fair* were open to new young artists of every stripe—Americans as well as Europeans. Besides the Picassos and Matisses, *Vanity Fair* carried in its pages artists as diverse as Jacob Epstein, Rockwell Kent, Kees van Dongen, Marie Laurencin, Arthur B. Davies and Nicholas Remisoff. Bucking the prevailing view that photography was not an art, Crowninshield willingly opened his pages to the avant-garde photographers. Some of these photographers were even added to the payroll, which later was a source of enormous pride to Crowninshield. *Vanity Fair*, he boasted, employed Baron de Meyer and Edward Steichen "when their work was branded as wild and absurd. They are now the highest paid photographers in the world."

Toward writers Crowninshield had a slightly less paternalistic fervor; yet he was encouraging and supportive of all kinds of writing from the traditional to the experimental. Robert Benchley, who became managing editor of *Vanity Fair* in 1919, claimed that Crowninshield would tolerate any kind of writing at all as long as it was dressed up in evening clothes. True, perhaps, if one does not stretch this to the conclusion that Crowninshield's only fare was veneered sophistication. A playful man, with a wry sense of humor, he liked youthful writers who were themselves playing around with the world, and he could tolerate most manners and forms of eccentricity and unconventionality. Like Mencken and Nathan at the *Smart Set* he set about to corral as many of the "literary bucks and wenches" that he could find.

Accordingly the number of writers discovered by *Vanity Fair* during its heyday is quite startling. Among the younger talents coming into magazine print for the first time were Donald Ogden Stewart, Nancy Hale, Edna St. Vincent Millay (who wrote her lighthearted pieces under the pseudonym Nancy Boyd), Claire Boothe, John Peale Bishop, Edmund Wilson, P. G. Wodehouse, Elinor Wylie, e. e. cummings, Compton Mackenzie, Aldous Huxley. Three young writers about to embark on illustrious careers in the 1920s also served briefly as staffers on the magazine and are deeply embedded in its history. They were Robert Benchley, Dorothy Parker, and Robert E. Sherwood.

The magazine, however, also published a wide variety of other writers already blessed with fame including Ferenc Molnar, F. Scott Fitzgerald,

Alexander Woollcott, Heywood Broun, Paul Gallico, George Jean Nathan, Anita Loos, Roger Fry, and Carl Van Vechten. Like the *Smart Set*, *Vanity Fair* was not a notoriously good payer, but it was a magazine that its writers took to with avidity, the kind of magazine every zestful or up-and-coming author loved to be associated with. Because of its openness of spirit and its experimental style, the magazine attracted some of the most vigorous writing in its day, usually putting to shame the acquisitions of the mass-market magazine giants such as the *Saturday Evening Post*, or *Collier's*.

In spite of its devotion to the avant-garde and often to exotic trends in the arts and literature, *Vanity Fair* found an enthusiastic audience fairly quickly under Crowninshield. As *Dress and Vanity Fair* the magazine had stumbled and lacked direction, but in its new format the magazine had hit the right target. It did not become a mass-circulation leader, of course, because frankly the appeal was to a sophisticated elite. The circulation at no time exceeded 100,000, this figure being attained as the decade of the 1920s began. In the late twenties, and with the coming of the depression, circulation began drifting downward. But the advertising picture was different from the beginning. A general circulation magazine that appealed mostly to well-heeled urbanites was naturally catnip to advertisers who flocked to buy even if they couldn't understand some of the editor's peculiar tastes. By the end of 1915, *Vanity Fair* was first in advertising lineage (although not total revenues) of all monthly periodicals in America—403,219 lines, as opposed to 355,025 for the second-place *System*.

Condé Nast was pleased but mildly dumbfounded by the instantaneous success of this eccentric offspring of his magazine empire. *Vanity Fair* would never replace *Vogue* as the biggest money-maker in the Condé Nast family of magazines (which by 1915 would also include the soon-to-be triumphant *House and Garden*), but in other respects it would be the brightest star in his firmament. *Vogue* was there for people to look at, the flagship of the fashion industry, but yesteryear's issues were always as dead as mutton. *Vanity Fair* was the magazine people talked about, included in their conversations, displayed at their parties. And it had all been accomplished against difficult odds that advertisers and others had warned against. He had produced a successful smart magazine with two editorial principles in mind:

(1) To accomplish it by devoting its entire editorial contents to the restrained, truthful and cultivated treatment of the arts, graces, and humors of American life, thereby strictly limiting its appeal to men and women of known means, and inferred high breeding and high taste; and, (2) to accomplish it without the aid

of the quickest of all circulation builders—fiction: a builder of large circulation, but because of fiction's indiscriminate appeal, a builder whose constant tendency is to dilute "class" circulation.

Above all, though, what seemed to have made *Vanity Fair* so rapidly and so eminently successful is that it mirrored to perfection its time and place. The decade of the 1920s had not yet arrived, but its spirit had already broken over the land by 1915. Already on hand were the Castle Walk, cafe society, cabarets, women's suffrage, the automobile, discussions of Freud and sex. America was poised on the edge of transcendental social change, a shifting of the rudimentary values from rural to urban society. And the mecca of this urban society was, of course, New York, sometimes seen as the great Gommorah by the Babbitts and mugwumps of the land, but by the young as the shining beacon of hope, the place where success and the pleasures of the universe were achieved and dramatized. On the eve of World War I, long before the twenties began to roar, New York had become the cultural showcase of America, and it called out for an organ of its most extravagant yearnings and triumphs. Everybody realized that *Vanity Fair* was that organ. *Vanity Fair* was New York.

The offices of *Vanity Fair* and the other Condé Nast magazines were located at 19 West 44th Street in New York—that part of the city already by 1915 devoted to the sybaritic side of commerce. In the mid-twenties the offices were moved to more spacious and elaborate quarters in the Graybar Building next to Grand Central Station. *Vanity Fair* was separately quartered, never a mere offshoot of the larger *Vogue* operation. The magazine was a highly personal enterprise, always something of a fiefdom of Frank Crowninshield, and not usually interfered with either by Condé Nast himself or any of his money men or advertising overlords.

On the other hand, the ambience of *Vogue* and the general relationships with the Nast circle of magazines overflowed into the *Vanity Fair* quarters. The office was run with much informality, with actresses, models, photographers, writers milling about and moving to and fro. Indeed *Vanity Fair* was generally thought to be the fun, easy-going place to work. *Vogue* was presided over by its very formidable editor Mrs. Edna Woolman Chase, whose remarkable thirty-four year term (1914 to 1948) got under way around the same time that Crowninshield took over at *Vanity Fair*. Mrs. Chase, a grand-duchess type, of far more humble origins than Frank Crowninshield (she was born Edna Alloway in Asbury Park, New Jersey, of Quaker parents), ran a tight ship with very little merriment. She tyrannized models, fashion designers, agents, all who came within her orbit. There was always an uneasy but fragile truce between Mr. Crowninshield and Mrs. Chase: *Vogue* editor regarded Crowninshield as a sophomoric and anarchic bad boy; the easy-going and antic Crowninshield regarded Mrs. Chase as an unbending old tartar, which, if it had not been for her high editorial competence and infallible taste, she might well have been.

There seemed to be no management style at *Vanity Fair*, only style itself. Mrs. Chase and her staff believed that *Vanity Fair* people were frivolous, spending all their time on extended lunch breaks and writing risqué articles. And, yes, extended weekly luncheons at *Vanity Fair* seemed to go on forever; lunches were brought up from the nearby Savarin and invariably consisted of eggs Benedict, kippered herrings, and *café special*. Nothing very much was accomplished at these luncheons, but everyone present seemed to have a hilarious time. It was not, however, the proverbial three-martini lunch; indeed, curiously Frank Crowninshield himself was a lifelong teetotaler who never took so much as a drop to drink. (In his exquisitely mannered way, he never objected to the drinking habits or excesses of others.) Even with *Vogue* models, photographers and their satellites present and enjoying the greater freedom of the *Vanity Fair* enclave, there was always plenty of joshing of "high fashion," which *Vanity Fair* people regarded as silly and offensive. A typical *Vogue* headline, such as "Why not spend your summer under a black sailor?" was always ripe for a *Vanity Fair* parody, or at the very least some unrestrained hilarity in the office.

Crowninsheild was hardly a fussy editor who lingered over copy; articles either won his immediate enthusiasm or they didn't. He seldom indulged in the deftly worded inspiring memos for which Mencken was famous, or the nitpicking critiques of Harold Ross, which for years drove *New Yorker* contributors to their wit's end. He had few long-range plans for the magazine and seldom made any kind of intellectual analysis of its contents. He was pretty good at firing up authors with ideas when they were in his presence and had a reputation for imaginative outpourings on a moment's notice, although such outpourings seldom survived transmission through the mail. Unlike most literary men he was not a loner or isolated worker, and thrived on social intercourse and interchange of ideas. Accordingly, the real work of *Vanity Fair* was carried on at luncheons, in club rooms, even in the drawing rooms of the city's elite.

To Crowninshield, editing a magazine was supposed to be fun. He believed that the magazine should be spun out of play, not the other way around. He did not believe that the editor of a smart magazine was the custodian of a lofty priestcraft, but rather that editing was one activity among others, part of the warp and woof of the everyday life of a clubman and city gentleman. Thus the mood in the *Vanity Fair* offices was always one of easy familiarity, of give and take, of flexibility, of leisured charm.

Crowninshield was a good talent scout when it came to assembling his own staff. Over the years he had some enormously successful writers and artists working as editors or staffers, and these were invariably awarded their positions on the basis of merit, not on the basis of membership in Crowninshield's own social circle. Clearly Crowninshield knew what was going on in the world of magazine and book publishing, and he was an effective stealer of youthful talent. Even *Vogue* was not immune from Crowninshield's raids, one of his most successful finds being Dorothy Parker, shortly to be a famous poet and short-story writer, but virtually unknown when she came to work for *Vanity Fair*.

Dorothy Parker had been working on *Vogue* since 1915, seemingly a strange apprenticeship to those who know her later work. Yet Parker was born to a wealthy New York family; her father J. Henry Rothschild, had been a successful garment manufacturer. Dorothy had attended a snooty girls' school in Morristown, New Jersey, which she found something of a refuge from a cold New York upbringing that had led her to despise her indifferent father and a cruel stepmother. In those days, a society girl was not supposed to go on to college, but to sit around the house until Prince Charming came along. This Dorothy Rothschild refused to do; instead she cut herself loose from her family and took cheap rooms on the upper West Side of Manhattan. As luck would have it, she fell in with a number of literary types in that spartan rooming house, including another soon-to-be humorist, Thorne Smith, who later became extremely popular for his fantastic and often ribald books such as *Night Life of the Gods* and *Topper Takes a Trip*. Precisely how these fledgling writers survived is not clearly known. "There was no money, but Jesus we had fun," Dorothy later recalled.

Dorothy's job on *Vogue* came about in a rather curious way. She had been sending some of her short, witty verses to magazines and a few were accepted by *Vogue*, where Mrs. Chase, recognizing real talent, offered her a staff job at twelve dollars a week. The choice was a rather peculiar one for the eagle-eyed Edna Chase, who would never have allowed a bohemian on her staff. But more than a little of that finishing school background had rubbed off on Dorothy Rothschild, and she remained throughout her life something of a fashionplate. Possessed of a quiet and ladylike manner, always covering up a strong undercurrent of rage and cynicism, the youthful Miss Rothschild must have seemed the very picture of an ideal *Vogue* staff member.

Dorothy Parker's considerable writing talent was evident from the beginning, as was her ascerbic and brilliant wit. For *Vogue* she wrote such delicious legends for fashions as "Brevity is the soul of lingerie, said the petticoat to the chemise." Sometimes her bilious effusions had to be killed by the editors, in spite of their cleverness. One adaption that didn't make it was, "There was a little girl and she had a little curl, right in the middle of her forehead. When she was good she was very very good, and when she was bad she wore this divine nightdress of rose-colored mousseline de soie, trimmed with Valenciennes lace."

Although she was highly fashion conscious herself and a very attractive young lady, Dorothy Parker was not really the stuff of a *Vogue* staffer. She looked the part but she mocked the faith and had to hide her contempt for the fashion game. When she entered the *Vogue* offices on her first day of work she was overheard to say in a loud stage whisper—a technique that became something of a trademark—"Well it looks just like the entrance to a house of ill fame." In any case, anyone with this degree of independence and skepticism could not have escaped the attention of Frank Crowninshield, who kidnapped Dorothy and added her to the *Vanity Fair* staff at twenty-five dollars a week. This was in 1917, the year the United States became engulfed in World War I.

Dorothy Parker's career at *Vanity Fair* was somewhat quixotic, and, as things turned out, not very long lived. Shortly after moving over from *Vogue* she began writing theatre reviews, replacing P. G. Wodehouse, the English-born humorist and later author of the many "Jeeves" stories who was then on one of several extended stays in the United States (finally leading to citizenship in 1955). Parker had few qualifications as a theatre critic, none, really except that high intelligence and ascerbic wit which gave her theatre pages a real sting and zest. Eventually her sharp tongue and endless malice would get her into trouble with Nast and Crowninshield, but her tenure began in the war years when good theatre critics male or female were in short supply. Dorothy's atrabilious comments on vaudeville, on commercial theatre and on second-rate actresses caught the fancy of many of the magazine's readers. Dorothy herself was in a bad frame of mind during these years. She had fallen hopelessly in love with a wealthy young man named Edwin Pond Parker who was drafted before he was able to inaugurate a Wall Street career, and she had spent most of the war chasing after him on weekends as he moved from one training camp to another. When the war was over, their marriage fell apart very swiftly; young Parker proved himself to be a mild, charming and agreeable drunk, who lacked the stamina or wit to keep up with a wife who had moved into circles of the city's intellectual elite. Dorothy's style could not have been an easy or long-lasting fit for *Vanity Fair* in any case, but her *Vanity Fair* years were also among the most traumatic in her personal life, filled with many unhappy memories.

Before Dorothy Parker left *Vanity Fair* she was joined by two other young writers with whom she formed an immediate and close-knit alliance. These were Robert Benchley and Robert E. Sherwood, two Harvard graduates who were hired immediately after the war. Sherwood had served in the Allied expeditionary force; Benchley, married and not subject to the draft, had spent the few previous years slaving in a Washington bureau attempting to keep the press in the dark about the doings of the Aircraft Board. Both were unknowns at the time they were hired by Crowninshield, but, like Dorothy Parker, they were taking their first tentative steps in their own remarkable literary careers. The presence of all three of these writers at *Vanity Fair*, even if only for a short time, created one of the most remarkable talent pools ever seen on any American magazine before or since.

Robert Benchley came to the magazine in May 1919 as Crowninshield's managing editor. Being the son of an old New England family with pronounced Republican sympathies would have been quite sufficient to endear Benchley to Crowninshield, but by the time he joined the staff Benchley had already developed a small but growing reputation as a humorist. A graduate of Harvard, Class of 1912, Benchley in his student days had been president of the *Lampoon* and a principal writer of the comic Hasty Pudding shows. He had been the leader of a small group of wits that formed the nucleus of a kind of golden age of humor at Harvard—a group that contained, among others, Gluyas Williams, Frederick Lewis Allen, Paul Hollister and Vinton Freedley.

Upon graduation, like most aspiring humorists, Benchley found few outlets for his college capers, and for a while he worked for a paper-making company in Boston and translated French catalogues for the Boston Museum of Fine Arts (an occupation that clearly would also have impressed Crowninshield). Later he drifted to New York, where he worked as a press agent and wrote advertisements for the Curtis Publishing Company. What's more important, he became associated with Franklin Pierce Adams ("FPA") on the *Tribune* and began contributing to Adams's column called "The Conning

Tower." Through his work as a press agent he also struck up an acquaintance with Heywood Broun and playwright George S. Kaufman. By 1914 he was contributing pieces to *Vanity Fair*, his first bearing the title, "No Matter from What Angle You Look at It, Alice Brookhausen Was a Girl Whom You Would Hesitate to Invite Into Your Own Home."

Crowninshield became acquainted with Benchley through FPA's column no doubt, but Benchley had also become pretty well known for prankish after-dinner speeches, and Crowninshield was in the audience when Benchley served as toastmaster at one of Adams's annual banquets, which presented his most prolific contributor with a "coveted timepiece." The recipient was Deems Taylor, but in the audience that night were, among others, Howard Dietz, Morrie Ryskind, Marc Connelly, Edna St. Vincent Millay, George S. Kaufman, Carolyn Wells, and Crowninshield. Taking advantage of the theme of the banquet, Benchley delivered a short biography of the watch, tracing its history from its invention by John W. Watch to the present day. It was the kind of youthful delirium that could only have delighted Crowninshield.

Robert E. Sherwood, Harvard '18, had had virtually no experience of any kind when he arrived at *Vanity Fair* a few days after Benchley. Coming from a patrician New England family known to Crowninshield, Sherwood had shown up at the *Vanity Fair* offices resplendently attired in his Black Watch uniform, perhaps a rather crude play for sympathy, but one that the mellow Crowninshield could hardly resist. At the age of twenty-two, Sherwood was to be strictly a junior staffer on a three-month trial basis at twenty-five dollars a week. Sherwood was already aware of Benchley by reputation when he was hired. At the Harvard of his day, the very name Benchley provoked peals of laughter among the undergraduates.

Sherwood had one other thing that recommended him to Crowninshield. Like Benchley, he had been on the *Lampoon* at Harvard, and had edited a *Vanity Fair* parody issue of the *Lampoon*, which was published April 6, 1917, the day the United States entered World War I. Sherwood's scholarly attainments had been spotty at best. As a student at the Milton Academy he had one of the worst academic records in the school's history and had actually been denied a diploma (the following fall he gained admission to Harvard merely on the basis of a certificate of attendance). But he had also been enormously well liked at Milton Academy, and the students elected him to give the valedictory address, even though his teachers considered him class dunce. At Harvard his record was no more impressive. He was thrown out for poor grades and readmitted twice. While waiting for the war to roll in,

Sherwood paid no attention at all to his studies but devoted his time to the glee club, intramural football, Hasty Pudding, and the *Lampoon*. An enormous youngster of six feet seven inches tall, Sherwood had his own highly individual charm and style, and if he had any defects they would hardly be noticed at a place like *Vanity Fair*, where a patrician sense of fun and devotion to highly individualized learning was always warmly welcomed. Few could have predicted in the spring of 1919 that Sherwood was about to embark on a career as one of America's most distinguished playwrights.

These three young writers almost immediately took to one another and formed an impregnable triumvirate in opposition to office bureaucracy and repetitive habits of life in any and all forms. Always addressing one another formally as Mrs. Parker, Mr. Benchley, and Mr. Sherwood, they shared an office that visitors could hardly distinguish from an unruly sophomore's rumpus room—an office always emitting peals of laughter throughout the day. Mr. Benchley was mostly the ringleader, but his constant ebullience never failed to provoke mischief on the part of the soft-spoken and lady-like Dorothy Parker. Although all of them personally liked and admired Frank Crowninshield, they took a childish delight in disrupting all vestiges of dignity and propriety in the office. Benchley, for example, was a subscriber to two undertaker's magazines and he kept them on display in the office (shades of Mencken and Nathan). Both were richly endowed with anatomical plates with arrows showing precisely where embalming fluids should be injected. Benchley would cut these out and give them to Mrs. Parker as interoffice memos and she in turn would hang them on the wall—a disheartening display to poor Crowninshield, who fastidiously displayed the latest prints of Braque or Picasso and wanted the office to be a model of modern elegance.

Nothing was sacred to these three "amazing whelps," as Crowninshield later called them. On one occasion a "Policy Memorandum" came down from Nast's accountants demanding that all employees fill out tardiness slips explaining their reasons for being late to work. Benchley took the card, and in the most minute handwriting filled it up over the course of the morning with a long and complex story about how on the way to work that morning some elephants got loose from the Hippodrome, down the street from the *Vanity Fair* office, and that he had helped to round them up. This escapade, which would have taken an hour for a reader to grasp, supposedly caused Benchley to be late by eleven minutes. No further tardiness slips were required.

Another "Policy Memorandum" forbade discussion among employees of salaries received. Benchley, Parker, and Sherwood countered this by having large placards painted up with their salaries in outsized lettering—and sauntered around the office with this vital information on display. (Parker and Sherwood were in fact drawing a pitifully small twenty-five dollars a week and Benchley, as managing editor, a more respectable hundred dollars a week.)

As three literary musketeers standing tall against the system, Benchley, Parker, and Sherwood almost always went to lunch together. These lunches have since become enshrined in the annals of cultural history in that they shortly led to the founding of one of the most celebrated institutions of the 1920s, the Algonquin Round Table. The Algonquin Hotel was only a few doors away from the *Vanity Fair* offices, but its hotel dining room would have doubtless been outside the means of at least the two junior editors. For some time, however, when the group went out to a small eatery nearby, Sherwood had been accosted by a group of dwarfs from one of the acts at the Hippodrome—these dwarfs would grab the six-foot, seven-inch Sherwood around the legs, calling to him with such jibes as "How's the weather up there," and other more ribald comments. Sherwood, who had been through the ordeal too many times, preferred to take refuge in the lobby of the Algonquin, on which occasion the trio decided to stay for lunch. Lunches at the Algonquin then became a habit, although in 1919 Sherwood and Parker could only afford to have eggs. But after a while, with a group of dedicated and witty conversationalists from publishing, show business and other fields on hand, owner Frank Case set up a large round table in the Pergola Room, which later became known as the Round Table—sometimes called by less flattering names such as "Wit's End" or "The Vicious Circle." Among the regulars during the twenties were Alexander Woollcott, Harold Ross, FPA, Heywood Broun, Irving Berlin, George S. Kaufman, Marc Connelly, Herbert Bayard Swope, and Donald Ogden Stewart.

Long before the name "Algonquin Round Table" became known to the general public, Robert Benchley, Dorothy Parker, and Robert E. Sherwood had left the employ of Condé Nast and gone their separate ways. Frank Crowninshield was hardly unaware of the high talents of all of them, but their antic behavior proved to be a medicine too strong for a periodical publication that had to be gotten out on a monthly basis. It may or may not have been clear to him that writers need to unfold their genius in lonely isolation. If the three "amazing whelps" failed to realize it in their earnest desire to earn a living, they certainly knew it by instinct.

They were all getting in trouble with management, however delightful and amusing that trouble might have been. Dorothy Parker, especially, was sailing into dark waters with her theatre criticism. She had written a number of acid-tongued reviews of plays as well as attacks on prominent actors and actresses, and these had brought strong complaints to Nast and Crowninshield from the Shuberts and other theatre impresarios who were major advertisers in the Nast magazines. Parker on one occasion heard Crowninshield apologizing on the phone to Florenz Ziegfeld, whose wife Billie Burke received a scabrous Parker review of her performance in the title role of *Caesar's Wife*. Parker probably sensed that her days were numbered. In any case, some time afterward, Crowninshield, who would avoid firing anybody at all costs, took Parker to lunch at the Plaza Hotel and patiently explained that she would now have to confine her writing to things other than the theatre because P. G. Wodehouse was returning to New York and wanted his old job back. In a pet, Parker ordered the most expensive dessert on the menu, went back to the office and resigned. Needless to say, neither Benchley nor Sherwood could countenance this insult to their comrade in arms and both immediately resigned also. Crowninshield offered an exaggerated display of sympathy but he made no strenuous effort to keep the trio from leaving, perhaps indicating that he was looking for a way to ease them out even though he was enormously amused by them.

However disagreeable the parting, and it was virtually impossible for Frank Crowninshield to leave any of his friends with bitter feelings, the three amazing whelps continued to remain in the chief's good graces, and he kept track of their literary careers, which were clearly in the ascendancy. They would be welcomed as contributors later on, and in 1924 *Vanity Fair* would honor Benchley in its "Hall of Fame" pages as "one of the most adroit and original American humorists." Dorothy Parker, who seldom forgave any one of her enemies, could never hold anything against Frank Crowninshield, and regularly sent him copies of her books of verse when they came out, inscribing one of them: "To Frank Crowninshield—He accepted my first verse—Please will he accept all these? With love and gratitude."

As Benchley, Parker, and Sherwood were moving out, indeed even before they left, Crowninshield had hired another young staffer also destined for fame in the years ahead. This was Edmund Wilson, the formidable literary critic and man of letters. Wilson was hired at twenty-five dollars a week—the same that Parker and Sherwood were making—but doubtless Crowninshield was comforted by his more serious demeanor. (Surely he was also impressed by Wilson's lineage; he had come from an old American family with deep roots in New Jersey and upstate New York. His father, a staunch Republican, had been an attorney general of New Jersey.) Wilson was not drawn into the uproarious atmosphere of the office, although he liked the departing trio who jokingly called him a scab, even as they generously showed him the ropes and helped him to become acclimatized. Wilson was especially attracted to Parker, who had called Crowninshield's attention to some of his pieces in her role as reader of unsolicited manuscripts. He recalled later that she was a very pretty girl and that he might have considered dating her but that he was ever so slightly repelled by her overly perfumed hand, the scent of which remained with him all day after they had shaken hands.

Wilson came to *Vanity Fair* in January 1920 and stayed for one year, after which he left for a better position on the *New Republic*. Clearly, *Vanity Fair* was not really his cup of tea; he found the offices a "madhouse," infiltrated by a kind of "sweet poison." He liked Crowninshield, but also harbored mixed feelings toward him. This was a type he had met before, a courtier who somehow lacked a court, a man living in a world that was not quite real. "In his well-pressed gray suits that harmonized with his silvering hair, Crowninshield would travel around the office with a gait at once strutting and mincing, with the upper part of his body bent forward."

There was something in Wilson's liberal makeup, his attachment to the simple virtues of a bygone Jeffersonian democracy that would not permit him to approve wholly of the club-going Crowninshield. If he was leery of Crowninshield, he detested Condé Nast—an antipathy shared by many of the *Vanity Fair* staffers. He found Nast to be a commercial bounder of the worst sort, a man "incapable of saying good morning without a formally restrained but somehow obnoxious vulgarity." Nast was a hopeless womanizer who would proposition any model or secretary who took his fancy; the vast majority of them found him repellent but ofttimes were in no position to resist the advances of the seignior. Crowninshield, on the other hand, was a tremendously powerful magnet to women of all ages, perhaps because he seemed so safe and avuncular. The secretaries in the office all idolized this editor who brought them flowers, always remembered their birthdays but seemingly never made a pass at any of them. They despised Nast, in spite of his smooth manners, regarding him as little more than a proverbial dirty old man.

In his extensive private diaries of the 1920s, Wilson addressed himself to the frequently asked question of whether Crowninshield was a homosexual. He had never married and formed few really intimate relationships except one with a dearly beloved brother. Wilson's belief was that Crowninshield was probably not a homosexual. "In spite of the not very attractive habit of seizing you by the arm in a way that seemed calculated to establish some kind of affectionate ascendancy, I do not believe that he was," Whatever his sexual preferences, there can be little doubt that Crowninshield was a highly discreet individual whose personal habits always seemed beyond reproach, a person whose individual style would suggest a homosexual orientation only to those determined to look for it. Doubtless his sexual tastes were complex and enigmatic.

Wilson did believe, however, that the atmosphere at *Vanity Fair* had a somewhat vaguely homosexual flavor about it. It was an atmosphere that emanated from the men's fashion department, where the regular staffers were invariably homosexual. Interestingly enough, the men's fashion department was never one of Crowninshield's strong interests; he largely ignored it. It had been instituted by Nast pretty much against Crowninshield's wishes. Crowninshield's view was always one of contempt for magazines that told men how to dress, and he was chagrined when that element had to be introduced into *Vanity Fair*. His belief was that "a gentleman knows how to dress," and that his was a magazine intended to be read by gentlemen.

But Wilson's raising of this issue does lead one to an interesting observation about the general appeal of *Vanity Fair* as a magazine. The public appeal certainly was to both sexes, and there were probably large numbers of both men and women who enjoyed the magazine and read it on a regular basis. Nonetheless, *Vanity Fair* always had what might be called a slightly more masculine than feminine appeal and ambience. A men's magazine? Too strong a term, perhaps, but, yes, always a magazine to tempt the masculine fancy. It was an essence or a perfume that would doubtless never have been detected in *The Smart Set*, edited as it was by those two robustious bachelors-about-town, Mencken and Nathan.

Perhaps there was something of a spirit of masculine frivolity and nonchalance that soured some of *Vanity Fair*'s staff members, if seldom the casual reader. Edmund Wilson left after a year to become a literary critic for the *New Republic*, where he told friends that at last he would be able to devote himself to more serious writing projects. Privately he was angry, like Bob Sherwood and Dorothy Parker, that he hadn't received a raise while a superficial and inexperienced young man was brought in to write on men's fashions at a much higher salary. Frank Crowninshield freely admitted that what the fashion writer was doing was inconsequential, but it would be hard to find someone else capable of writing on men's fashions, while young men wanting to write about literature were always easy to find.

If these erosions from the staff during the early years diminished in any

way *Vanity Fair*'s potential as a great magazine they were probably not in-
jurious in any substantial way. A style and direction for the magazine had
been discovered and laid down, and it would move forward briskly and
cheerfully during the 1920s. Readers and contributors would continue to
come tumbling in. And they all loved the magazine.

A look at a run of *Vanity Fair* during the period just after World War I
shows a magazine that by the standards of today would seem to offer a rather
eccentric mix of materials, but certainly a rich and tasty smorgasbord. The
magazine carried no short stories or novelettes in the usual sense, but it did
publish satirical sketches and what it liked to call "literary hors d'oeuvre,"
and in these classifications were often found some modest effusions of the
imagination. By 1920 the magazine had settled down to a format whose
table of contents began with a section called "In and About the Theatre"—
a section that invariably contained the largest number of items. *Vanity Fair*,
after all, wanted to leave no doubt that it belonged to the tradition of
"Broadway" magazines, and its pages were always filled with profiles and
pictures of actors and actresses, pieces about drama, playwriting and the
like. Most issues also contained materials under the sections "The World of
Art," "The World of Ideas," "Poetry and Verse," and "The World Out-
doors." Under "Miscellaneous" the magazine invariably offered something
for the businessman on the financial situation and the columns on men's fashions.

It is important to remember, too, that *Vanity Fair* was a generously large
folio, an illustrated magazine, whose prime appeal was to the visual senses.
In this it differed from the *Smart Set*, and more closely resembled the old
Life with its full-page drawings and cartoons. Indeed, few if any magazines
today run such large and beautiful pictures on their pages (postal rates, of
course, have shrunk their page size), and few editors today would be willing
to devote an entire page to a handsome photographic portrait of a single
prominent individual. It hardly needs to be said that in this male-oriented
magazine, the most beautiful, and tastefully suggestive portraits, are of
women—stage and screen actresses, poets, opera singers, artists; always
women prominent in the arts, never women prominent only in society. They
are women of excitement and glamor, certain to stoke up the flames of the
male imagination. And there are a number of smaller photographs also,
many of comely women usually portrayed in a mood of dignified and highly
restrained eroticism.

Looking at the issue for September 1921—a nice effort is being made
here as socialites return to New York for the season—we find a typical mix

for the editorial content of the magazine during this period. (Benchley, Sherwood, and Parker are now long gone; Edmund Wilson departed seven months ago; the masthead lists Heyworth Campbell as managing editor.) The cover, by "Fish" ("Fish" was, in fact, an enormously clever Englishwoman), shows a highly stylized early flapper sitting in a dainty porcelain bathtub and showered from above. This is followed by eight pages of full-length ads all elegant in design. These, and other full-page ads elsewhere in the magazine, are *Vanity Fair*'s usual and best supporters—Arrow Soft Collars, Whitman's Chocolates, Keiser Cravats, Stetson Hats. The most brisk spenders amongst the advertisers seem to be the makers of luxury automobiles—the Pierce Arrow, the Packard, and others, invariably the builders of large sedans, limousines, touring cars, phaetons, roadsters and the like. There are a number of pages of small display ads here and at the back of the magazine—theatre agencies, dancing schools, mouthwash, golf balls, shoes, fountain pens, and so on, most of these with a strong masculine appeal.

Embedded in the front matter and worked in among the shorter ads is a regular column entitled "The Financial Situation," by Merryle Stanley Rukeyser, a newspaper financial writer, the only nod to the world of commerce that Crowninshield would allow—nothing serious about business ever seeping into the heart of the magazine. The magazine itself begins with a serious essay by St. John Ervine entitled "The Economical Bernard Shaw," and this faces a beautiful frontispiece, "A Peasant Madonna in France," which is an etching by English artist Lee Huntley. Turning the page one finds another serious essay, this opposite a series of woodcuts made behind the lines of the recent Great War by French artist J. E. Laboureur. The next page contains an article for the theatre buffs, "The Well-Made Revue," by Heywood Broun, with a portrait of Lynn Overmann in evening dress and top hat, and containing an extensive discussion of the *Ziegfeld Follies*. Facing this page is a triptych of three lovely actresses appearing in comedies on Broadway. (Readers of Heywood Broun's piece will be gratified to find several pages later a glorious full-page picture of one of Ziegfeld's hottest stars, Fannie Brice.)

There follows two humorous sketches, one on the Model T Ford by Donald Ogden Stewart and another called "Rollo's Weekend in the Country," by George S. Chappell. Then, poised between the lighthearted and the serious, is the fifth in a series that *Vanity Fair* has been running on "Latter Day Helens." (*Vanity Fair* is ever teasing the feminine spirit.) There is "A Railroad Adventure" by the Hungarian playwright Ferenc Molnar, using the familiar He/She dialogue then so commonplace in humor magazines. And there is another such on the next page, "Powder, Rouge and Lip-Stick" by Nancy Boyd. Nancy Boyd, of course, is Edna St. Vincent Millay, then still struggling down in the village, and using "Nancy Boyd" as her pen name on articles that might detract from her more lofty reputation as a lyric poet. (Millay was more or less being kept alive by Crowninshield at this time, a good example of his generosity to writers, and a clear indication that he knew talent when he saw it. He was also regularly running Millay's poems in his magazines under her own name.)

There is next a funny piece by Canadian humorist Stephen Leacock, "How I Succeeded in Business," followed by a tongue-in-cheek "Hymn in Praise of the Critics" by French composer Erik Satie—one never ceases to wonder how Crowninshield managed to wheedle so much lighthearted fare out of serious artists. Facing these and the aforementioned essays are some deliciously varied full-page plates. There is a page of humorous sketches of girls in burlesque. But there is also a page devoted to the sketch books of the celebrated English artist Augustus John. There is a page devoted to a new parlor game invented by younger French artists showing how some "modern art" curves can be created in three minutes. Facing Leacock's lightweight piece on business is a somber but still mildly erotic portrait of Kyra, a dancer at the Winter Garden, executing a classic snake dance.

There follows a series of articles and plates mostly related either to Broadway or Hollywood, introduced by a glorious full-page cartoon by Ralph Barton entitled "When the Five O'Clock Whistle Blows in Hollywood." There are, of course, attractive pictures of actors and actresses, but also several serious essays, including "The Irish Players" by Ernest Boyd and a large number of frivolities such as "the Monstrous Movies" by Charles Hanson Towne, and "The Flapper—A New Type" by Alfredo Panzini. In this section too, is a double-page spread of cartoons by the issue's cover artist "Fish," illustrating "Wild America: A Few of its Follies." (All of the follies, it seems, are of high society.) Also in this section is a page devoted to photographs of "The Younger School of Italian Composers." There are a few more gorgeous photographs of women, "Eleanor Painter—A Prima Donna of Comic Opera," this in a distinctly classical mood and setting, and a demure and sweet Frances Starr, then working under the direction of David Belasco. Interspersed here, too, are a regular photographic feature, "We Nominate for the Hall of Fame," and a regular bridge page (auction bridge was then the rage among society folks—contract bridge had yet to sweep the country).

The realm that one traverses is decidedly masculine in its atmosphere. There are articles on sport, on yachts, on automobiles, and the regular section "For the Well Dressed Man." The sports section contains an especially good piece by Heywood Broun on the recent Dempsey-Carpentier fight, and facing this page a beautiful boxing lithograph by George Bellows. There is also an article by Grantland Rice on the French tennis player, Mlle. Suzanne Lenglen. All these parts are richly illustrated, the motor cars and speed boats photographically, men's fashions by pen and ink sketches. From here, one dreamily turns the final pages of the magazine, running to one hundred pages, concluding with the usual complement of small and large ads taken by makers of expensive motor cars, top hats and cutaway coats, golf wear and golf equipment, cigars, jewelery, and all the rest.

This is *Vanity Fair* in its prime—an utterly charming magazine. Never frivolous, never shallow as one might suspect from the vantage point of a more harried and troubled America. Entertaining, yes, for magazines are there to entertain. But never trivial. Always wafting about is the assumption that the sentient social being, the "whole man" is a person of wide-ranging interests and tastes, a person curious about the world, even that which is esoteric, even that which may be outside the current mainstream of thought and value.

Many, many magazines have since attempted to fabricate just such a clever admixture of diverse attractions—of rock stars and French countesses, of polo players and mathematicians—but in *Vanity Fair* the potpourri was never such as to cause indigestion. A magazine should never be a full meal, but perhaps more like an hors d'oeuvre that creates excitement for what is to follow. There was more than a little of the French spirit in Crowninshield. His appetizers led on and never detracted from the main course, but they were quite capable of being savored by themselves; you never got the idea that you were being tied down to a quick martini and a dismal cheese dip. There was always something here on the side table to draw you onward to deeper pleasures, to the real thing. There was always a kind of civilized agreement between the magazine and its readers, an agreement of shared pleasures and a call to more profound opportunities. There were many things to view through the windows of *Vanity Fair*, but they weren't intended to be viewed passively. That would have been an abhorrence to Frank Crowninshield. These rich offerings were an affectionate gift, tempting you to be not another onlooker but a participant, a co-creator.

If *Vanity Fair* was one of the best magazines ever published in America, or, at the very least, among the most charming and magnetic, it must also be admitted that it never became, nor could it ever aspire to become, a mass-circulation magazine. In the 1920s the magazine was clearly a proud possession of Condé Nast Publications, Inc., but at no time did it rival its sister publication *Vogue* either in readership figures or advertising revenues. In 1920 the circulation of *Vanity Fair* stood about 90,000, a figure that would remain more or less constant during the next decade. It had a healthy group of dependable advertisers during the 1920s, but there were almost no opportunities to augment their number. *Vogue*, on the other hand, began the 1920s with a circulation of about 137,000, not a great deal larger than *Vanity Fair*, but its advertising revenues per year were nearly three million dollars. At this same time, the annual advertising revenues from *Vanity Fair* were only about a half million dollars. Neither circulation nor advertising revenues were particularly worrisome during the years of the great Coolidge prosperity, but with the coming of the depression *Vanity Fair* would get into severe difficulties. These would be much less serious at *Vogue*, where, miraculously, neither circulation nor advertising revenues sagged dangerously. (After World War II, *Vogue*'s fortunes shot into the firmament: by 1963 its circulation had grown to 500,000 and its annual advertising revenues to well over eight million dollars.)

During the 1920s, *Vanity Fair* changed but little in style and format; it was essentially a conservative institution with its own hardy and loyal band of readers. Which is not to suggest that the magazine fell behind the times during these years—in some ways it might be more accurate to say that the times caught up with *Vanity Fair*. In one domain, however, *Vanity Fair* always remained supreme, and this was in its high production standards and visual beauty. As a member of the Condé Nast family of magazies, now also including the very successful *House and Garden* (which Nast had bought in 1915), the magazine had the regular advantage of connections with the best photographers and commercial artists; it remained in the forefront of all the leading commercial magazines in all fields of the graphic arts and print technologies.

These were the phases of magazine production in which Condé Nast himself proved especially proficient and skillful and in which he took a special pride. His attitude had always been that he would spare no expense to make his magazines the most beautiful and richly produced in America. To this end, a great stride forward was made in 1921 when a splendid company printing plant was planned on the Boston Post Road in Greenwich, Connecticut. Prior to this time Nast had dealt with commercial printers—always the best that he could find—but World War I paper shortages had rankled him, as had a nasty strike by his major printer in 1918.

At first the venture in Greenwich was expected to be on a rather small scale, Nast merely having bought up a tract of land and a small printing plant owned by the typographer Douglas C. McMurtrie. But the site was lyrical and awe-inspiring, partly rocky and partly unused swampland. Nast finally decided to hire a firm of landscape architects to make over the grounds so that they could serve as a setting for a gigantic printing establishment that would enjoy a sylvan and noncommercial environment. The printing plant was expanded many times in size, eventually covering some 300,000 square feet. It contained all the latest in printing and typographical equipment, and Nast brought to it the best artisans he could find from Europe and America to operate slow but highly discriminating flatbed presses. To please these workers, and give them a setting worthy of their talents, Nast's landscape architects designed elegant driveways, cascading fountains, beautiful flower beds, formal gardens with works of sculpture (many imported from Italy), the whole surrounded by fine New England elm trees. So pleased was Nast with what he had done, that he also had an office building built in 1923, and this eventually housed most of the business operations of all his maga-zines. Only the editorial offices remained in New York.

Here in this setting of sylvan grandeur the Nast magazines continued their quest for typographical beauty and excellence. The press regularly published books of typefaces it used, many designed in Greenwich for the company's publications but later adopted by advertising and typographical designers everywhere. In 1929 a sumptuously bound *Condé Nast Type Book* spread the gospel of fine typography to the fraternity of commercial design. Back in the Greenwich plant, all the aesthetic principles were put into effect in *Vanity Fair* as well as the other company magazines, and, even more importantly, Nast's principal production men slaved over the design tables and presses to make sure that every issue was perfect. Unlike the typical mass-market magazine, the Nast publications were printed only on flatbed presses that offered high ink viscosity, greater gloss, and higher definition of both illustrations and type images. The process was a slow one that required pressmen to monitor constantly the feeding mechanism and the page quality, but Nast was convinced that nothing less was acceptable for his magazines. In time new and faster printing lines would have to be added; however, in the early 1920s *House and Garden*, with a circulation of about 100,000 requried a two-week press run with men working day and night to get the magazine to the bindery.

By the late 1920s, Nast was venturing into another field that would eventually record one of his finest achievements in the realm of printing. This was the new domain of color printing. During the mid-twenties there had been rapid strides in the technology of color photography, and Nast had become convinced that color photography would be the wave of the future in the best magazines, most especially in fashion magazines. By 1928 he had bought a photoengraving company in New York and began experimenting with the possibilities of four-color engravings. By the early 1930s Condé Nast Engravers had developed a process for color separations that was unmatched anywhere in the world until the introduction of Kodachrome by Eastman-Kodak in 1935. This led to the first color photograph in *Vogue* in its issue of April 15, 1932, and its first photographic color cover in July of the same year. This latter effort, a photograph by Edward Steichen, pictured a woman in a striking red bathing suit, sitting cross-legged while holding a beach ball above her head. The picture and the cover were a benchmark in the annals of American magazine publishing and design.

Vanity Fair, of course, was not neglected in these various advances; it had had a distinguished history as a showcase of art photography. And when color photography made its entry in the magazine field, color photographs began having an impact here also. Perhaps the last major advance made in this field during Nast's lifetime was the introduction of high-speed color photography, the first example of which appeared in *Vanity Fair*'s September 1935 issue. The photograph in question was another Steichen marvel, a portrait of the corps de ballet at the Radio City Music Hall taken at a speed of a thousandth of a second with synchronized flashbulbs.

So excellent and so renowned were the various Condé Nast production companies by the mid-twenties that publishers of other magazines, even competing magazines, were anxious to make use of their matchless facilities for engraving and printing. Eventually the operation at Greenwich became a mammoth one, with many large press lines running, enabling Condé Nast Publications to print not only *Vogue*, *Vanity Fair*, and *House and Garden*, but other magazines looking for superlative production standards. Among the magazines that would eventually be rolling off the presses at Greenwich were *Scientific America*, *Modern Photography*, *Field and Stream*, *Mademoiselle*, and, yes, a magazine that would bear much of the responsibility for bringing *Vanity Fair* to its untimely end — the *New Yorker*.

Vanity Fair's disappearance from the publishing scene presents us with what is surely one of those sad and inexplicable twists of fate to which the print media have been exposed since the time of Gutenberg. While the magazine had never been a circulation leader or a tremendously big moneymaker, it managed to purr along over the years at a high level of respectability. It had its avid and devoted readers and was always the kind of magazine in which any publisher could take deep pride. When it finally stumbled, however, one can attribute its woes to no single blow from exterior forces, no obvious inattention on the part of management; rather its sad decline can only be attributed to a slow accumulation of adverse circumstances none of which by themselves should have proven fatal.

Old-time readers of *Vanity Fair* are surely likely to ascribe most of the blame for the magazine's decline to the economic debacle of the 1930s. It is an easy assumption to make, because the early years of the depression killed off a great many once prosperous magazines in a single deadly coup, just as a hard frost kills off so many tender blades of grass. But *Vanity Fair* wasn't precisely in this category; it staved off the effects of the darkest years of the depression and was not really moribund in 1936 when Condé Nast decided to bury it in the pages of *Vogue*.

In a larger sense, of course, the great depression had much to do with *Vanity Fair*'s demise. The mood of the nation had changed, and so, too, had the class of people who were the regular readers of the magazine. Not that the moneyed class had been wiped out—much old wealth remained, some coupon clippers now being possessed of more leisure than ever before. But the very wealthy had never formed the nucleus of support for the magazine—no magazine ever in existence in America had lived on the support of the wealthy alone. The changes, in any case, were not in people's pocketbooks as much as in their mood and frame of mind. *Vanity Fair* had been created in those halcyon days before World War I when few real skeptics of social progress were afoot in the land, and it had been polished to its permanent lustre during the affluent and smarty atmosphere of the Coolidge prosperity. Somehow the magazine had too much gaiety, too much brio, too much youthful innocence to survive in the hard-questioning environment of the depression. Still, with just a little luck, it might well have survived, either pretty much intact or with slight modifications in format.

When it finally came time to make crucial decisions about the fate of *Vanity Fair*, Condé Nast was not in a good position to make them. While his magazines themselves were never in serious jeopardy, he and his company were. Portents of the coming troubles were present in the years of the great bull market. Like all of his moneyed, socialite friends Nast had allowed himself to become ensnared by the passion for speculation. Already a very wealthy man, he became deeply involved in a number of dubious investment opportunities. In 1928, for example, he bought a controlling interest in the Park-Lexington Corporation in New York, which owned a whole block of choice Manhattan real estate just north of Grand Central Station, including Grand Central Palace and the Park-Lexington Building. This investment would later prove to be a disaster.

An even more fatal step had been taken the year before when Nast, looking for funds to make yet further improvements in his Greenwich operations, had been tempted to put his company on the big board. This act led him into the clutches of the investment banking firm of Goldman, Sachs & Company, which now became a major shareholder in Condé Nast Publications. All went well for a while, with the holding company paying handsome dividends as the stock market bulled its way upward. When the stock market crashed in 1929, Goldman, Sachs stock plunged from four hundred dollars to five dollars; the stock of Condé Nast plummeted from ninety-three dollars to four dollars. Condé Nast had been wiped out. He did not lose his magazines, but in the financial cyclone that followed, control of them passed to bankers and financiers. His neatly managed little corporation had taken a joyride on a giant's back and had suffered a nasty fall from which it would never entirely recover during his lifetime.

The first several years after the stock market crash were pure agony for Condé Nast. In 1928 at the age of fifty-five he had married a twenty-one-year-old debutante and had every expectation of finishing his life as a satiated and leisurely country squire with all his magazines running themselves in perpetuity like well-oiled music boxes. But the financial disaster of the early thirties eventually broke his health and ruined his marriage. Before the decade was over he would regain a large measure of control over his empire; in the meantime he was not really able to give the attention he would have liked to the day-to-day operations of his magazines. And the weakest link in the chain turned out to be *Vanity Fair*.

The most pressing problem at *Vanity Fair* during the early 1930s was advertising. Advertising revenues steadily declined, especially those derived from the full pages once purchased by makers of fine automobiles (many of these had gone under during the first cruel wave of the depression), jewelry, men's golf attire, yachts, and so on. Things looked up slightly with the repeal of Prohibition when pages of liquor ads began pouring in, but in the long run this was not sufficient to stop the eroding revenues. In the mid-twenties the magazine had taken in over a half million dollars in advertising a year; by 1935 this was down to about a quarter of a million.

When the depression began in 1929 Frank Crowninshield was nearing sixty, and he was little disposed to change either the appeal or the format of *Vanity Fair*. He believed (as editors frequently do) that his magazine was a sacred institution not to be tampered with. He himself had not been touched by the depression to any great extent—his had been one of those voices raised in opposition to the unbridled speculation and risk taking of the late twenties. As far as he was concerned, New York society had not changed; he met his same old friends at his usual clubs—few of his acquaintances belonged to the class of financial freebooters, and not many individuals he knew had jumped out of the windows of tall office buildings at Broad and Wall streets. Were there apple sellers down in the financial district? Were there soup kitchens and unemployment lines? If so, they were passing aberrations, and the pains they symbolized could probably be assuaged by the very sort of balm offered by his lighthearted and upbeat magazine.

Unfortunately at this very time experience was proving otherwise. The country was in a wholly different mood as the clouds of economic woe descended, and none of the old remedies seemed to work. All magazines were struggling for survival, even the giants, but magazines that were essentially lighthearted and gay had grave difficulty convincing people that the cures for all the sorrows of the world lay in laughter or fun. Even readers with the leisure and affluence to have fun—and there were still many—were cautiously pulling in their wings, believing apprehensively that the old social order might crumble and that a total realignment in their way of life might be necessary. Even the rich were looking for new kinds of printed matter for their drawing room tables.

Magazines of high society and of humor seem to have been particularly vulnerable in those early years of austerity. The *Smart Set* had died at the first whiff of the depression in the summer of 1930, but for years it had been resting on its laurels. *Life* and *Judge* began a dizzying downward plunge from which they would never recover. Both were seen to be far too frivolous for these times. In any case, all of these magazines, including *Vanity Fair*, were now suffering from strong competition from the *New Yorker*, which seemed ready to seize the monopoly on all the readers who might be interested either in humor of the gentle phantasms of urban society.

The *New Yorker*'s ever-growing popularity during the early years of the depression must have seemed surprising to some, especially since it had been inaugurated only in 1925 and limped along pitifully during its first few years, many seeing it then as nothing but a feeble imitation of *Life* or *Judge*, with a little cafe chatter thrown in. Somehow, as if by a kind of miracle, the *New Yorker* had transformed itself into something different, something with staying power. There were new young writers, a new style of humor, a new and subtle approach to art and design. Above all the magazine's interest in high society became nothing but a mannerism, a gloss, which shortly would permit the development of a new style and mood that had been unknown in any of the previous smart magazines.

The first few years of the depression dragged on with little response from *Vanity Fair* to the inroads made by the *New Yorker*, by changes in magazine marketing, or by economic conditions generally. Crowninshield had little impetus toward change and Condé Nast was distracted by financial affairs as his empire unraveled. Surely by 1930, with advertising revenues sagging badly, it must have been obvious to Nast that something should be done, but his own preoccupations and his lack of desire to wound his old friend Crowninshield kept him in a state of inertia.

Change was inevitable, however, and not surprisingly it came from the prompting of younger staff members. Not surprisingly, also, their suggestions did not really cure the magazine's ills and perhaps even added to them. One of the newcomers was a bright and beautiful young blonde named Claire Boothe Brokaw, a *Vogue* staffer whom Nast had impulsively hired at a cocktail party. Her talents were soon noted by Frank Crowninshield, who purloined her as an assistant editor during one of his frequent raids of *Vogue* personnel. Mrs. Brokaw was not only bright and full of ideas, she was bold and aggressive in action, not at all hesitant about suggesting sweeping changes in the format of the magazine.

Mrs. Brokaw immediately began working her wiles on the magazine's managing editor Donald Freeman, who apparently promptly fell in love with her, and she proposed that present economic conditions demanded a much stronger political orientation for the magazine—not, of course, a shift to the leftward since Mrs. Brokaw was a wealthy woman and a staunch Republican, but a shift in the direction of advocacy journalism—what the magazine had always avoided in the past. With this new orientation, the magazine solicited articles on international peace, war reparations, the gold standard, and so on. Joining the regular list of contributors were men who surely must have seemed far too intense to the laid-back Crowninshield. Seen now on the pages of *Vanity Fair* were pieces by Walter Lippmann, Drew Pearson, John Maynard Keynes, John Gunther, and George Sokolsky. There were discussions of Hitler and Mussolini, of fascism and communism, of war, of international banking, of economic turbulence.

Mrs. Brokaw, who could be as reckless as she was beautiful, conceived a number of innovations that proved disastrous. The magazine had run for many years a page called "We Nominate for the Hall of Fame"; now Mrs. Brokaw suggested a department to be entitled "We Nominate for the Hall of Oblivion." Funny perhaps, and in some ways more suitable for the grim depression years than the older page of honored luminaries. Nevertheless, it added a downbeat note to what had always been a happy and genial magazine. Worse than this, though, the idea got the magazine into difficulties. One of those nominated for oblivion was Bernarr Macfadden, whose *Dance Magazine* was printed by the Condé Nast Press in Greenwich. When Nast lost the fifty thousand dollar contract that was involved he insisted on seeing all the names of individuals proposed for "oblivion." Eventually the feature was dropped.

Late in 1932 Donald Freeman was killed in an automobile accident at the age of twenty-nine. He was succeeded by Mrs. Brokaw, who continued her campaign to make over the magazine. In her first issue as managing editor *Vanity Fair* contained a piece by William Harlan Hale. "The Germans Are Marching Again," which accompanied some small news photos laid out in a style that was usually only employed by newspapers. Even before this time, however, the magazine had lost much of its old visual appeal. Pictures had shrunk in size, and gone were the playful drawings of artists like Fish and Benito. Artwork in the magazine became decidedly political. Sometimes, as with some very incisive cartoon covers of Hitler and Mussolini, the work was every bit as brilliant as what had come before, but it was not in keeping with the original mood of the magazine. Among the new artists coming to work for *Vanity Fair* was the brilliant German, Georg Grosz, whose talents were indisputable. Whether his vitriolic sketches belonged in a magazine like *Vanity Fair* poses an altogether different question.

Even before Claire Boothe Brokaw had become managing editor, she and other younger staff members were asked by Condé Nast to make suggestions about an entirely revitalized format for *Vanity Fair*. "He did not ask Crowninshield," Mrs. Brokaw recalled years later, because "he was too devoted to the magazine as it existed and insisted that it go on just as it was." Crowninshield raised no strong objections to changes being made in the magazine that were to match the spirit of the times; his tactic was to busy himself with the few parts of the magazine that still appealed to him—the art and theatre sections, all those parts that still held their charm for his clubby friends.

The most inspired suggestion made by Mrs. Brokaw was one that doubtless would have worked under the proper auspices. In a memo to Nast in 1931 she had suggested that Condé Nast Publications, Inc, buy up the faltering *Life* magazine and make it into a picture news magazine. Nast's best designers actually made up a dummy of such a magazine, and the publisher was very taken by the idea. It sat on his desk for several months, and at one time he appeared ready to have a sample version printed up for insertion inside the traditional *Vanity Fair*. But the suggestion had come to Nast at a time when his mind was beclouded with financial worries; he held the idea in abeyance and it was never implemented. Needless to say, Mrs. Brokaw never abandoned the notion, and when later she became the wife of Time, Inc. publisher Henry Luce, a revamped *Life* magazine became one of the greatest commercial successes of American publishing history.

It may be true that nothing could have saved *Vanity Fair* from its fateful slide during the early years of the depression. With the Nast magazine publications company in a confused financial condition, with Crowninshield having little motivation or interest to reshape or reformat his magazine, the last chapter in the magazine's history may have been a foregone conclusion. In later years some hindsighted magazine critics suggested that *Vanity Fair* might have had a chance for survival if it had been pushed firmly in the direction of the "masculine-interest" magazine—the kind of thing that was to be done with smashing success by Arnold Gingrich with his *Apparel Arts* and *Esquire*. The fact that Gingrich's magazines, born as they were in the darkest years of the depression and spectacularly successful, suggests that *Vanity Fair* may have had a route of escape had management been alert and open to change. On the other hand, as great a magazine as *Esquire* was to become, it is hard to imagine Frank Crowninshield visualizing it or wanting to serve as editor of it. Personally he was scornful of the idea of allowing men's fashions to get a stronghold in his magazine, and thought of that dimension as a mere obligatory appendage to his concept of a smart magazine. Too, the kind of masculine boldness and jauntiness so well exploited by *Esquire* was probably far removed from his conception either of a general magazine or a masculine-interest magazine. It was just not his cup of tea.

Whatever might have been done to keep *Vanity Fair* alive would be too late by the mid-thirties. Advertising revenues were continuing to fall, and Nast had countered these losses by trimming the magazine's budget—expenditures for artwork and articles were down to a mere $16,680 for the month of February 1935. The magazine now looked thin, a pale shadow of its former self. Circulation drifted downward also, but not drastically, to about eighty thousand. Even though some were believing that the depression might wear itself out with Roosevelt's New Deal in full swing, the year 1935 was a particularly bad one for the Nast magazines. Nast himself knew that the prospects for *Vanity Fair* were not bright, but he kept hoping that some magic formula for the magazine might be found. Claire Brokaw had long since departed, and the present managing editor was a beautiful and highly intelligent young lady named Helen Brown Norden (later known thruogh her writing as Helen Lawrenson). Although she had won her position because she had been Condé Nast's lover, Norden was a gifted and clever editor. She doubtless would have been open to any good suggestions for remaking the magazine. In the end, sorrowfully, nothing happened, although as late as the fall of 1935 Nast was attempting to solicit ideas from his friends for a refreshened *Vanity Fair*. But all such suggestions seemed either to do violence to the original intent of the magazine (and too much violence had already been done to it), or requried expenditures of money that the company simply didn't have.

The final blow came in December 1935 when Nast announced to his staffers that *Vanity Fair* would be merged into *Vogue* with the issue of March 1936. The basic idea was to be presented in an upbeat way to subscribers who were told that all of the best *Vanity Fair* features would be carried in *Vogue* (*Vogue*, naturally took up the subscription lists of *Vanity Fair*). It was a crushing blow to Crowninshield, who couldn't imagine himself working for his pompous arch-rival Edna Woolman Chase. It was naturally a blow to younger staff members, most of whom were laid off. Even Helen Norden got her pink slip in spite of her intimate relationship with Nast.

Frank Crowninshield left for his winter home on Boca Grande, Florida, to look back nostalgically on a forty-year career in publishing now abruptly ended. His old friend Condé Nast had no intention of letting him go, however, and he later returned to the office as an editorial advisor to *Vogue* in the areas of literature and the arts. In this reduced capacity he served with distinction, and naturally his fautless manners forbade any serious altercations with the imperious Mrs. Chase. Crowninshield also acted as a kind of advising editor to all the Nast publications—a gentle sinecure suitable to a man of retirement years. And in this capacity he proved himself more than a little valuable through the World War II period. In 1939, when Nast was contemplating the introduction of a junior version of *Vogue* for young working girls (this in response to Street & Smith's highly successful *Mademoiselle*) and was planning to call it *Glamor*, it was Frank Crowninshield, his taste never deserting him in such matters, who suggested that a *u* be added to the word, so that the magazine finally appeared on the newsstands as *Glamour*.

But in a twinkling, as it were, *Vanity Fair* was dead and gone. Some of its best features were carried over into *Vogue*, and in an editorial Condé

Nast expressed the bright but not very realistic hope that something of the old magazine's spirit would live on in the surviving sister publication. "We feel confident," he wrote, "that this richer *Vogue* will please *Vogue*'s readers. And although it may not completely fill the place of *Vanity Fair*, we hope that this larger and more varied *Vogue* will give *Vanity Fair* readers a sense of being at home in its pages." But as is so often the case, when two magazines merge, one is submerged, and in this case, the spirit of *Vanity Fair* slowly disappeared in the months that followed. Only a few of the old features were retained, and eventually even they lost their identity and flavor. Within a few years there would be nothing left of *Vanity Fair* except the memories.

When their subscriptions ran out, *Vanity Fair* readers got a chance to renew with *Vogue*. A few took the opportunity, but not many. The story is told that an elderly gentleman was looking for *Vanity Fair* in his club, and when he didn't find the latest issue on the library table he became incensed and demanded that an attendant bring him the magazine forthwith. "But, sir, that's a woman's magazine now," blurted the attendant. "We just throw it away as soon as it comes in."

Condé Nast Publications Inc., kept ownership of the name, and, yes, a new magazine using it appeared under their imprint in the 1980s. But the namesake was mostly just tinsel, a faint and brummagem imitation of the original. By the time that the new *Vanity Fair* appeared, all vestiges of the original were lost to public consciousness. The principal players, too, were long dead, Condé Nast having died in 1942, Frank Crowninshield in 1947, the latter holding fast to a faith that his much beloved New York was still the civilized and charming place he had once helped to make it.

It has been said that nothing is as dead as yesterday's newspaper, and perhaps the same thing can be said about yesterday's magazines. There are few people today with strong recollections of the original *Vanity Fair*, and many of those now must look at it through a heavy veil of nostalgia. Nonetheless, *Vanity Fair*'s twenty-two year reign is worth getting nostalgic about. It was one of the great American magazines. It brings us back an older and happier America. It reminds us of a side of ourselves that today is sorely neglected, the ability to entertain ourselves in lofty material ways. Critics from abroad have often complained that we Americans lack our own distinctive aroma and flavor—except that of anxiety and the sweated brow—that we don't know how to amuse ourselves in an adult fashion. We spend too much of our time making our world and not enough time savoring it. Our only play is the play of adolescence. In *Vanity Fair* we find an America at ease, a reflective America not bedeviled by debt, by cheap merchandise, by demagogic politicians, by nuclear holocaust, by world hunger. It was, however, a generous and outgoing America. *Vanity Fair* was a magazine of high style and an intelligence to match that generosity. It encouraged Americans to spin out a world of creative play and amusement, a world where it was still possible to get a breath of fresh air and laugh at the elemental absurdities of life.

The Rise of the New Yorker

When the *New Yorker* first saw the light of day on February 21, 1925, it looked to all the world like just another humor weekly, not much different from *Life* and *Judge*, except that at first glance it seemed to be markedly inferior to those old standbys. The *New Yorker* was a puny weakling at birth and seemed destined for an early grave, like so many other competitors of *Life* and *Judge* over the years. Roughly fifteen thousand copies of the first issue were bought up by the curious, most of whom doubtless shook their heads in mild amusement at this skinny imposter. And those in the know would have been even more inclined toward pessimism had they known that this magazine, which said it was trying to reach sophisticated New Yorkers, was being guided in its destinies by a former hobo newspaperman from Colorado named Harold Ross, a man once described by the maliciously mirthful Alexander Woollcott as looking something like a dishonest Abraham Lincoln.

And, yes, the *New Yorker* immediately took the road of failure. The third issue sold a mere 12,000 copies, the fourth, 10,500. By April of 1925 the magazine was selling only 8,000 copies and losing eight thousand dollars a week. The end seemed to be just around the corner. Nonetheless, all the sages and wicked fairy godmothers were wrong. The *New Yorker* would go on to be one of the most phenomenally successful ventures in American publishing history. It would hit its stride in the 1930s when all of the earlier smart magazines were dead or dying. It would in fact become something that none of them had ever succeeded in being—a big money-maker. Magazines like the *Smart Set* and *Vanity Fair*, and even the humor magazines in spite of their devoted followers, had always been marginal ventures in the world of commercial publishing, rarely enjoying circulations above 100,000 and usually far below. The blue baby *New Yorker*, when it finally took its first breath, made the moguls of Madison Avenue sit up and take notice. When its first quarter century was out, the *New Yorker* was selling 400,000 copies a week—mass circulation by any standard, even though still a dwarf in comparison with the great popular giants like the *Saturday Evening Post* and the *Ladies' Home Journal*.

Four hundred thousand copies a week! And this a magazine that editor Ross at first hoped would reach only a small elite of city sophisticates. (In 1925 he projected, or rashly aspired to, an eventual circulation of seventy thousand.) Four hundred thousand when everybody knew that the cream of New York society contained but four hundred persons. What occurred to bring about this transformation is one of the most inspiring mysteries of publishing history. Of this we can be certain: when the *New Yorker* finally stood upon its legs, it reached for a far broader audience than any that Harold Ross had ever dreamed of. In a prospectus for the magazine attendant upon its birth, Harold Ross had stated that "The *New Yorker* will be the magazine that is not edited for the little old lady in Dubuque." This remark, borrowing the name of H. L. Mencken's favorite provincial town, has, of course, been Harold Ross's most frequently quoted prophecy, and was, like a lot of things he said, totally mistaken. The *New Yorker was* produced for the little old lady in Dubuque, or at least for her upwardly mobile and city-bound daughter. Whatever its pretext, whatever its announced goals, the magazine would get a grip on middle America. To be sure, the *New Yorker* would seldom be found stashed behind the egg stove in some lonely Kansas farmhouse. It would be found on only a few of those same gaslit parlor tables graced by the *Saturday Evening Post.*

Still, the magazine clearly found its level somewhere, and not just one level really; its appeal would be broad and pervasive. It would reach out to a great many Americans who everywhere were yearning for the joys and benefits of metropolitan life—this in a nation that was being rapidly transformed from a rural to an urban society. The *New Yorker* would assemble a group of writers and editors most of whom represented the ethos of middle-class America. To be sure, in the beginning there were not a few "socialite" writers and artists on the *New Yorker,* but some of these added more style and aroma than direction and substance to the magazine. Snobbery of the old kind was not Harold Ross's dish; he himself was as out of place in high society as an atheist at a Bible seller's picnic, and in the end if he sought "smartness" at all it was not the smartness so beloved of Col. William D'Alton Mann, a smartness of countesses, dukes, dowagers and bluebloods of old Gotham. There would be a new "smart set," a new elite, a new manner and mode of sophistication, but it would be something the *New Yorker* magazine would create from scratch. By a strange miracle of gestation, the *New Yorker* discovered itself by slow degrees mainly by assembling a group of writers and artists who, one by one, dropped in on editor Ross as if the nation had been tilted on end, the appropriate talents, happily landing, however often painfully, on Mr. Ross's lap.

Harold Ross began with a vision of the *New Yorker,* but it was largely indistinct, a kind of skeleton. In the first year or so of the magazine's existence he did not really know what the *New Yorker* would be like in its mature form. The magazine built itself up by a series of inexplicable accretions until it became, in the 1930s, a miracle of the magazine industry. This miracle, of course, has often been attributed to the sorcery of H. W. Ross, the mysterious and unlikely editor who guided, shook, cajoled, wheedled his assembled writers, editors, and artists into shape by means of mysteriously organized good taste and the possession of a mercurial temperament that seemed to force the best out of people.

In a sense there developed over the years a kind of Ross mystique, aided and abetted by several generations of *New Yorker* writers who knew him in the old days and went on to write books about him. These many writers, including James Thurber, whose *The Years with Ross* was perhaps the best of the lot, took a kind of impish delight in creating a figure so enveloped in paradox and confusion that he was beyond definition and ordinary mortal comprehension, thus making the *New Yorker* a much more arcane and esoteric enterprise than it actually was. It suited *New Yorker* staffers and insiders to make the goings-on in the editorial precincts mysterious to the heathen, to outsiders, to those who hadn't yet made the grade, to people trying to figure out the *New Yorker* formula—above all, to advertising people and the money men who were always kept at arm's length in the early days—this distancing certainly being one of Ross's great inspirations and triumphs.

Whether Ross was really as inscrutable as has been alleged, there can be no doubt that "by the book" he was a totally inappropriate figure to head a magazine of high sophistication and literary excellence. Possessed of an inferior education, weighted down by huge pockets of ignorance, Ross had to be coddled and gingerly outmaneuvered by staffers who were either genuinely shocked or merely convulsed by his editorial queries, his gaudy displays of misinformation ("Who was Moby Dick? The man or the whale?" "Willa Cather. Willa Cather—did he write *The Private Life of Helen of Troy*?"). These same people were perplexed by Ross's preoccupation with punctuation marks as he became alternately rhapsodical or frenzied over commas, periods and semicolons. How, they all wondered, these many young lads fresh from Yale, these girls from the best finishing schools, how could such an individual have gotten to a place where he could be making proclamations by fiat in matters of grammar, art and literary taste? Was it largely the possession of a mercurial personality always ready to disarm or derail any adversary by dint of a dramatic and emphatic style of talking, an itinerent newspaperman's vulgarity striking his more timid and mellow writers at an odd angle? Well, perhaps there is no one answer, no coherent explanation of Ross's editorial gifts. Perhaps, after all, we shall have to settle for an explanation of him given by Paul Nash, an English painter, taken to see the editor by James Thurber in the early thirties. Nash merely threw up his hands: "He is like your skyscrapers. They are unbelievable, but they are there."

It is clear that Ross did not exactly create the *New Yorker:* the magazine did not emanate from his vision or his intelligence the way that the universe emanated from the God of Plotinus. The magazine was created by the unique collection of talents who gravitated to its orbit at a time when the older smart magazines were blindly groping toward their graves; indeed the *New Yorker* was a beneficiary of the demise of those older magazines and inherited many of their best writers. But the *New Yorker* acquired a staff of much greater diversity and potential than those enjoyed by the earlier smart magazines, and by the late twenties and early thirties it would find itself blessed with a rich treasury of talent, the best in the field. How precisely it was put together is a matter for debate—perhaps it was the pinch of the depression, perhaps it was the result of some social alchemy beyond easy description—but, as if out of nowhere, there was a totally new magazine style, one that owed some of its initial impulse to the magazines of the previous generations but would now present the world with something altogether new and strikingly different.

All this is not to denigrate Harold Ross's role at the *New Yorker*, merely to say that in truth he was not identical with the *New Yorker* either in spirit or embodiment. Nor did he simply push forward a vision he had of the magazine in the mid-twenties, for that vision existed at first only in the form of a fuzzy and indistinct outline. Still, the story of the *New Yorker* can't really start anywhere else, since Ross was the magazine's founder; he did set the ship upon the seas, and his predictions about the magazine both as an editorial entity and as a business enterprise were remarkably astute and uncannily accurate. In the beginning the magazine didn't look very novel to most casual observers—or to keep observers as well, for that matter. But Ross intended it to be different. Without those intentions the magazine would probably never have clicked. So, yes, the story of the *New Yorker* has to begin with Harold Ross and the idea upon which he launched his new magazine. If everything has to start somewhere, the *New Yorker* clearly started with Harold Ross.

Ross was not without an enviable load of journalistic experience by the time he established the *New Yorker* at the age of thirty-two. He had been born in Aspen, Colorado, in 1892, but grew up mostly in Salt Lake City, Utah, where his family moved when he was seven. His father, George Ross, a Scotch-Irish mining engineer who had arrived from the old sod, was a man of forthright, some would say combative, character, with a gift of gab and not a little Irish wit. Harold and the elder Ross apparently didn't get along too well and experienced more than the usual number of father-son clashes, with the result that Harold developed something of a truant disposition and ran away from home a few times during his youth. But the son did not have entirely unpleasant recollections of this father and credited him with having bequeathed him a sense of humor, a trait that would remain an undeniable part of the character of the editor.

His mother, Ida, was a sweet, simple, upright woman, a Scotch Presbyterian, a very Victorian lady with the usual inhibited characteristics. Some of Ross's friends who met Mrs. Ross years later when she came East while her son was editor of the *New Yorker* believed that Ross was a mother-dominated individual, if not precisely what is usually called a momma's boy.

A man accustomed to the language of the pool hall or the saloon, Ross was nonetheless afraid to use profanity or sexual innuendo in front of women, an inihibition that not only influenced his editorial philosophies in later years, but also made him uncomfortable in working with women around the office. Women needed to be sheltered and protected from profanity Ross believed, yet he couldn't quite function in his daily life without it.

Ross attended West Side High School in Salt Lake City, where he was an uninspired student, but never without a large curiosity and sense of adventure. He did read, but seldom the classics; he developed a large appetite for dime novels and the characteristically rugged adventure stories of the day. All his life he liked authors such as O. Henry, Joseph Conrad, Jack London and others who seemed to enjoy the turbulance of life. During his high school years Ross developed an itch to become a newspaperman and served with relish on the staff of the school paper. *Red and Black*, where one of his close acquaintances was John Held, Jr., whose career in big-time journalism would flourish long before Ross got started in New York, and whose work Ross would buy during the early years of the *New Yorker*.

Dropping out of his junior year of high school, Ross took a job on the Salt Lake City *Tribune*, where Held was already drawing a regular cartoon. This began his career as a wandering newspaperman; he never returned to the classroom, a choice that left him with strong feelings of inferiority, covered up in later years by a scoffing attitude toward people overly stuffed with formal or systematic learning. The possession of a college degree, even a high school diploma, invariably invoked in him a contempuous smile or wave of the hand.

In the years that followed, Ross worked for a number of newspapers, mostly in the West, where he was considered a competent and reliable reporter, although hardly a star. It was the era of the tramp newspaperman, just as it was the era of the boomer railroad brakeman or telegraph operator, and shifting around from place to place was no disgrace. Over a period of several years he managed to do stints in Sacramento (where he hoped that he would be able to follow in the footsteps of Mark Twain), Atlanta, Panama City, New Orleans and San Francisco. At one time he even attempted to storm the bastions of the great metropolitan dailies in New York, hoping to be taken on by one of the glamor papers of the day, the *World* perhaps, or the *Sun* or the *Herald*—but the city was overrun by tramp newspapermen from the boondocks, most of whom, including Ross, had to retreat licking their wounds.

In San Francisco some of his newspaper colleagues took to calling him

"Rough House Ross," probably because of his fast-talking, hard-swearing roustabout manner, his disheveled style of dress; perhaps his poker playing and his occasional hard drinking. He also enjoyed for a time the nickname "Hobo Ross," this not because he was a hobo newspaperman, which would hardly have been a rarity in those days, but because of a practical joke once played on him by his city editor at the Sacramento *Union*. Ross was told that he should hop a Southern Pacific freight to Truckee where he was instructed to get a good feature story about the high Sierra. Unbeknownst to Ross, the editor had another reporter check out which freight car Ross was riding on and then called ahead to a local Sheriff of his acquaintance, asking him, as a joke naturally, to grab Ross off the train and throw him in the calaboose.

Annoyed and swearing, Ross was hauled from his box car and locked up without any charges being filed. After strenuous protests that he was a Sacramento reporter, and while enduring the scornful laughs of the jailers, a call was put through to the paper in Sacramento, which denied any knowledge of a "Harold Ross." Now, of course, Ross knew that he had been had, so between night and morning he made the best of the situation. He alleged to his captors and all the petty criminals in the jug that he was a notorious criminal, wanted for three murders in Salt Lake City. Throughout his life, Ross was an incomparable practical joker and could seldom be bested in such situations.

By the time the United States entered World War I in 1917, Ross was looking for new adventures and he almost immediately signed up for service with the 18th Railway Engineers Regiment, whose posters proclaimed that the unit would be the first to go overseas. Landing in France, but with no desire to be put in a trench, he quickly made a move that would ultimately bring about a radical change in his career and later lead to his founding of the *New Yorker*. Spotting a notice in a Parisian English-language newspaper that a publication for enlisted men was being contemplated and was in need of experienced journalistic talent, Ross immediately left his unit without so much as an explanation or goodbye to officers or friends and swung aboard the next truck to Paris—he was AWOL, of course, for which he could have been court-martialed or even shot.

The first issue of *Stars and Stripes* was already off the press when Ross arrived at its makeshift offices in the old Hotel Sainte Anne. There was a pressing need for men to churn out copy and Ross was immediately put at a typewriter, his new commanding officer promising to take care of the paperwork and arrange for his transfer from the 18th Engineers. In the weeks that followed Ross found himself being joined by a number of other literati who had been assigned to the new enterprise, one being John T. Winterich, a bookworm type who looked even less the soldier than Ross, another being Alexander Woollcott, who had already made his mark as drama critic for the New York *Times*. Ross greeted Woollcott scornfully, laughing in his face upon hearing that this fat Eastern dude was passing off among his credentials a college degree (from Hamilton College), and a stint on the supposedly effete *Times*. Woollcott was not offended apparently by Ross's jibes and the two became uneasy friends. (Woollcott seemed to have no difficulty abiding the rough and crude-mannered Westerner who mocked him, just as he was lustily drawn to those who fawned over him, but apparently could tolerate few people in between.)

Although he was probably the roughest and crudest of the newsmen who eventually gathered to put *Stars and Stripes* together, indeed perhaps *because* he was, Ross was soon selected to be editor of the GI paper. The office gave him no perquisites and throughout the war he remained nothing but a private first class, but he was out of the trenches and he did have an uproariously good time. Above all, he learned how to be a magazine editor, at least by his own strange lights. All day long he hunched over copy, fussing over commas no doubt and fuming over the dearth of facts, while in the evenings he and his colleagues sat around swapping stories, drinking and playing poker.

He even had time for a little romance. He fell in with a dark-haired girl named Jane Grant who had formerly worked on the *Times* with Woollcott. Grant had wheedled her way abroad with a movie company after she failed to gain a berth on any paper as a war correspondent. Hailing from Joplin, Missouri, she had earlier elbowed into New York journalism in the company of a hardy band of women who were the first to crack the bastion of male-dominated newspapers during the years just before the war. Woollcott some-how had come to the conclusion that Grant and Ross would make a likely couple and introduced them. And Grant, like Woollcott, was convinced that Ross ought to come to New York when the war was over and try to reach for something big there. In any case, the romance flourished and, in 1920, two years after the armistice, Jane Grant became the first wife of Harold Ross.

After the war Harold Ross did head straight for New York, now con-vinced that magazine editing would be his métier, but unclear how to break in. War's end had actually given him a tidy bankroll because he had put together a little collection of GI jokes from *Stars and Stripes*—nothing but a scissors and paste job really — but the book, called *Yank Talk*, became something of a best seller, and put a nice piece of change in his pocket. Furthermore, he was offered a job almost immediately by the Butterick magazine group, whose management thought there was something to the idea of a stateside version of *Stars and Stripes*. The magazine, which was called *The Home Sector*, also signed up the talents of Winterich and Woollcott and a few other staffers of *Stars and Stripes*, and there was a quick blaze of interest in it, which, unfortunately, subsided all too quickly. A printer's strike and lack of advertisers killed off the magazine after a few months, and Ross began to turn his mind to other magazine ventures.

He accepted a good paying position with the American Legion, editing a magazine for veterans. But this publication, nothing but a house organ really, convinced him of the necessity of finding his own magazine concept, a notion that occupied him and his new wife for the next several years. Jane Grant by this time had resumed her work on the *Times*, using her maiden name, an unheard of practice at the time; in fact Grant, along with another newspaperwoman, Ruth Hale, who was married to Heywood Broun, had been among the founders of the Lucy Stone League, a pioneering feminist group that kept alive the suffragette causes that many thought were dead in the wake of the Nineteenth Amendment. Jane and Harold now spent many evenings hashing over the various possibilities for some kind of magazine formula that might occupy the attentions of one or both of them.

Even though Ross was frittering away his time on inferior editorial assignments and seemed to be going nowhere he had formed lasting relationships with a number of figures prominent in journalism and publishing in New York. He became a member, of sorts, of the Algonquin Round Table, introduced there, no doubt, by Woollcott, although he was also known to Franklin P. Adams, who similarly served out the war years in Paris, even though he had a pair of captain's bars on his shoulders. How "Roughhouse Ross" could have been made to fit in at the Round Table is something of a mystery since, as Edmund Wilson said, the group was made up of people from the suburbs and provinces "who had been taught a certain kind of gentility, who had played the same games, had read the same children's books," all of which they were now able to mock from a snobbish altitude of New York sophistication. Ross would scarcely have been able to share this lofty plateau since he did not share the genteel upbringing; yet clearly he added a certain gritty texture to the group by his very crudeness and naiveté. Certainly the acid-tongued Woollcott and Adams took a fancy to the crude Westerner who was every bit as ready to sling barbs and insults as they were.

Undoubtedly Ross was strongly influenced by the Round Table bunch in more ways than one. As a former journalist he was especially impressed by Adams's column "The Conning Tower," which was a regular and highly influential feature in the *World*. This column, and a few others like it, was filled with tidbits, clever sayings, ditties, rumors, witticisms and innuendo by and about the literary wits of New York. Adams was able to take in so much of this material that he came to believe he was a kind of Knickerbocker Samuel Pepys. While Adams's material was invariably rather thin, often the result of shameless logrolling of material passed from one newspaper chatterbox to another, Ross came to believe that New York society was big enough and probably stratified enough to support a magazine devoted entirely to local news reporting and features. This assumption was the seed idea that led to the concept of the *New Yorker* when it eventually went on the drawing board.

Truth to tell, though, the seed idea for the *New Yorker* went back even a little further, to the war years, when Ross was sitting around with his poker-playing cronies in the Hotel Sainte Anne and taking Jane Grant out for an occasional stroll. Ross had entertained the idea, and talked about it from time to time, of establishing a high-class tabloid newspaper directed to the upper crust of New York society. The tabloid idea may seem strange in hindsight, but the notion must have been powerfully reinforced in Ross's mind in the years immediately after the war when the tabloid concept caught fire in American journalism, quickly giving rise to such highly successful daily newspapers as Joseph Medill Patterson's *Daily News*, founded in 1919, and Hearst's *Daily Mirror*, founded in 1924. To be sure, the daily tabloids became notorious for wading through troughs of sex, crime, sensationalism, and other emaciated forms of human-interest reporting; still, tabloids were the wave of the present in journalism, so why not a high-class tabloid?

The high-class tabloid was not Ross's only idea during the early twenties; at one time he seriously thought about a shipping magazine of some kind—he was living in the port of New York, after all, so why not report on ship movements, news about the shipping industry with articles dealing with technical innovations and the like. And doubtless a few other ideas crossed his mind as well. Anything that would get him away from the drudgery of the *American Legion Weekly*. But he continued to be drawn again and again back to the idea of some kind of magazine or paper directed to New York society, and containing local news and reporting. Jane Grant took it upon herself to raise the idea of the high-class tabloid to her editor at the *Times*, the legendary Carr Van Anda, but Van Anda pointed out that no such paper could be gotten off the ground without the investment of huge sums of money, which neither Ross nor Grant could hope to round up. Still, the dream didn't die.

Ross became fairly well aware of the competition; he had been introduced to Frank Crowninshield and had a certain admiration for *Vanity Fair*, but felt that *Vanity Fair* was hemmed in my its simplistic formula and by the dominance of its oleaginous publisher Condé Nast. He was aware that Mencken and Nathan had achieved a certain amount of editorial independence at the *Smart Set*, and were able to run the work of many unconventional or avant-garde writers; still, the *Smart Set* hadn't made money for years and had never succeeded in targeting a vast commercial audience.

Then there were the humor magazines, *Life* and *Judge*. Ross believed that there was some reason for optimism along those lines if the stale formulas of those old boys could somehow be scrapped. And as luck would have it, shortly after having his own hopes for a society tabloid dashed by Carr Van Anda's gloomy assessment, Ross got a chance to work on *Judge*. Early in 1924 the firm that did the printing for the *American Legion Weekly*, and that also printed *Judge*, took a financial interest in the failing humor magazine and maneuvered a position for Ross as a kind of co-editor with Norman Anthony. (Since both magazines were housed in the same building, Ross merely moved down the hall to his new office: John T. Winterich took over as editor of the American Legion's magazine.) Ross accepted the assignment with the hope that the tired old *Judge* might be resuscitated and made into the kind of magazine he had been dreaming about. Ross's brief tenure at *Judge* was a dismal failure except in one respect. The experience reinforced his own ideas about the kind of magazine that he wanted to put together and strengthened his faith that it could succeed. By 1924 *Judge* was floundering, and Norman Anthony's charge as editor had been to look around for newer forms of humor that would appeal to a broader audience. He opted, as he was later to do also at *Ballyhoo*, for the lowest common denominator— bethroom jokes, sexual innuendo and the like. The magazine's traditional he/ she jokes had been bad enough in Ross's estimation, but now he found himself buying "Krazy Kracks" from readers and laying out "Funnybones"— jokes inside little boxes shaped like a dog's bone.

Above all, Ross came to perceive that the trouble with the old humor magazines was that they were casting their nets too widely in attempting to reach a national audience. What was needed was a really smart humor magazine that would appeal only to a sophisticated and educated elite and in a narrowly circumscribed geographical area. His keen business savvy had led him to the same conclusion. *Judge* was no longer attracting many advertisers, and Ross thought that he knew why. Who precisely would the advertiser be targeting in a nationwide humor magazine? On the other hand, if a somewhat similar magazine were put out directed mainly to people living in New York City and vicinity, it might well pick up numerous ads of the kind that were overflowing in papers like the *Times* and the *Herald Tribune*—ads from posh restaurants, theatres, automobile dealerships, polo clubs, furriers, couturiers, and so on. Ross had read the wave of the future astutely in the advertising field and correctly surmised that the way to pull in ads was to have a very well-defined audience that can be spotlighted. He knew that most of *Judge*'s ailments stemmed from failure to do this. And as he strolled through the magazine's mailing room looking at the ominous piles of back issues returned from all over the country, he became fortified in his resolve to publish a magazine that was not making these same mistakes.

All that Ross needed to try out his ideas was the money to get under way. He had talked to a number of financial backers but all of them had shied away from a project that seemed to be working a vein that had already run dry. Suddenly, however, a backer appeared in the person of young Raoul Fleischmann, heir to a modest yeast and baking fortune who had become one of the irregular hangers-on at the Round Table. Fleischmann, a good-looking habitué of the demimonde and of art circles, had decided that he wanted nothing to do with his family business or any of the straight and wide avenues of commerce; accordingly he was open to persuasion by Ross, always a convincing talker. He listened eagerly when Ross argued that the magazine could be gotten off the ground for a relatively small amount of money. (Fleischmann was hardly what would have been called filthy rich even in the twenties—but his nest egg of approximately three-quarters of a million was enough to get a new magazine off and running.)

If Fleischmann had known how much of his fortune would follow his initial investment out of the window in the next few years he almost certainly would never have entered into any agreement with Ross. But the projected investment was bearable. Ross had said that fifty thousand dollars would do, and Fleischmann was required to put up only half—the rest coming from the savings of Ross and his wife Jane Grant. Ross agreed to plow back most of his salary in return for stock. The new magazine, still unnamed, was now ready to go into the planning stage. It was the summer of 1924.

The *New Yorker* began its period of gestation in a shabbily furnished suite of offices at 25 West 45th Street, in a building owned by the Fleischmann family. Besides Ross as editor, the editorial staff consisted of Tyler

(Tip) Bliss, a veteran of *Stars and Stripes*, and Philip Wylie, a young son of a New Jersey minister who had started a public relations business in New York but had found it ruined by the nasty publicity surrounding his accusation in a paternity suit. Wylie had agreed to do a little publicity for the magazine and act as a kind of copy boy and general factotum. Bliss, with more magazine experience under his belt, was Ross's principal assistant. The rest of the staff consisted of Helen Mears, Ross's secretary, a switchboard girl, and an advertising salesman and his secretary.

There were some part-time helpers, however. One, of course, was Jane Grant, who usually came over in the evenings after her assignments were finished at the *Times*. Raoul Fleischmann dropped in occasionally also, although his experience in the magazine field was absolutely nonexistent. (In time, Fleischmann would take over the business side of the magazine, but at the beginning he was really little more than an investor: Ross was actually president of the F-R Publishing Company and Fleischmann vice-president.) But there were on hand in the beginning a few part-timers who would play key roles in the growth of the magazine. The most important, undoubtedly, was Rea Irvin, former art editor of *Life* who came in one day a week and would have much to do with the appearance and overall design of the magazine for a number of years. Also making important contributions at the beginning were James Kevin McGuinnes, a veteran of the humor magazines who suggested the title "Profiles" for a series of silhouettes of important people, and Howard Brubaker, a newspaperman whose material Ross had used at *Judge* and who agreed to get up a section entitled "Of All Things." A young man-about-town named Charles Baskerville was hired to write about night life.

Of course this was a staff that could hardly be relied upon to put out a weekly magazine for city sophisticates. Ross was going to have to depend on soliciting contributions from outsiders. He believed in the beginning that he had thought this through: following the practices of men like FPA, Alex Woollcott and Heywood Broun he believed that he could fill his magazine by logrolling. He was sure that at the Round Table, the Thanatopsis Club the many loquacious dandies of cafe society would give him enough material to put out a fresh, current and topical humor magazine. To this end, and with the urging of Raoul Fleischmann, Ross put together a list of "Advisory Editors," mostly names of Round Tablers, hoping to use this list in a dummy version of the magazine, thus selling the idea to advertisers.

In later years Ross ruefully admitted that this was the "only dishonest thing I ever did," but at the time his chagrin was more due to the fact that he had a rude awakening when he found that it was not going to be easy to shake regular material out of his old friends at the Algonquin. Some of them were under contract to competing publications (such as Benchley, Sherwood and Adams); others simply didn't believe that Ross's venture would ever get moving. Still others, such as Dorothy Parker and Alexander Woollcott performed only in a desultory and unreliable manner. Very early in the life of the magazine Ross came to the realization that he could not depend wholly on his old friends from the Round Table, but had to develop his own youthful staff of writers and artists.

The Round Table did contribute one important thing to the new publication: its name. There had been a lot of discussion on the point during many luncheons, and the only name that kept coming to Ross was *Life* and that was already taken. Ross promised a share of stock to anybody who would put forward an especially fitting name. John Peter Toohey, a publicity man who many have alleged to have started the Algonquin luncheon table before the more glamorous figures arrived on the scene, had been eating and not paying attention to the banter over the magazine's name. But when he perked up his ears and inquired what kind of magazine this was to be, somebody replied: "A metropolitan magazine."

"Then call it the *New Yorker*," said Toohey. And so it became.

Toohey probably did not know, Ross certainly did not know, that the name had been used once before, way back in the 1830s by Horace Greeley, who put out a rather short-lived weekly of the same title. But that was hardly of concern at this point. Ross had no time at all to think about past failures of old magazines. His main concern now was to keep his *New Yorker* from being stillborn.

At this stage the only thing that seemed to forestall this grim possibility was Harold Ross himself and his capacity for hard work. Like so many desk-top publishers of the 1980s, Harold Ross *was* indeed the *New Yorker* during its first few years and especially in those late months of 1924 when the magazine was in the planning stage. Ross had his hand in everything, and no detail of organization escaped his attention. He was negotiating with printers and typographers; he fretted over design, subscription rates, circulation and distribution problems, paper stock, the myriad details large and small that invariably make or break a magazine.

Most important, he was now up against the crucial decisions about what precisely would go into the magazine—how specifically he could translate his dream for an urban smart magazine into concrete realization. What kind of artists and writers did he want? What departments and regular features would there be? To address these problems and to satisfy potential advertisers he sat at his typewriter one day and drafted a prospectus for the magazine, one that turned out to have prophetic powers of a high order. It described with uncanny accuracy what kind of magazine the *New Yorker* would eventually become, even though Ross was hazy about exactly how his objectives could be immediately achieved. Among the items in his prospectus were these:

> The *New Yorker* will be a reflection in word and picture of metropolitan life. It will be human. Its general tenor will be one of gaiety, wit and satire, but it will be more than just a jester. It will not be what is commonly called sophisticated, in that it will assume a reasonable degree of enlightenment on the part of its readers. It will hate bunk.
>
> As compared to the newspaper, the *New Yorker* will be interpretive rather than stenographic. It will print facts that it will have to go behind the scenes to get, but it will not deal in scandal for the sake of scandal nor sensation for the sake of sensation. Its integrity will be above suspicion. It hopes to be so entertaining and informative as to be a necessity for the person who knows his way about or wants to.
>
> The *New Yorker* will devote several pages a week to a coverage of contemporary events and people of interest. . . . The *New Yorker* will present the truth and the whole truth without fear and without favor, but will not be iconoclastic.
>
> Amusements and the arts will be thoroughly covered by departments which will present, in addition to criticism, the personality, the anecdote, the color and chat of the various sub-divisions of this sphere. The *New Yorker*'s conscientious guide will list each week all current amusement offerings worth-while — theatres, motion pictures, musical events, art exhibitions. . . . Readers will be kept apprised of what is going on in the public and semi-public smart gathering places — the clubs, hotels, cafes, supper clubs, cabarets and other resorts.

Ross also promised that the *New Yorker* would contain reviews of books, editorials "in a manner none too serious," prose and verse; he expected it to be distinguished for its caricatures, sketches, cartoons and humorous and satirical drawings. Now it was, too, that Ross promised not to produce a magazine for the little old lady in Dubuque. But he drove much more brilliantly and incisively to the point when he concluded that "the *New Yorker* is a magazine avowedly published for a metropolitan audience and thereby will escape the influence which hampers most national publications. It expects a considerable national circulation, but this will come from persons who have a metropolitan interest."

In this prospectus, whether wittingly or unwittingly, Ross had laid the foundation stone for the great institution that would become the *New Yorker* magazine of the 1930s and 1940s. In his mind's eye he had conceived of a magazine that would appropriate some of the best features of the earlier smart magazines, of the *Smart Set*, and *Vanity Fair* and the humor weeklies, but that would sidestep their weaknesses.

The *New Yorker* would have the light touch of the humor magazines, but it would avoid their stale jokes and their perpetual superficiality and graininess. It would have some of the bite and hardness of the *Smart Set* without its iconoclasm and without the monolithic stamp of personality evoked by the ideologies and intellectual crusades of Mencken and Nathan. Too, with its art work and cartoons it would avoid the dreary visual format of the *Smart Set*. It would be a slick magazine like Crowninshield's *Vanity Fair* but it would take a giant stride forward in an area where Crowninshield strangely missed out; Crowninshield, the archetypal man-about-town with global cultural pretensions, failed to cover the city of New York he loved so well. So desirous was he to teach the world about avant-garde art and European philosophy that he let slip through his fingers the quirky and often colorful happenings of his hometown. His magazine was current, but only in the big things, never the little things that gave the city color and irony and variety. *Vanity Fair* was gay and glamorous but it could also be ponderous and stuffy. Ross was determined to be gay and light without being frivolous and inconsequential—admittedly a hard-to-achieve combination.

The *New Yorker*, in brief, would be a magazine of familiar lineage, but if fully realized it would be unlike any magazine known to Europe or the Americas. Could it be pulled off? Eventually it was, and splendidly. But in the short run Harold Ross would first have to face the agony of failure and defeat.

The first issue of the *New Yorker*, which appeared on February 21, 1925, was an emaciated looking affair of thirty-six pages. There were six pages of ads—full-page ads for Caron Parfums, Elgin watches and the publishing house of Boni & Liveright. There were a number of smaller ads for bookstores and theatres. The design of the interior of the magazine looked like a jerry-built collection of fashionable typographical faces not yet thought out for their aesthetic harmony. Luckily a last-minute change had been made in the cover of the magazine—Rea Irvin, who would later go to work on the interior, designed a cover showing a dandified gentleman of the

Beau Brummell era peering at a butterfly through his monocle. Ross in one of his later spasms of unpredictability claimed that he wasn't fond of the drawing, but it has endured through the years and appears over and over again on the magazine's anniversary issue cover.

Leading off the editorial segment of the magazine was a section of two pages containing short news items most of which were intended to reflect life in New York. The section was called "Of All Things." This was followed by a department called "Talk of the Town," which contained somewhat longer items of the same nature. Then there were signed pieces by some easily recognizable names—Fairfax Downey, Corey Ford, Ernest F. Hubbard, Arthur Guiterman. (Ominously, perhaps, only one member of the Round Table appeared in the magazine over his own signature: FPA.) There were short departments covering music, books, movies. There was a "profile" of the opera impressario Guilio Gatti-Casazza, a kind of journalistic innovation that no one would have attached importance to at the time, but that was to become one of the *New Yorker*'s boldest achievements.

The magazine did a little better with its sketches, satirical drawings and cartoons. On the other hand, Ross, who had passionately determined to avoid the *Judge* style of humor, nevertheless tolerated a cartoon showing two people standing near a poster advertising a movie called *Wages of Sin*. The caption read:

> Uncle: Poor girls, so few get their wages.
> Flapper: So few get their sin, darn it.

The *New Yorker* clearly had a long way to go if it was to purge itself of the stale frivolities of *Life* and *Judge*.

In the second issue of the magazine there were two contributions by Dorothy Parker: a poem and a satirical sketch of a typical clubwoman. In the third issue there was an unsigned profile of the *New York Time*'s Carr Van Anda by Alexander Woollcott, but it must have been obvious to all readers that not much fresh stuff was coming in. In the second issue, "Talk of the Town" appeared on page 1; the following week it was moved to page 13. Thereafter it returned to page 1, where it has remained to the present day. Ross was desperately struggling to find a formula that would work, but as the weeks wore on he was not attracting much material and both advertising revenues and circulation were beginning to slump badly.

By the spring of 1925 it was apparent to almost everybody except Ross that the magazine was not going to make the grade. To keep the ship afloat in spite of all the adverse signals, Raoul Fleischmann pumped more of his inheritance into the project. Fleischmann brought in, although hardly with Ross's blessings, a consultant named John Hanrahan, sometimes popularly called a "magazine doctor." Hanrahan's initial assessment was that there was little reason for optimism, but he pitched in anyway. Although Ross was cold to his ministrations, Hanrahan's advice proved to be of some value later on as things began to pick up. In April the situation looked desperate, with financial losses mounting and circulation failing. Ross did everything he could to spur contributions; he put notices on newspaper bulletin boards asking reporters to submit human-interest stories; he called everybody he knew. But the *New Yorker* was not in a position to pay generously for anything, least of all squibs, so that its issues remained thin and scrawny. The Round Table was silent about the fate of the *New Yorker*. Worst of all, its members came only grudgingly to Ross's aid. He was forced to the realization that his original plans for filling up the pages of his magazine had come to naught. On the morning of May 9, a small group assembled at the Princeton Club for what looked like a wake for the *New Yorker* magazine. Among the group were Ross, Fleischmann, Hanrahan and Hawley Truax, a friend of Ross's who had taken a liking to the magazine and had been advising Ross on business matters. Fleischmann expressed his desire to abandon ship, and certainly his insistence that a tourniquet he applied to stem the flow of his cash into this rapidly failing venture. While no absolute determination was made to close down the magazine and lay off the staff, the situation looked bleak. When the little band broke up and were walking across the street, Fleischmann heard Hanrahan say, "I don't blame Raoul, but he's killing a living thing." The remark apparently cut Fleischmann to the quick and he momentarily wavered in his resolve to pull out. The next week he agreed to wait just a little longer if Ross could find a few more outside investors.

No new big investors were located, but Hawley Truax, son of a wealthy New York lawyer, agreed to put something in the kitty. Truax also attempted to use his persuasive powers on a few other wealthy individuals that he knew but without much luck. He did obtain a little help from his brother-in-law, the celebrated trial lawyer Lloyd Paul Stryker. The investments of these two were hardly bounteous, however, and in the months ahead Fleischmann would be prevailed upon to sink still more of his money into this project, in which he had come to take a kind of paternalistic pride.

With the summer coming on, the *New Yorker*'s situation was almost exactly identical with that of the old *Life* back in the 1880s when the young chums from Harvard who founded the magazine discovered themselves on the edge of oblivion but had one last desperate chance to make good during the drowsy summer months when magazines usually provided only meagre fare. And the same thing happened to the *New Yorker* that happened to *Life* in 1883. The magazine did not die, but it picked up just a jot. Circulation did not fall below the deathly figure of ten thousand that had been reached in May.

In the fall of 1925 advertising revenues were up ever so slightly. But legend has it that the corner was turned for the *New Yorker* when a young lady of high society, Ellin Mackay, whose father was considered one of the wealthiest men in New York, sent in an article entitled "Why We Go to Cabarets," which eventually appeared in the *New Yorker*'s issue of November 28, 1925. The piece was atrociously written, clearly by a rank amateur, although it had arrived at the *New Yorker* offices bound in a sumptuous leather cover. After the hand script was deciphered it was decided that massive rewriting was necessary, but the article was immediately perceived to be an important one and its thrust was not altered. Miss Mackay's explanation of why the demure young ladies of high society frequented cabarets was somewhat shocking. The high society functions planned for debutantes were boring and mostly fraudulent. The young males in attendance were either under the complete control of their dowager mothers or else they were imposters who had pushed their way in without being bluebloods, only having learned to dress and act like such. In a cabaret, therefore, a girl was free of the heartless stag line and could choose the kind of partner that interested *her*.

Miss Mackay's article created quite a stir in New York society, and this magazine, which heretofore had been mostly neglected on Park Avenue, came to be thought a product that might just possibly provide a little amusement and perhaps edification. Miss Mackay wrote other articles, but these turned out to be less important than her private life, about which the *New Yorker* was also able to provide some information. (She was, by the way, a peripheral member of the Algonquin Round Table.) While following her own prescriptions for life, and to the horror of her parents, she had fallen in love with a Jewish songwriter, Israel Baline, better known to the world as Irving Berlin. The ensuing courtship, a temporary enforced separation, and finally the marriage of the couple became hot news to which the *New Yorker* would be privy in the months ahead—in fact, for a time Jane Grant and Harold Ross had been hiding Miss Mackay from the press in their own apartment.

However much this fortuitous liasion and the article on cabarets may have played a role in the *New Yorker*'s reversal of fortunes, at the end of 1925 advertising revenues were up sharply and so was circulation. The *New Yorker* continued running in the red for a long time. It did not actually turn a profit until 1928, but as the year 1925 came to a close, it was apparent to all concerned that the magazine could survive.

Even as the circulation of the magazine began to pick up, Ross knew that his product was still mired in mediocrity and that he would have to cast about vigorously for new talent if he were to eradicate the magazine's reputation for being either old hat or superficial. He had discovered, as editors of smart magazines had in the past, that you could not depend on people from the tuxedo and champagne set to drop into the office with well-crafted articles, or even tidbits of news. An even more shocking discovery was that he couldn't even depend on his old friends from the Algonquin Round Table.

One of the Algonquin bunch that Ross was able to harness occasionally in the early years of the magazine was Dorothy Parker, now doing some of her best work, and decidedly rising above the level of most of her erstwhile cronies at the Round Table. Parker had no other full-time commitments and so was able to send in some of her clever, acid-edged verses, which seemed so suitable to the twenties' mood of brassy cynicism and hard sophistication. But Parker's personal problems and her alcoholism tended to make her sufficiently elusive that Ross never succeeded in converting her into a regular staff member, although he had wanted to do so. One day when she was supposed to be churning out copy in the *New Yorker*'s offices, Ross found her sampling the wares at a local speakeasy. Why wasn't she at the office? "Someone was using the pencil," was her sarcastic response.

To fill up a substantial magazine week after week Ross needed to locate somewhere a wholly new vein of talent, and for the next several years the personnel situation at the *New Yorker* would be in a state of perpetual flux — some would say chaos. Writers, artists and editors would pass through the magazine's editorial offices as if through a revolving door. Ross would have to fire over a hundred people during the early years, accumulating a certain amount of ill will and an undeserved reputation for harshness and arbitrariness that managed to get distorted by later historians of his magazine. In his desperate search for a formula for the *New Yorker*, though, he had little choice but to try out all kinds of new people.

Probably the most important early recruit from the social register was Ralph McAllister Ingersoll, recently of Hotchkiss and Yale, who had been recommended by Mrs. Franklin P. Adams. Ingersoll dropped in for an interview, made Ross so nervous that he spilled ink on Ingersoll's spotless suit, but was hired on the basis of his relationship to Ward McAllister, who, after all, had invented the "Four Hundred." Ross didn't have the slightest idea of whether Ingersoll would work out, but the lad had had some newspaper experience on the New York *American* and seemed willing to try anything. As things turned out, Ingersoll was one of the best additions to the staff that Ross ever made. A resourceful manager, Ingersoll became and remained for a number of years, the magazine's de facto managing editor, handling deftly and with aplomb a great many administrative functions in the office. Ingersoll would never quite receive the credit that was his due, and with the passage of time the two editors rubbed one another the wrong way, but Ingersoll was the great organizer, or "Jesus" that Ross long claimed to be looking for. Later on, probably annoyed by Ingersoll's arrogation of power, Ross appointed other "official" managing editors, but while he remained on the staff Ingersoll was the magazine's most skillful executive, perhaps the only naturally gifted one. In the thirties Ingersoll would be lured away by Henry Luce to be editor of *Fortune*, and later he became a highly successful newspaper publisher, but his stamp on the early *New Yorker* has probably always been underestimated.

There were not to be a great many socialites, however. Ross was suspicious of them—certainly he was always suspicious of Ingersoll, even as he privately admitted his talents. He knew that a magazine intending to reach the salons and drawing rooms of high society would need a few genuine specimens on the premises, but what he was looking for was a wholly new kind of talent, possessing characteristics yet unknown. But where would it come from? Mostly, as things turned out, beginners would just drop in from the subway—a group of young writers and artists who had seen the magazine on the newsstands and felt some kind of kinship with it.

Ross was especially interested in recruiting from the ranks of New York newspapermen, and his first important catch, the first writer to turn out the kind of material Ross was looking for, was a twenty-five-year-old rewrite man from the New York *World* named Morris Markey. To begin with, Markey was the kind of fellow that Ross could warm up to. Hailing from Richmond, Virginia, where he had dropped out of high school in his junior year, Markey had worked in a soap factory and then had spent a few years as a wandering newspaperman—had even spent some time on the Atlanta *Journal* where Ross had done a turn. Ross had noticed some of Markey's feature stories in the *World* and appreciated his ability to get a grasp on significant stories behind the news and to lay them down with clarity and without the embroidery used by the typical feature writer. Markey began writing a column for the *New Yorker* called "Behind the News," a title later changed to "The Reporter at Large." Under Ross's careful eye, Markey began creating a new mode of journalism characterized by "casualness," by a leisured story line. A strong sense of narration in reporting that was also accurate and precise would become a *New Yorker* trademark in the years ahead. The idea was to avoid "hard news," the urgency and pressure of the city room, but stay rooted in fact. But the facts that were wanted were not those of the morgue or the hot telephone line, rather those found between the interstices of the hard-news network. If a building was to be torn down on Fifth Avenue making room for a skyscraper—well, the solid news was there for all to read in the daily newspaper. But was there something to be had in the conversations of the sidewalk superintendents? Do we learn that the old building now tumbling down once housed the library of the New York Antiquarian Society, and what happened to that library? Is a frieze above the door of the old building being removed to the Metropolitan Museum of Art? Come to think of it, had anyone ever noticed that old frieze, so long covered with the grime of automobile and bus exhaust? A look at such things would be the heart and soul of a new kind of reporting.

By the early 1930s Ross's hunt for young writers who could write casuals and other "Talk of the Town" material had paid off handsomely. By that time the front pages of the magazine contained the most sprightly and crisp journalistic prose to be found anywhere in America. The brilliant, almost childlike simplicity and *joie de vivre* of these pages come as a surprise to the reader who has endured the care-hardened end of the twentieth century. Here is a characteristic piece from the issue of November 14, 1931, entitled, "Up in the Air":

Millionaires and peddlers get their balloons from the Airo Balloon Corporation, in Third Avenue. The William Thaws ordered colored balloons, made to look like ripe fruit, and white balloons with electric lights inside them—quite a trick—for their daughter Virginia's coming-out party. The Eugene Meyers spent several hundred dollars on the balloon-work for a party they gave in Washington. These were gold balloons which were hung in clusters in trees. Incidentally, this was the party both the Ganns and Longworths stayed away from; but the balloons didn't have anything to do with that.

Mr. Charles Heitman, head of the company, says many interesting people are customers of his: several department stores, Ruth Nichols (who released her balloons from the Empire State Building), Nicholas Roberts (who releases a lot every year at the barn party he always gives for the Yale football team), Fred Stone and Eddie Cantor, Sheffield Farms, Warner Brothers, the Gulf Refining Company, and Witherbee Black of Black, Starr & Frost, etc. Mr. Black was so pleased with his balloons that he ordered some for the thirtieth reunion of his class at Princeton. The feature number was a balloon made in the shape of a tiger and painted like a tiger. "Humorous, very humorous," Mr. Heitman told us.

Balloons sell from a penny apiece, for the ones you blow up yourself, to whatever you want to pay. Airo recently filled a three-hundred-and-fifty-thou-sand-dollar order for some big concern. Mr. Heitman wouldn't say what concern. The balloon business can be very secretive. Airo has a special inflating place in Newark. Helium is used there. Of course the bulk of their business is advertising-balloons. The company will print anything you want on a balloon excepting, of course, profanity and the like. They do political balloons, circus balloons, Halloween balloons. A balloon in the shape of a cat's head is a popular number. You could get a thousand of them very reasonably, with your name printed on each one, and set them loose over the city, if you were a mind to. You don't have to get police permission to release balloons, as you do to drop roses on a building from a plane.

The Airo company takes special pride in doing the balloon-work for parties. You can have a small party done for as little as twenty-five dollars. The balloon people usually work with the decorators and florists. All seem to get along well. Mr. Heitman, who is only about thirty, but an old hand at balloons, is very fond of an arrangement whereby balloons come trickling down the ceiling of a drawingroom or ballroom while an orchestra plays "I'm Forever Blowing Bubbles." He frequently suggests this number to clients.

A few weeks later, another piece from "The Talk of the Town" entitled "Bus Stop":

Habitual travellers on Fifth Avenue buses know that Thirty-sixth Street is specially honored by conductors, who call out plainly: "Thirty-sixth Street." It is the only street so honored. The reason, we have discovered, is that the Union Motor Coach terminal is in that street, No. 59 West Thirty-sixth, and the Union Motor Coach Company, which operates long-distance buses, is owned by the Fifth Avenue Coach Company. The terminal is the one that used to be in the old Waldorf before that inn was razed.

Not only does the F.A.C.C. honor the U.M.C.C. by hollering out "Thirty-sixth Street," but a week or so ago conductors on all buses handed out to passengers a book called "Travelers's Mother Goose" urging the advantages of travelling by bus. This we found engaging, largely because it answered that question: "Where are you going, my pretty maid?" It turns out that the maid (who intimated that she was simply going a-milking) was actually going to Montreal, by motor coach.

The exact style of writing sought by Ross was slow to develop and it did not blossom at the *New Yorker* overnight. There would, of course, never be anything like a single and monolithic *New Yorker* fact piece or story, but a wide latitude of things that fit in under a shiny new umbrella. What had to be done in the months and years ahead was to assemble a staff that could be relied upon to produce solid material, diverse in variety, that would satisfy Ross. In his book *Ross and the New Yorker*, Dale Kramer assumed that Ross marched forward knowing only what he *didn't* want—he didn't want the formulas of *Life* and *Judge*, or *Vanity Fair* for example—not what he *did* want. But that is not wholly accurate; Ross may not have known what he wanted in advance, or may not have been able to articulate his wants, but there was no question that he knew what he wanted when he found it. So the early years at the *New Yorker* were painful ones, a time of sifting the wheat from the chaff, which was an often excruciating process and earned Ross a reputation for being much more irascible, quixotic and changeable than he actually was.

There is no doubt that the *New Yorker* style had to be won by slow and painful steps, and for the first five years of the magazine's existence, Ross was almost weekly tampering with the formula, the layout, the placement of departments, the relation of fiction to fact, the length of casuals, talk pieces, theatre reviews. With horrifying regularity and with traumatic consequences to his associates, Ross would regularly tear up the magazine, even right up to press time, hoping for some emerging style, some new aroma that wasn't there before. Above all, though, if he recognized fresh young talent, he would do whatever he could to develop it.

A good example of Ross's ability to get the right person in the right job was his recruitment and direction of a high-spirited Vassar graduate, Lois Long, whose work he had noticed at *Vanity Fair*, where she was being paid a pittance to fill Dorothy Parker's old job as drama critic. Long was brought on board to take over Charles Baskerville's department, "Tables for Two," when the latter went to Paris late in 1925. Long chose the pseudonym "Lipstick" in place of "Top Hat," and she covered the cabarets, nightclubs and restaurants of New York with dash and sparkle. She was, from the very beginning, a writer of great force, precision and honesty. The beat was a terribly exhausting one, however, and after two years, Ross, fearing that

Miss Long might drink herself to death, shunted her into a job that would be much more enduring. Perhaps sensing the demise of the cabaret era even before it arrived, Ross gave Miss Long a column on fashion, which at one time he had vowed not to have. Doubtless he was responding to some unspoken demands of local advertisers, but even more important, he had intuitively figured out that Lois Long possessed precisely the right skills to make a success of such a department. He was right—Miss Long stayed with the *New Yorker* until 1970, writing several million words of deft and pungent commentary on fashion, an area usually noted for its timidity and banality.

By the late 1920s there may still have been some doubt on the part of many close observers as to precisely where the *New Yorker* was headed and what it was looking for from its writers. In the field of art, however, there seemed to be little doubt that the *New Yorker* had already produced a revolution in its design, its aesthetic standards, and, above all, in the quality of its cartoons and drawings. Much of the success of the *New Yorker* in this area was due to the steadying influence of Rea Irvin, the magazine's part-time art director. Irvin was a product of the humor magazines, having been the art director at *Life*, but he was flexible, he was well trained, and he shared Ross's belief that the *New Yorker* should be looking for new and better styles and approaches. Because he was a somewhat older man, because he only came in one day a week when decisions were being made on art work, he and Ross seldom crossed swords. Furthermore, Ross, far more ignorant about art than about the written word, came to lean implicitly upon Irvin's judgment in aesthetic matters.

None of which means to suggest that Ross was passive during the regular weekly art conferences—Ross was seldom passive and never inert. To discover what he wanted for his magazine he was forever thumbing through the pages of current magazines, even European humor magazines such as *Punch* and *Simplicissimus*, trying to find novel ideas and approaches. These he pointed out to Irvin, and through a process of dialectic the artistically naive editor and the sophisticated art director were able to steer the magazine along a new course. Ross did have his own primitive sense of what was right, and his ideas had a lot to do with the art revolution that was getting under way at the *New Yorker*. Ross despised the long legends, especially the two-line captions used at *Judge* and *Life*, and he pushed for drawings in which nearly all of the humor or punch would be in the picture itself and not in the literary element. Although never completely abandoning or ruling out longer legends (he/she two-liners *were* ruled out), Ross ingeniously enhanced the *New Yorker*'s visual style by insisting on the predominance of the one-line caption. (In the 1930s Ross became especially delighted by Otto Soglow's completely uncaptioned cartoons.)

Ross and Irvin were looking for a good deal more from their artists than cartoons. At the *New Yorker* cartoons were invariably called "drawings," indicating that the art form commonly called by this name was only one among many being considered by the magazine's editors. The *New Yorker* was looking to buy sketches, spot drawings, caricatures, paintings that could be used on covers, and numerous other art forms, and it would not be unfair to say that in its first few years the art work of the *New Yorker* was much more rich, more eclectic and more variable than its writing.

Very early on Ross had hoped to identify and showcase the work of artists who could do for the "town" of New York the same sort of thing that Morris Markey was doing in the casuals and in "Reporter at Large." When such artists began arriving on the scene, they were invariably youngsters who hadn't yet identified their own distinctive style, but found out where their strongest talents lay while working for the *New Yorker*, often doing so with a little prodding from Ross and Irvin. A good example of the newcomers discovered by the *New Yorker* was Helen E. Hokinson, a shy willowy girl from the Midwest who had been submitting cartoons to *Life* and *Judge* but without success. Coming from Mendota, Illinois—not too far from Dubuque—Hokinson, or Hoky as she came to be called around the office, had left home abruptly after high school and moved to Chicago where she did fashion drawings for Marshall Field. Later she gravitated to New York and got a job on Hearst's newly established tabloid the *Mirror*, drawing several cartoon strips, one called "Sylvia in the Big City"—about a young lady not unlike Miss Hokinson. It didn't wash, however, and it looked as though Hoky's career as a cartoonist would come to an end. On her own, however, she was doing some stuff that gave her a great deal of pleasure—sketching amusing and realistic pictures of life in and around New York—people coming up from the subway, cab drivers hanging out the window, women pushing babies in carriages or carrying groceries, people looking up at skyscrapers.

Hokinson started sending some of her sketches to the *New Yorker*, and at one editorial meeting Philip Wylie held up a drawing of a plump middle-aged woman standing at a pier of New York harbor waving goodbye to her friends. The ship and the friends were actually out of view, but the woman's gestures told the whole story. Ross believed that this was the kind of thing he was looking for, and the drawing was bought—but used only as a spot illustration. After a few more submissions, Hoky was brought to the office and soon sketches from her voluminous notebooks were turning up as two-page spreads in the *New Yorker*. Only later did she find her métier and her enduring fame as a cartoonist, rendering with delicious perfection those now-famous middle-aged clubwomen with their outrageous hats, their indiscernible waistlines and half-size fashions.

By the mid-1930s the *New Yorker* would have on hand its own stable of artists, many of them known throughout the land. The cartoonists are probably the best remembered today, and surely old-time *New Yorker* readers will recall that during the depression years such giants as George Price, William Steig, Chon Day, Whitney Darrow, Jr., Richard Taylor, Robert Day, Charles Addams, Sydney Hoff and others began their long careers, giving the *New Yorker* unquestioned leadership in this field. On the other hand, cartoonists of the first rank started coming in during the magazine's first few years. Even before the *New Yorker* found itself in the profit column the magazine had featured the talents of Garrett Price, Gardner Rea, Barbara Shermund, Ralph Barton, Carl Rose and Mary Petty. Coming over from the old *Life*, and more than willing to abandon old formulas, was the highly talented Gluyas Williams. Another figure well established in 1925 was John Held, Jr., Ross's old high school chum from Salt Lake City. Ross wouldn't allow Held to do flappers—of which he had drawn thousands for every major magazine in the country—but he was permitted to do many other kinds of drawings.

Surely the most brilliant cartoonist to arrive at the *New Yorker* during its first five years was Peter Arno. The son of a prominent New York judge, Arno had been born Curtis Arnoux Peters, but changed his name to Arno professionally so as not to give offense to his family. He had already brought sufficient grief on his family even before arriving at the *New Yorker*. Dropping out of Yale in 1923, he had—seemingly like all Yale boys of the period—started a band, and in a nightclub called Rendezvous, played the piano for the well-known shimmy girl Gilda Gray. When the *New Yorker* started, Arno began to submit drawings, fully expecting them to be rejected out of hand, but their dash, their high-spirited and saturnalian elegance and top-hatted sophistication encapsulated the very qualities the *New Yorker* was looking for and they were accepted with alacrity.

Arno was a highly skillful and original artist who developed his own individual and immediately recognizable style. An impeccable draftsman who worked almost entirely in charcoal and wash, his bold and simple lines made him a cartoonist in the original and classic sense of the term. He tackled a number of subjects during his brilliant career, but in the early days of the *New Yorker* he captured with shimmering delight a worldly ambience that could not fail to appeal to a smart readership—a mood of jaded sophistication that was sometimes tinged with ennui, sometimes with ebullience. There was always a strong tincture of eroticism in Arno, usually kept somewhat in check for the *New Yorker*, but still there in his drawings of voluptuous females reminiscent of Renoir and Matisse. Only a certain smart-aleck quality, only a sense of satire and aloofness, allowed Arno to sidestep Ross's prohibitions against sex. Always deliriously present were his many curvaceous cuties lying in bed, bursting the seams of their nightgowns while attempting to spark the interest of inert, indifferent, and bloodless stockbroker husbands. And these same pneumatic creatures brought the New York cabarets and speakeasies alive as they whipped their top-hatted but usually inconsequential escorts into a state of effervescence much like that of a newly opened champagne bottle.

Like so many artists and writers who came to prominence with the *New Yorker* in its first few years, Arno evoked a mood that was totally familiar to New York high society, but at the same time his own alienation and playful detachment from that society allowed him to offer something new and refreshing—a new style, a new kind of cleverness. Arno had roots in what had come before, but the flowering of his art was something that had not quite been seen before. So it was with the *New Yorker*, which followed the lead.

Long before the great stock market crash of 1929 the *New Yorker* had turned the corner and edged its way into gentle prosperity; its balance sheets were now all showing in the black and it seemed to have found its own distinct audience. And it was not, apparently, an audience that would blow away with the first whiffs of the depression like other magazines whose appeal was to the affluent and the well fixed. Ross would continue to act, for now and for many years to come, as if the whole operation was on the brink of catastrophe. But by the time it was three years old the *New Yorker* had prepared itself for the long haul, and the depression years would actually mark the apogee of its long and stable history.

Before the onset of the depression, the *New Yorker* would move its offices from 25 West 45th Street to another building at 25 West 43rd Street, where they remain to this day. This building, like the first, was owned in part by the Fleischmann family, but there was more room here for the expansion that would be needed in the years ahead. Once officially known as the National Association Building, it is an especially nondescript piece of Manhattan real estate—of red brick facing, and with faint touches of Georgian detail in the upper stories. The *New Yorker* eventually became the largest tenant of the building, taking over three floors for the editorial department and two floors and a good deal of other miscellaneous space for the advertising and business departments.

The editorial quarters of the *New Yorker* have not been upgraded very much over the years—doubtless Harold Ross wanted it that way. The offices have always suggested a magazine that was just struggling to get by. The ambience of the hallway that leads from the elevator, and that of the main reception room on the nineteenth floor, are not at all suggestive of Col. William D'Alton Mann's "grand editorial chambers," but rather that of some third-rate literary agent or perhaps the headquarters of the steamfitters' union. The offices of Harold Ross and of William Shawn in later years always seemed more suitable for the managing editor of a provincial daily newspaper than of a celebrated smart magazine.

Surroundings were a little spiffier in the advertising and business departments; indeed after the first few years of the magazine's existence there was little if any direct intercourse between the two domains. This again was Harold Ross's doing. Before the decade of the twenties was over the relationship between Ross and Raoul Fleischmann had become strained and it was something of a tradition that there were two separate fiefdoms each keeping to its own affairs; editorial people never went on the business floors, and vice versa. As time went on Ross had fewer and fewer contacts with Fleischmann. This he felt was the only way that editorial autonomy could be achieved. Furthermore, with a frame of mind that could only have been a mystery to the modern businessman, Ross would sell more of his stock in the magazine every time some further strain developed between he and Fleischmann—when he died he owned no stock at all. This, he insisted, gave him a comfortable feeling that he had no ties to the business office and the financiers. There continued to be a few thin strands linking the separate domains over the years—Hawley Truax, for example, remained on good terms with both Ross and Fleischmann and acted as something of a conduit between them for a long time; but probably no major magazine in American (not even the *Smart Set*) managed to enjoy such complete editorial independence as did the *New Yorker* under Harold Ross. Theoretically Ross could have been unseated as editor at any time by Fleischmann, but for practical purposes Ross's quixotic and legendary rule was so firmly entrenched by the time the magazine emerged from infancy that the removal of Ross would have been unthinkable.

The *New Yorker* quickly became a staff-written magazine—never wholly so, of course, and in the early days, during the process of discovery of the magazine's formula, turnover in the staff was so rapid that its pages seemed open to all comers. As time went on, however, Ross and his fellow editors identified a group of contributors who would be thought of as *New Yorker* writers, and who developed a fierce loyalty to the magazine that they had created, and, in a quixotic way, to its mercurial editor. The distinction between a staff-written magazine and a magazine that depends heavily on outside or occasional contributors is an important one—most mass-circulation monthlies then and now tend to rely heavily on contributors who drift in and out of their pages, except, of course, for certain departmental editors and columnists.

It was perhaps inevitable that the *New Yorker* would become largely a close-knit editorial family. As a weekly, heavily dependent on obtaining hard news, there was little choice but to develop a group of people who could write news breaks, casuals, talk pieces in conformity with house standards. Furthermore, Ross had very exacting standards for what he hoped to see in his magazine, and he wanted his principal contributors to be on the property so that they could be regularly exposed to his editorial queries and to the general atmosphere and style of the office. To be sure, the *New Yorker* always had readers of unsolicited manuscripts, and new blood was pumped into the magazine, especially during the formative years. But from the early days the magazine developed its coteries, its reliables, its unannounced hierarchies. (In more recent years the relative rigidity in the pool of contributors and the sameness of the formula have been sources of some complaint against the magazine.) In no small measure the *New Yorker* owed its excellence and its professional polish during the 1930s and 1940s to a highly trained and loyal band of artists and writers.

It is more than a little interesting that a large number of the *New Yorker's* big guns, its best known and most characteristic figures, came to the magazine during its first five years. Some just dropped in, came out of the subway, so to speak; others were drawn to it because they had been reading the magazine and had come to the conclusion that the formula, although it had not yet jelled, offered something that was just right for them.

Probably the most important writers to join the staff of the *New Yorker* in the early days were E. B. White and James Thurber. White became a regular (but also maddeningly irregular) member of the staff in 1926; Thurber in 1927. For a time the two shared a small cubbyhole office together. It was probably one of Ross's great achievements that he spotted both of these writers quickly and allowed the magazine to build itself along the axis of their quite distinct but still harmonious talents.

White began contributing to the magazine shortly after it began publication. In later years he recalled buying the first issue at Grand Central Station, found himself amused by the cover drawing of Eustace Tilley and the contents inside, not because they had any high merit, but because the items were short, relaxed and sometimes funny. White was working in a bread-and-butter advertising job at the moment, but he wasted no time sending in things to the *New Yorker*. He considered himself a "short" writer, and accordingly contributed a number of short poems and squibs for which he was delighted to receive a check or two.

Born Elwyn Brooks White in Mount Vernon, New York, this "short" writer was nearly twenty-six years old when the *New Yorker*'s first issue hit the newsstands. His father was a well-to-do piano manufacturer and White grew up in a commodious home in this affluent "near-in" suburb of Manhattan. A quiet, loner type, who often preferred the company of snakes, mice, turtles, pigeons and rabbits, White's childhood and adolescence, like his own nature and his later literary style, were mostly sunny and benign.

After graduating from Mount Vernon High School in 1917, White matriculated at Cornell, capturing there the attentions of some of his English teachers—most of whom, surely, could not have failed to be charmed by his graceful prose style. As a senior he was the editor of the *Cornell Daily Sun*, and made the acquaintance of a number of other soon-to-be writers including Gus Lobrano (also to be an important figure on the *New Yorker*), Howard Cushman and Morris Bishop, a Cornell alumnus who would shortly return to the campus to teach.

White's college years were interrupted by the war, like so many youths his age, and after graduation he seemed to drift aimlessly for a few years. He had a job with the United Press that didn't work out, then one with the American Legion News Service where he spent time in the same building as Harold Ross, then editor of the Legion's *Weekly*. He didn't like this job much, bought a Model T Ford and began a trek across the United States with his college classmate Howard Cushman. During a vaguely planned *Wanderjahr* he held a few short-term newspaper jobs in Seattle, San Francisco, then jumped a ship to Alaska on which he was given a job as a mess boy.

Back in New York late in 1923 he began working as an advertising layout man, a job that gave him few satisfactions. But he did return to his first love, writing, sending light verse and occasional short pieces here and there. He was ecstatic when a few of his things were accepted by FPA for "The Conning Tower" — without pay, of course. In his spare time he wandered around New York simply observing the passing show, the delicate and often humorous nuances of urban behavior in all of its bewildering complexity. He sat in Grand Central Station and watched the commuters puff up the ramps to their stultifying office jobs. He rode the El, looked out to sea at Battery Park, spent long hours at the Bronx Zoo watching the animals. His own job was a mere mechanical function, so he devoted himself undistractedly to the gentle arts of observation and imaginative reconstruction of the phantasmagoria of city life.

White's first contribution to the *New Yorker* came in the magazine's ninth issue — a tongue-in-cheek piece that was titled "New Beauty of Tone in 1925 Song Sparrow," gently joshing what an advertising copy writer would write if he took over the "Vernal account." A few weeks later he was in the magazine again with a hunorous four-hundred word essay, "The Bronx River Rises in Valhalla and Flows South to Hell Gate," based largely on observations he had made from the window of the New York Central commuter train that he regularly took to his parents' home in Mount Vernon — as always, E. G. White was seeing things out the window that wouldn't even be noticed by the busy commuter with his face buried in the *Times* or the *Wall Street Journal*.

For over a year White would send in occasional short pieces or poems to the *New Yorker* — some of them would be published and some of them wouldn't. In the spring of 1926 he wrote two somewhat longer "casuals," as they were known at the *New Yorker*, and he received a letter from Harold Ross asking him to stop for a chat. When White arrived at the office he was greeted by an attractive dark-haired lady with a classic profile and a patrician manner, who enquired, as she stepped into the reception room, "Are you Elwyn Brooks White?" The lady was Katharine Sergeant Angell, who had been hired some months back by Ross as a reader of unsolicited manuscripts. It was this lady who had urged Ross to offer White a full-time job on the magazine.

White could not have known it at the time, but Mrs. Angell had already become a formidable force on the *New Yorker* magazine. He could also not have known that this lady would in a few years become Mrs. E. B. White, and that the two of them, singly and jointly, would play a monumental role in the shaping of this still-struggling weekly. All that White noticed was his future wife's classic profile and her intelligent, well-modulated voice. Still he was delighted to be offered a job on the *New Yorker*, even though he hesitantly asked to be taken on only for half-time work—he was still skeptical of the wisdom of giving up the solid footing of an advertising job.

But White did agree to go on the payroll, at thirty-dollars a week for half time. He continued with his advertising job at the same salary for a number of months and then joined the *New Yorker* full time. Eventually he would do almost everything there was to do on the magazine, although he began as "an orderly," as he liked to put it—writing kick lines for news-breaks. White never truly became a regular nine-to-five worker at the magazine, and no amount of prompting from Ross, Katharine Angell or any of the other editors could keep him from taking off abruptly for the zoo or for a stroll over to Times Square; he was a totally reliable worker who invariably got his copy in on time, but he remained the persistent introvert and solitary worker who no one, not even Ross, could imagine tied down to a meeting or an editorial conference.

In later years, when White's connection with the *New Yorker* had become somewhat more remote—although never broken—he came to be firmly identified in the public mind as a first-rate writer of children's books (*Charlotte's Web*, *Stuart Little* and others), and perhaps as the best familiar essayist we have in America. He also became known to millions of American college students through his contribution to *The Elements of Style*, a revision of a short treatise on writing originally written by his old Cornell professor William Strunk. But for a good part of his first decade on the *New Yorker* he graced the pages of the magazine as the principal writer of the "Talk of the Town" and "News and Comments" sections, and accordingly, was the primary force behind the style and mood of those departments.

Marc Connelly, a close observer of the *New Yorker* and a Round Table regular, once said that it was White who brought the *New Yorker* its "steel and music." He did this, of course, mainly through his clear, precise, but graceful prose style. White's pieces for the *New Yorker* were so close to perfection that he became the only writer on the magazine whose copy Ross couldn't find ways to improve, whose ideas were so lucidly and forcefully expressed that they needed no editorial tampering. But there was more to White's "music and steel" than lyricism and well-honed and highly crafted prose. White was a hard thinker, a thoughtful man, a philosopher perhaps, but in keeping with Ross's insistence that the *New Yorker* be light, White garbed his penetrating and rigorous thought in language that was blithe, sprightly, often childlike in its simplicity. His ideas were never expressed, as those of a philosopher must be, in a march of airtight syllogisms, but rather reduced always to metaphor and simple narration. White's comments on life were never theses pounded down and out, but rather playful musings, ideas in liberation, ideas rooted in sensation and immediate perception.

This accounts, no doubt, for White's obvious high suitability for Ross's *New Yorker*. The *New Yorker* had been intended as a smart magazine, was to possess a certain aloofness of spirit, an unconcern for the sweated brow of the intellectual or social reformer. In White, and the *New Yorker* style generally, sophistication emanated from an ethereal unconcern for the intellectuality of theses, propositions, the strivings of the ideological mind. It came from a delicate handling of life's little ironies, the relaxed, meandering and ineffable quality of things. Ross, the city editor type, known to be fanatical about facts—the exact address of somebody, the precise number of people who worked in the Chrysler Building—was never interested in facts as dead weight, but rather because they were fun, playful and intrinsically interesting. He did not want facts for their solidity but because of their joy of handling. He wanted a magazine that made molehills out of mountains, not mountains out of molehills—which, after all, was what every other magazine was purporting to do during the grim 1930s. And in White he found a writer who was light but not insubstantial, serious but bemused, knowledgeable but not glutted with ideas and theories. With White providing the spirit of the *New Yorker* in the darkest years of the depression, the country had a magazine that saw that the world had not yet been suffocated; that somewhere there was still a faint tinkle of bells, a play of lights on the darkened streets of New York—proving that one could continue to laugh and enjoy the same eternal but simple truths that had always made life worth living.

Unquestionably, one of White's most important contributions to the *New Yorker* was that he breathed a spirit of refinement and high good taste into the magazine. Earlier smart magazines had been clever, witty and intelligent, but at times they skirted the properties. To be sure, a social elite might well be amused by the bumptiousness of Mencken and Nathan; they might have tolerated the ribald snooping of old Colonel Mann; they could probably have had some appreciation for the crackerbarrel jokes of magazines like *Life* and *Judge*, but in the *New Yorker* they would have at last a magazine that was sophisticated in a genteel way, with a sense of humor that was subtle, laid back, finespun.

Getting these qualities in the *New Yorker* involved a slow process of discovery and the eventual engagement of a number of talents. White, of course, was the fulcrum of this innovative and powerful thrust of the *New Yorker* in the twenties and thirties. But discriminating historians have given an almost equal amount of credit to White's wife-to-be, Katharine Angell,

The New Yorker's formula was vague and tentative in the first few years. By 1931 it had discovered its essence and a path to lasting success.

Katherine Sergeant White thought she had the best editorial job in New York—keeping the steady hand on the helm of the New Yorker.

Peter Arno's "real" cartoon style gave the New Yorker the kind of punch and image that it needed in the thirties.

Wolcott Gibbs, whose talents both as writer and editor fit the New Yorker to perfection.

OPPOSITE. It was the guiding light of E. B. White and James Thurber, more than anything else, which gave the New Yorker its style.

THE TALK OF THE TOWN

IS THIS:

"See you Triangling* on the PARIS August 8

or the FRANCE August 15!"

THE August temperature in the west Atlantic averages 69 degrees. The August temperature ashore averages ever so much higher. Our Statistical Division adds that the longest gangplank in the world is really the short-

> *Triangling*— from v.t. to triangle: viz., to move in a French Liner in a triangular manner, as from New York-to-Bermuda-to-Halifax-to New York. Synonyms: to *rest*, to *relax*, to *sit-and-sip*, to *swim-and-shop*, to *dine-and-dance*, to *make* (fun), to *make* (envious, as in neighbors), to *make* (money, e. g. *save*).

est, and suggests that if we were to pack a toothbrush, a bathing suit, and a cake of cocoa butter, we would be in a position to take eleven steps from Pier 57 on board the *Paris* or the *France*, thus landing us in France itself, popularly supposed to be 3,000 wet miles away.

EVERYONE, apparently, is booking for these two new triangle cruises. It is either because they "come at the right time," or because "we aren't going to the shore this year," or because any French Line addict needs no more than the flimsiest excuse to get under a red funnel with a black collar on it, especially for six sublime days with Bermuda and Halifax thrown in. The moot question the Line hears is "What sort of people are booking?" The answer is of course "people"—the sort of people who make up any smart ship's-company: recognizable names

and unobtrusive names; nice young people and nice old people; Detroiters, East Seventies, a girl in a red dress, a jigger of Broadway, a few feet of film, and without any doubt a duenna from Dubuque. So that nice

social problem is solved, and is (as our French Line informant tells us) jake. On a French Liner everybody minds his own business anyway, and has a swell time doing it as the guest of the ablest hosts afloat.

FACTS. A lot is being done to *Paris* and *France* to make them gay and extra-special. Two salt swimming pools on deck. Clay-pigeon shooting (special prize if you bring down a schooner). Three special orchestras (one of them Lopez's). A true Montmartrois nightclub with dancing to sun-up *after* you've danced on the trick colored-

glass floor of the bright salon of the Paris. Movies for the afternoon. No change; of course, in the *famed* (*Time*) cooking of the French Line; no change

in the list of oh-so-inexpensive vintages; no change in the French Line habit of *rouge et blanc* on every table free.

Time ashore? But yes. A day of golf in Hamilton, and swimming, and a bit of British shopping. Halifax ditto. Venturesome souls will leave the ships at Halifax and come home by the St. Lawrence for not-very-much extra.

THE ships have booked much faster (report our secret agents) than even the ingenious French Line had expected; there are good cabins still to be had for reasonable prices. About twice the minimum will take you triangling like a king and queen. If you go, please send no postcards to this department.

Lucky so-and-sos will find it easy to book by calling the French Line, 19 State Street, New York—or any authorized French Line agent.

*Robert Benchley, of course, wrote for all
the smart magazines at one time or another.*

Publisher and editor of Esquire *were
David A. Smart and
Arnold Gingrich (left).*

OPPOSITE. Judge *hoped to parody the* New
Yorker *out of existence in 1931, but without
success.*

Esquire *flashed across the horizon like a meteor in the dark days
of the depression. Issues were immediately sold out at the unheard
of price of fifty cents.*

George Petty, whose early, highly stylized
Esquire *girls were restrained but frolicsome.*

The largeness, generosity, and high style of
Esquire's *early art and the large-folio*
format gave the magazine much
of its visual appeal.

The Esquire man, jaunty in his years, but never a mere overage playboy. The superb blend of editorial matter and advertising was an Esquire breakthrough.

the lady who pointed out White's talents to Ross in 1926. The Whites together—for many years they were referred to around the office as "the Whites" since they seemed to represent somehow the same spiritual power— provided a harmonious, Apollonian dimension to the magazine that Ross appreciated, and desired, but could not supply himself. Mrs. White, more than her husband, had the force and authority to make this dimension endure.

Mrs. White was an altogether remarkable woman in the *New Yorker's* history. She was really the only woman who held a top editorial position at the *New Yorker* during the Ross years. There were, to be sure, women contributors, but they were invariably not around the office day in and day out. Mrs. White was. Indeed, the only reason she did not become the titular managing editor of the magazine is that Ross with his old-fashioned ways could not abide the idea of a woman holding such a title. The truth was Mrs. White probably came closer than anybody to being the "Jesus" Ross always said he was looking for. She had her fingers in every pie, could always be depended upon to lay to rest all office uproars (and there were many), and above all, she was a constant and unrelenting presence of refinement and good taste.

She seemed to have been made for the job. Born to the patrician Sergeant family, Katharine was the daughter of an executive of the Boston Rapid Transit System, had attended Byrn Mawr, probably the most determinedly blue stocking of the great Eastern women's colleges, had served her term as a society matron (she had married a Cleveland lawyer, Ernest Angell, from whom she would later be divorced), had done social work in hospitals during the war, and later wrote for magazines like the *Atlantic Monthly* and the *New Republic*. When she showed up at the *New Yorker* offices shortly after the magazine was born, Ross hired her without much hesitation, doubtless impressed by her pedigree, her Boston accent and her highly refined manner (Ross could tolerate a patrician manner in a woman much more readily than he could in a man. He was ever suspicious of the highly talented Ralph Ingersoll but accepted Mrs. Angell without skepticism.)

Most important, from her very earliest associations with the *New Yorker* Katharine Angell seemed a perfect foil for Harold Ross, the ideal counterweight. Nobody understood this better than her future husband E. B. White, who years later, in an interview with the *Paris Review*, explained the relationship in his own deft and incisive prose:

I have never seen an adequate account of Katharine's role with the *New Yorker*. . . . She was one of the first editors to be hired, and I can't imagine what would have happened to the magazine if she hadn't turned up. Ross, though something of a genius, had serious gaps. In Katharine he found someone who filled them. No two people were ever more different than Mr. Ross and Mrs. Angell; what he lacked, she had; what she lacked, he had. . . . She was the product of Miss Winsor's and Bryn Mawr. Ross was a high school dropout. She had a natural refinement of manner and speech; Ross mumbled and bellowed and swore. She quickly discovered in this fumbling and impoverished new weekly, something that fascinated her: its quest for humor, its search for excellence, its involvement with young writers and artists. She enjoyed contact with people; Ross, with certain exceptions, despised it—especially during hours. She was patient and quiet; he was impatient and noisy.

Still, the *New Yorker* was in no sense a mere reflection of the tastes of the Whites any more than it was a direct reflection of the raucousness of "Rough House Ross." As it grew to maturity in the late twenties and early thirties, the magazine offered the world a rich diversity of styles and moods—indeed in all fairness to Katharine White, who served as the main editor of fiction in the 1930s, it ought to be remarked that the *New Yorker* did not manifest in those years (as has sometimes been complained since) a characteristic New Yorker story, or a *New Yorker* style. She was, it is true, a guardian of the gate, and fought tenaciously to keep material out of the *New Yorker* she deemed not appropriate, but her power to recognize an enormous diversity of talent was never stunted. John Updike, who came to know her a number of years later, said that she was "gifted with that terrible clear vision some women have (the difference between a good and a bad story looked like a canyon in her vision), yet not burdened by it, rather rejoicing in it and modest and humorous in her firmness." In spite of her regal exterior she possessed the zestful feeling of discovery and enjoyment of creation shared by so many wildly different *New Yorker* contributors during the early days.

In any case there were so many youthful voices being heard at the *New Yorker*, so many clashing personalities demanding an outlet for their talents, that a monolithic style would then have been well nigh an impossibility. If E. B. White's gentle, familiar style represented one of the *New Yorker*'s several voices, quite different styles were being cultivated by other writers whose temperaments and personalities were equally forceful and pervasive. A very obvious contrast to White was James Thurber, who became, after a somewhat agonizing apprenticeship, one of the magazine's top writers and clearly one of America's most brilliant humorists. Thurber and White were close friends for years, in an uneasy sort of way, and each contributed a great deal to the talent of the other, yet there always remained a deep temperamental gulf between them.

James Thurber, born in Columbus, Ohio, in 1894, came on the magazine in 1927 at which time he was thought of as one of the rare number of "gray heads." Coming from a large and solid middle-class family in Columbus, Thurber had attended Ohio State University, and, like White, had served his time on the usual student newspapers and humor magazines. Because of poor eyesight Thurber had been unfit for duty during World War I, and had spent time instead as a code clerk in the foreign service in Paris. After the war he married a respectable, solid and no-nonsense Ohio State coed and got a job as a reporter on the *Columbus Dispatch*. Tiring of this, he moved to New York in 1924, hoping to support himself as a free-lance writer. But for a long time nothing he did clicked; he sent short pieces to "The Conning Tower," but they were rejected. As soon as the *New Yorker* was founded he began sending in short items there also, but they too were speedily rejected. But he persevered, and eventually broke through.

Harold Ross would certainly have had reasons for taking a liking to Thurber even though in the beginning there was absolutely no indication where he might fit in. Like Ross, Thurber had been a working newspaperman; he had a somewhat extravagant manner and a propensity for mimicry and practical jokes. Perhaps because he didn't quite know what to do with Thurber, perhaps because of some characteristic and inexplicable logical lapse, Ross tried to make Thurber into an editor for a few years—indeed, even gave him the title managing editor, a role for which he would have been no more suited than E. B. White. But slowly, Thurber the writer (and later Thurber the artist) got discovered. After writing hundreds of "talk" pieces that Ross rejected, Thurber got the knack of it, greatly aided by White, who had immediately grasped the newcomer's essential genius, and by the early 1930s Thurber was one of the magazine's shining talents.

Thurber's humor was a good deal more pungent and biting than White's, and there was to his personality a certain spirit of maliciousness and a decided suspicion of the world, perhaps even a kind of gloominess. But he developed a light touch to disguise and soften his feelings of hostility and despair—much of this lightness, and also the seeming childlike simplicity of his writing style, he attributed to the influence of White. "Until I learned discipline in writing from studying Andy White's stuff," he explained, "I was a careless, nervous, headlong writer. . . . The precision and clarity of

White's writing helped me a lot, slowed me down from the dogtrot of newspaper tempo and made me realize a writer turns on his mind, not a faucet."

Thurber, like White, was a limpid stylist but as a humorist he elevated American comic writing far above the stale and repetitive formulas of the old humor magazines and thereby imparted a new kind of smartness and sophistication to the *New Yorker*. Humor was now cut to a pattern of intelligence and refinement. "Humor," Thurber once explained, "is a kind of emotional chaos told about calmly and quietly in retrospect." Thurber's many humorous sketches and his fantastic drawings are now known to all the world, but once they had to be "discovered" and championed by E. B. White at a time when no one took them seriously—they had once been nothing but "doodles" on the memo pads and even the walls of the *New Yorker* offices. Thurber's dogs, his predatory women, his timid, ineffectual men populated a wholly fresh world that on the one hand seemed infused with melancholy, but in their airy, abstract quality, in their innocence and stoic resignation they seemed to brush aside the dead weight of things and conquer adversity through flights of fancy and the imagination, much like that of Thurber's later fictional hero Walter Mitty.

But there was more to the *New Yorker*'s comic vein during its first decade than Thurber and White. Among the most important movers and shakers during this period was S. J. Perelman, whose comic muse was anything but innocent, and whose prose style was often outrageously ornate and convoluted. By the time he arrived on the *New Yorker*, Perelman, still in his twenties, was a veteran of *Judge*, where he was both cartoonist and writer. He had published several works of humor and had been engaged by the Marx Brothers as a script writer, a role for which he was eminently suited. Gravitating toward a surrealistic style, somewhat influenced by James Joyce, Perelman showered the *New Yorker* with brilliant lampoons of advertising, motion pictures, romantic fiction and other imbecilities of popular culture, seasoned with extravagant wordplay and delicious non sequiturs. Perelman's narrative line might fall apart or run for the trees at the drop of a hat, and he studiously avoided the kind of clarity in writing that Ross admired, but once again his presence on the magazine proved that where Ross was concerned, no one can argue with genius.

Perelman was not an in-house writer, and thus wasn't required to rub elbows with Ross very often. Another comic genius who *was* an in-house writer, and a person of real value to management, was Wolcott Gibbs, who came to the magazine in 1928. Gibbs shortly became as important as Katharine White in the weekly running of the magazine. Gibbs was possessed of a sharp, sarcastic wit and a satiric gift that would have been the envy of Dr. Swift. His importance to the *New Yorker* was that he seems to have been able to do everything on the magazine that needed doing. He was a superlative editor of the cut-to-the-bone school, whose skills with the blue pencil could not have escaped Ross's attention. In very short order he was as highly regarded on the staff as Katharine White, but since he possessed a somewhat atrabilious personality, he was hardly as well loved.

Gibbs's talents as a parodist were nearly equal to those of Perelman, but he did a little bit of everything on the magazine. He wrote excellent stories, verse, profiles (his acid-filled profile of Henry Luce and of "Times-tyle" was one of the best of that genre to appear in the *New Yorker*'s long history), book reviews, movie reviews, play reviews—everything. In the late thirties, when E. B. White complained that he was tired of writing the "Notes and Comments" page and retired to a salt water farm in Maine, Gibbs took over that chore also, and in his own inimitable fashion did it just as well.

While the *New Yorker* was never a humor magazine, and never wanted to be seen in that light, the fact remains that by the depression years, the magazine had corralled nearly all the best humorists available in the land. Regular staff members and editors—men like White, Thurber and Gibbs—provided the backbone of the magazine and established its style, but by the time they had done this, Harold Ross had managed to bring on board nearly every humorist worthy of the name working in America at the time. Ross had recruited Ring Lardner, Robert Benchley, Dorothy Parker, Frank Sullivan, Ogden Nash, Clarence Day, and yes, even some of those hesitant Round Tablers who a few years before scoffed at Ross and his scraggy weekly. Alexander Woollcott took a column entitled "Shouts and Murmurs," and occasional contributions were accepted from FPA, Heywood Broun and Marc Connelly. Some may have had ulterior motives as the older humor magazines now stood dead or dying, yet the fact remains that the early years of the depression represented something of a renaissance for humor writing in America, and probably a high-water mark in the history of the *New Yorker* magazine. Such a formidable array of talent on a single magazine had probably not been seen before, and certainly has not been seen since.

By the mid-1930s the *New Yorker* had weathered the hard depression years and was now making its stockholders rich. It had established itself as far more than a humor magazine, far more than a "comic book for adults," as it had once been derisively labeled. It was an acknowledged leader in

American journalism through its excellent short stories, its regular departments (some of which—the "Letters" from here and there—were even occasionally grave in tone), its splendid theatre and book reviews. The "Profile," of course, had been a striking innovation in journalism, and probably in American literature. It was, said Clifton Fadiman (who became the magazine's book review editor in the mid-1930s), a new and incisive form of biography, perhaps every bit as specific a form of composition as the familiar essay, the sonnet or the one-act play. The "Profile" was especially beloved of Harold Ross because it called for hard news reporting, extensive and painstaking research and checking of facts, and concise and sharply pointed writing.

Again, this does not mean to say that the *New Yorker* was a simple and direct result of Ross's imagination and foreplanning. He was really more a midwife than an architect, although this is hardly a distinction that diminishes his achievement as an editor. Clearly he was one of the great magazine editors of the twentieth century. A good part of his genius stemmed from his unblinking dedication to the magazine, to his vast reserve of energies and good spirits. He knew how to separate the gold from the dross. That, in the final analysis, is all that can be asked of a great editor.

Much has been written about Ross in the years since his death in 1951, and a great deal of it has been conflicting or even contradictory. Some later contributors to the magazine, especially some of the younger ones who were never close to Ross personally, have leaned heavily on the capriciousness and crudeness of the man. Those who were close to him in the thirties, however, remember him as a very helpful and even kindly individual with boyish good spirits, interesting himself in everything that was going on in the magazine. He hated meetings, conferences, the stale workings of the group mind, but staff members from the thirties never recall Ross as a remote individual— even though he always seemed to be thinking of ways to sneak down the elevator or to the men's room without being seen. Whenever anything about the magazine was concerned, he did not stint of his presence; old-time staffers recall that they were supposed to keep one chair in their offices uncluttered in case Ross ambled in, clinking the coins in his pocket and running his hands through his disheveled hair.

Ross's dislike of organization (of course he always pretended that he was fanatically interested in it) was surely one of the great blessings to the magazine. The atmosphere at the *New Yorker* was always that of a multitude of loner types pounding typewriters in grubby individual warrens. There were few meetings of any substance (except on matters of art), no long-term policy making, no office politics, as little office romance as it was possible to get by with. All energies were devoted to putting out a good magazine.

A great deal has been written, much in an unflattering way, about Ross's heavy-handed style as editor—his often annoying habit of covering every page of manuscript with extensive notes, queries, complaints, discourses on comma usage, some of these said to have been unwarranted or even ignorant. But those closest to Ross knew that those queries were never intended to be taken as sacred pronouncements; rather they were the playful scribblings of a gadfly who often took a certain amount of mischievous amusement in showing the bright "college" kids who worked for him how careless they could be. The truth is he was neither rigid nor tyrannical about those things. He always knew when to give way to a person who was better informed than he—or to anyone who had taken the business of writing seriously. He simply wanted to make sure that his writers were kept on their toes, kept in a constant state of tension.

Katharine White, who was probably as close to Ross as anybody in the early years, admitted that Ross's editorial critiques were mainly goadings; still, they could never be taken lightly. "He delegated work to me with complete freedom," she said, "and when he sent me back a short story with two or three pages of his famous notes he told me to omit any I thought were foolish. This I did but I could sense the queries that he felt were really important and if I didn't agree with them I would just go to his office and argue it out." Ross would sometimes swear, and sometimes he would concede a point and then end a conversation insisting, "I am surrounded by women and children," but Mrs. White, the very proper Bostonian lady, learned to swear back and to hold her ground. She had learned that Ross was never pigheaded where important things were concerned.

Ross was a great editor because he created an air of tension and keen expectancy—it was not an air of ulcer-breeding tension, however; rather it was of a sort infused with playfulness and give-and-take banter. He might occasionally have to accept things that were second best, but only after a lot of howling and jibing. This quest for excellence was passed along to the other editors, and through them to contributors, newcomers, apprentices, so that the prevailing spirit in the office always was that stuff turned out in a careless and perfunctory way would be subjected to Ross's barbs and raspberries.

There is no doubt, too, that Ross knew what he wanted for the magazine. His sense of the *New Yorker*'s style was unerring. And such governing editorial policies as he had—his insistence on material that was light, well written, not grim, not intellectually pretentious, meticulously checked and researched — were quite sufficient to keep his contributors' minds focused on the prevailing policies and the predilections of the magazine. And this gave the *New Yorker* a cohering force and unity seldom seen elsewhere in magazine journalism.

By the middle of the 1930s, the *New Yorker* had elegantly and decisively moved out of its juvenile period and had become a giant among magazines. During the thirties the *New Yorker* would be as good as it ever would be. It would become the quintessential American smart magazine, the one against which, today, all the others are judged. And this great achievement was attained at a time that seemed inappropriate for the survival or luxuriant prosperity of any smart magazine, especially one born amidst the flamboyance of cafe society, of flappers, of spats and walking sticks, of all-night parties and uninhibited laughter — a culture that now seemed stale, even counterfeit. Most of the other smart magazines seemed to have no place in the depression and were on their way out. The *New Yorker*, however, had discovered a formula that miraculously lasted through storm and stress, even as the class of individuals to whom it was originally intended to appeal became as passé as the top hat and the hip flask.

One could engage in a fruitless discussion as to whether the *New Yorker* succeeded because it appealed mainly to an urban elite, or to a mass audience yearning for the zest and sophistication of the great metropolis — a social phenomenon that has become peculiarly American in the twentieth century. The *New Yorker*'s eminence, though, was due neither to its stated pretext nor to its surface appeal, but to qualities that it developed, nay created, on its own. With cafe society quickly fading into the thin and delicate air of the past, and with the *New Yorker* no longer having a smart set to appeal to — no smart set it could have wanted to appeal to — the magazine really had no alternative but to enunciate its own kind of smartness, its own style. While this style was never monolithic, the magazine continued to play upon all the old delights of smartness and sophistication: a patrician detachment, an insouciance, a refusal to assume the responsibilities of steamy social thinkers, rapturous reformers or world savers. This last was the road that every other magazine in the land was taking, and the *New Yorker* refused to take it. The *New Yorker* continued to laugh at the world at a time when laughter seemed inappropriate, even cruel. Freedom to laugh has sometimes been thought to be the last preserve of the privileged class — whether that privilege was the gift of money or of intellect no longer seemed to matter.

The *New Yorker* continued to provide entertainment in high style. It

insisted on remaining light, but it was not at the same time thin — the wealth
and diversity of its talent made superficiality impossible. So, yes, the *New
Yorker* became a mightier and more substantial magazine than, say, Frank
Crowninshield's *Vanity Fair*. To be sure, *Vanity Fair* was perfect in its own
way, a consummate experience, like that provided by an exquisite sauce or
meringue, a sheer delight to the palate — in such a way *Vanity Fair* has to be
judged every bit as good as the *New Yorker*. But the *New Yorker* was so
much more skillfully edited, so much more painstakingly thought out, possessed so many more reserves in its talents, so much more substance in its
offerings, that even with its essential lightness it would have to be seen, in its
best years, as comparable to the grave and serious journals of opinion of the
nineteenth century. It dared to be big and thoughtful. It dared to be important. Still, in its glorious years it never lost sight of the nature and goals of
magazine journalism, and was the highest product of the journalistic craft.
That was the way that Harold Ross wanted it. The *New Yorker* was solid
and instructive, but it never failed to amuse and entertain.

T he *New Yorker* has enjoyed a long and enviable history and an enduring
popularity and mystique that are probably unequaled among American
magazines. There have been complaints about the *New Yorker* in recent
years, certain grumblings from this quarter and that, some of them more than
a little strident and vituperative. Still, it would be a bit silly to argue with
the *New Yorker*'s continuing success and prestige over the years. A great
many have insisted that the *New Yorker* is vastly inferior to what it was in the
years of Harold Ross's editorship, yet curiously, the circulation, which for
years hovered around 400,000, reached an all-time high of 531,382 in
1986, at which time some prophets of gloom were insisting that nobody was
reading the magazine anymore. To be sure, the recent past has been less rosy
for the *New Yorker* in other ways. There was a sharp drop in the number of
advertising pages during the 1980s — down from 4,309 in 1981 to 2,772 in
1986. By the mid-1980s all the world knew that there was a major shift in
management in the offing since William Shawn, who had been editor of the
magazine since Ross's death in 1951, and had thus held the top editorial
post longer than Ross himself, was nearing retirement. Equally serious jitters
were felt before Shawn's retirement when the Fleischmann family, which had
owned the magazine since 1925, decided to sell out in 1985 to the giant
Newhouse media empire. The sale of the magazine in turn produced a few
tremors and shocks among the magazine's regular readers, its advertisers and

above all its writers and contributors, who anticipated the possibility of an editorial coup or revolution, perhaps a sacking of the magazine's traditions. Needless to say, no such house revolution took place.

It would be hard to deny that the *New Yorker* remains a high-quality magazine, though there have been no shortage of critics troubled by this or that slackening tendency or alleged evidences of decline. As might be expected with a magazine blessed with such a long life (and the *New Yorker* is now definitely an oldster in the family of American magazines), there are going to be the inevitable complaints that the magazine "is not what it used to be." It is also no wonder that the actual evidences of these complaints are vague, and even contradictory. Sometimes the complaint is heard that the *New Yorker* is not like its old self, that the old reliables have departed; sometimes the complaint is that the magazine hasn't changed enough and keeps doing the same things over and over again.

As early as 1958, not many years after Ross's death, James Thurber was grieving that the *New Yorker* had become too smug, perhaps too repetitive. In an article that appeared in the *New Republic* entitled "Everybody Is Getting Very Serious," Thurber lamented that the *New Yorker* had taken on a grim visage in recent years—there was that word *grim*, the word Harold Ross used for much of the material he didn't like. The magazine, said Thurber, had increased in size, wealth, and "matronly girth" but not in amiableness and nimbleness. There was lacking a certain *joie de vivre*, an effervescence, qualities that marked the *New Yorker* in the dark days of the depression.

There have been similar kinds of criticisms leveled at the *New Yorker* in recent years. Shawn as editor took much of the brunt of this criticism, especially in his later years. During the 1960s he was the object of an extended attack in a two-part profile appearing in the now-defunct *New York Herald Tribune*, written by author Tom Wolfe. A highly satiric and iconoclastic writer, Wolfe made the charge that Shawn had essentially "embalmed" the magazine, and drained it of all its literary juices. He derided the magazine itself as "the most successful suburban woman's magazine in the country," and complained that it was now a "national shopping news," with the literary content of the magazine nothing more than "thin connective tissue" holding together the fancy ads for cognac, furs and ritzy places. Wolfe's charges were heavy handed—many would say cruel and careless—but numerous times in the last few decades the complaint has been made that there is now something somnolent about the *New Yorker*. Late in 1986 a *New Yorker* parody arrived at the bookstores. It was entitled *Snooze: The Best of Our*

Magazine. The charges against the *New Yorker* may have gotten so repetitive that they, too, have become sleepy and have lost most of their effectiveness or relevance.

The fact remains that throughout Shawn's reign the *New Yorker* remained a first-rate magazine. It has not floundered in the few years since Shawn's departure. Many fine writers and artists were added during Shawn's tenure. One thinks of John Updike in fiction and John McPhee in nonfiction. The *New Yorker* continues to have the best cartoonists in the land. The charge that all of the humorists have disappeared is certainly unjust. Garrison Keillor and others continue the *New Yorker*'s tradition for superior humor and light material. There is no reason to think that the *New Yorker* has completely lost its light touch or its capacity to be entertaining on a sophisticated level. The sources of its appeal have seemingly remained constant, and for the most part it has been able to renew its readership appeal year after year.

No magazine can live sixty years and more without changing its face. It would be foolish to expect that the *New Yorker* of 1990 would have the same flavor and personality of the *New Yorker* of 1930. One can regret the passing of the really first-rate casuals of Ross's day and that highly entertaining and incisive journalistic prose that once graced the opening sections of the magazine. One misses perhaps "the silvery laughter of the mind" and the kind of fey indifference to the heavy burdens of the world that once gave the magazine much of its charm. But we now live in a much more complex world and a wholly different America. There was no way that the *New Yorker* could have remained precisely its "original" self whoever was at the helm.

The most important truth about the *New Yorker* is one that is hard to deny. It took its roots in the robust and fancy-free decade of the twenties and quickly established a base of quality on which it has been able to build handsomely from that day to this. It survived where so many other magazines failed because of solid tradition, continuity of personnel and editorial excellence. The pool of talent available to it continues to be awe-inspiring. Some may be critical of the fact that the *New Yorker* can no longer reflect an era over which we have grown nostalgic. But that it is rooted in those times, and has survived at all, we can only have reason to rejoice.

· 7 ·

Esquire—
The Early Years

Esquire was born during the darkest year of the depression—1933—an ill-chosen time, it would seem, to launch a smart magazine, or any kind of magazine for that matter. But *Esquire* was born under a lucky star and became an overnight sensation. It was the kind of success from its first issue that Harold Ross could only have dreamed of in 1925 when he launched the *New Yorker*. The press run for the first issue of what was planned as a quarterly was 105,000, and all 105,000 copies were quickly sold in spite of many dire predictions to the contrary. The first issue was labeled "Autumn," and arrived at the newsstands on October 15, 1933. The publishers were hoping to begin preparation for another issue in the spring, but so great was the demand for the magazine that a month later a second issue, dated January 1934, rolled off the presses with a considerable increase in the number of pages and advertisements. Both these issues were splendid. *Esquire* was born a great magazine. During this its first year it was probably as good as it would ever be, an extraordinary achievement for any fledgling magazine of that day or ours.

Esquire was a magazine for men. But it differed from all previous magazines for men as the Parthenon differs from the chicken coop.It was a large and grand folio, printed on fine paper stock, plump with advertisements, large, full-page color cartoons, a rich mix of articles for the urban male— articles on fashion, fishing, yachting, manners, dining, style, intrigue. Among the contributors of the first issue were Ernest Hemingway, Ring Lardner, Jr., John Dos Passos, Dashiell Hammett, George Ade, Morley Callaghan, Erskine Caldwell, Charles Hanson Towne, Gilbert Seldes and Montague Glass. The magazine sold for fifty cents at a time when most of the large-circulation magazines were still selling for a dime.

Those who saw the magazine when it first appeared may have been struck by a clear resemblance in style to another large-format magazine then enjoying tremendous popularity—*Fortune*. Henry Luce's original *Fortune* magazine, inaugurated in 1930, was a far cry from the *Fortune* of today, which is to say, it was not a crimped, pint-sized, run-of-the-mill business news magazine on coated paper, but rather a handsome, lush-looking folio that seemed to lisp a paean of praise to the genius and achievements of American business and society—there were sections of pictures devoted to the glorification of commerce and manufacturing, dignified portraits on matte paper of captains of industry, and long articles devoted to the manifold glories of some particular industry or great American family fortune. *Fortune*, of course, was rich, grave and dignified. Priced at a dollar a copy, the magazine clearly relished its appeal to affluent grandees. Still, it had gained a very respectable circulation.

Esquire was not grave, dignified and pretentious. It was *Fortune*'s playful younger brother, a much brighter, more amiable, more uninhibited brother who seemed to jump out into the sunlight with a gleeful yelp. Not that *Esquire* was a mere smirking kid, nor was he a sex-besotted adolescent. The *Esquire* man, or so one would assume from looking at the advertisers' drawings, had the fullness of maturity—was even a little gray at the temples— and thus he himself could have stepped from one of those board rooms that Henry Luce was celebrating. But he was out to prove that when one grew up one didn't abdicate one's animal spirits; one didn't stop savoring life in all of its gusto and diversity. *Esquire* was for the intelligent man, man at his leisure, but it was an expansive and adult leisure informed by curiosity, imagination and good taste. *Esquire* was for the man who wanted to live well, not for the man who wanted to taste all of the world's dubious pleasures in one orgiastic weekend. *Esquire* glorified the masculine world and the masculine style, but it did so with understatement and restraint. *Esquire* was a magazine for smart men. It was a smart magazine. It didn't pretend to appeal to the poseur or the upstart.

The initial good fortune attendant on *Esquire*'s birth was largely due to the previous success and wide experience of its two publishers and its editor, each of whom had extensive background creating publications for the men's fashion industry. *Esquire* was the brainchild of two crackerjack advertising men, David A. Smart and William H. Weintraub, and a bright young writer and editor named Arnold Gingrich, all of whom had had considerable luck in producing magazines and brochures for the men's fashion trade. To be sure, none of the three had experience editing or publishing general magazines, but the concept behind *Esquire* had already been tried in a rudimentary form and been found wildly successful. This was in an earlier quarterly publication called *Apparel Arts*. And before this, Smart and Weintraub had put out another magazine, or trade paper, entitled *National Men's Wear Salesman* and had followed this up by turning out a series of lavishly illustrated brochures featuring men's clothing that they syndicated to retail clothing stores. These brochures, with titles like *Gentleman's Quarterly*, *Club and Campus*, and *Observer*, were intended to be given away by owners of retail clothing outlets. They were all enormously successful.

By a curious irony, the depression, which hit the fashion industry hard, had a great deal to do with the founding of both *Esquire* and its predecessor, *Apparel Arts*. With money tight, many retailers balked at buying syndicated brochures to give away to customers, and these brochures had been the mainstay of the David A. Smart Publishing Company. But Smart and Weintraub, never at a loss in coming up with new things to sell, conceived the idea of putting out an oversized fashion quarterly that could display the latest men's fashions — a much more expensive item than their old brochures, to be sure, but the idea was that retailers could put the magazine, filled with impressive-looking pictures of the latest fashions, out on their counters for customers to thumb through. From the magazine's pages they could order things they liked that in those astringent times the store owner might not be able to include in his inventory. The idea worked marvelously; the only trouble was that customers frequently found the magazine itself irresistible and walked out of the store with it — little thefts that bothered Smart and Weintraub not in the least since they merely dramatized the popularity of their magazine.

Apparel Arts made its first appearance as a quarterly in the fall of 1931, and even more than *Esquire*, it showed the influence of Henry Luce's recently successful *Fortune*. With its large size, its format, its paper stock, its use of art work and photography, some might have thought the magazine a shameless imitation of *Fortune*. *Apparel Arts* seemed to be something of what one would have expected if *Fortune* had decided to add a fashion section to its regular offerings. *Apparel Arts* itself didn't stray far from the world of men's fashion, and there was little about it that would suggest the leap to *Esquire* two years later, but these were tumultuous and troubled times only safe for survivors. Smart and Weintraub were nothing if not survivors. Their drift to the *Esquire* venture is an epic chapter in the annals of American publishing history.

All of the magazines that emanated from what was originally called the David A. Smart Publishing Company were born in Chicago, a city that played a significant role in the men's fashion industry. Furthermore, the great Midwest, and the wide-open spaces beyond the Mississippi, represented a vast and inviting wonderland for the gifted merchandiser or resourceful seller. It is not easy to forget that some great merchandising empires, those of Mr. Sears and Mr. Roebuck and of A. Montgomery Ward, had Chicago as their capital. Their tentacles reached out into millions of farmhouses through the agency of the Grange, the railroad freight agent and the general store. That a smart magazine would arise anywhere but in New York, the capital of the nation's culture, might seem something of a surprise, but that the Midwest was not poverty stricken in its entrepreneurs was never a matter of doubt.

David A. Smart was a Midwesterner born and bred, and were it not for his tremendous verbal dexterity, inventiveness, panache, and unstoppable cascade of ideas it might be easy to think of him as nothing other than a superlative freshwater booster and drummer. He had been born in Omaha in 1892 (the same year as Harold Ross) but grew up on the West Side of Chicago. While still in school he got a job selling hats at a store called The Hub, and he established immediately and with seeming ease a phenomenal ascendancy over even the most successful salesmen in the place. It was said that he developed a technique of presenting a hat to a potential customer that both amused and confounded all who saw it performed. Suddenly bringing a hat out of its box he flipped it under and over his arm in a kind of somersaulting motion that, in the process, gave the hat a perfectly neat crease. With a flourish, Smart would then hand the magically produced hat to the customer with some glad refrain such as "There! Try that on for size." It was a bravura performance that very seldom failed to sell a hat. All of the other boys (and men) who sold hats at The Hub tried to learn the trick, but without success, naturally leading them to conclude that Dave Smart was something of a smart aleck. He was.

Smart quickly moved on to more challenging opportunities in the selling field, however. Before long he was hawking classified advertisements for the *Chicago Tribune*, becoming the ace salesman in that field, after which he moved on to other ventures, all of them also immediately profitable. Invariably, though, he found his superiors jealous or covetous of his achievements, and some time after World War I he decided that he would never again work for anyone but himself. He quickly established himself in a business that required no great capital outlay but only other aggressive salesmen like himself. To bankers and other businessmen he sold booklets, memo pads, calendars, wall and window display posters and the like. This business grew apace and eventually spawned several curious offspring. Rather than remaining merely a job-printer, which is how he got started in the business, Smart discovered some demand for him to actually publish material and create copy for businesses, especially banks. Under the guise of a subsidiary enterprise called the "Thrift Syndicate," Smart began producing booklets for banks — the kind of thing that bankers give to customers extolling the virtues of saving, how trust accounts work, and so on. One of his products that enjoyed a roaring success was a little booklet entitled *Getting On*, which was distributed by the thousands all over the country, and which demonstrated the virtues of thirft and frugality à la Benjamin Franklin, establishing the lesson with a series of homilies or anecdotes. Getting deeper and deeper into this sort of thing, Smart eventually had to hire copywriters since his own experience with the written word was virtually nil.

Smart's promotional abilitiess didn't go unnoticed in the Chicago area, and sometime in the mid-twenties a friend brought him in contact with a gentleman who was trying, but with very little success, to produce similar booklets for the men's fashion trade. The gentleman was William H. Weintraub, a virtuoso salesman in his own right, who dropped out of college to become a traveler in the retail men's clothing and furnishings field. Later, Weintraub had started his own syndicate, which produced a trade paper called *The Man of Today*, but he had had virtually no knowledge at all of printing and publishing, and his effort was a visual monstrosity. When a friend suggested he look up David Smart, Smart confirmed the diagnosis, telling Weintraub that *The Man of Today* had "about as much appeal as a copy of the *Congressional Record*." Eventually, the two must have seen the wisdom of linking up, and they established a partnership called the Men's Wear Service Corporation (Smart continued individually with his old printing company). The joint resourcefulness of these two remarkable individuals in time made the Men's Wear Service Corporation a large and highly successful enterprise.

Together Smart and Weintraub seemed to be an unbeatable team, although they were not precisely harmonious personally. With two such hard-hitting, "never-take-no-for-an-answer" salesmen there was bound to be friction; sessions in the office could on occasion be heated and vituperative. Luckily the two were not required to rub elbows on a daily basis: Smart, with his other business to run, became something of an inside man, while Weintraub had as his essential responsibility the routine selling of the company's publications to stores and retailers. It was probably the correct division of labor since Weintraub was surely beyond compare as a convincing talker and vanquisher of all resistance.

Arnold Gingrich, who later worked for both men, liked both, and frequently acted as an intermediary in their various squabbles. He believed that Smart was the more imaginative and inventive of the two, the idea man extraordinaire, but that Weintraub was the more consistently successful salesman. Smart was basically a kind of loner, which fact was covered up somewhat by his aggressiveness, and he more quickly tired of arm-twisting. Both men were short, with the tenacious bulldog quality often associated with short men, but Weintraub's tenacity was unrelenting and unremitting. "Although they were both past masters of persuasion," said Gingrich, "Dave was at his best in the tête-à-tête, or in a group of no more than three or four in a small room, having a tendency to become laconic in large gatherings, whereas Weintraub was a spellbinder, with a commanding voice like the bark of a mastiff, and as a speaker he was always 'on,' whether addressing one person or a thousand."

The story of Arnold Gingrich's eventual proximity to this dynamic pair is an amusing saga. Neither Smart nor Weintraub, for all of their verbal dexterity and flair for human communications, had the slightest gift for the written word. Without immediate feedback, without social interaction, both of them drifted aimlessly in dark and quiet waters. But now they were attempting to produce brochures on men's fashion, specifically a successor to the drab *The Man of Today*, a regular and syndicated publication that was called *Gentleman's Quarterly*. The first issue of this appeared for the Christmas season in 1926. *Gentleman's Quarterly*, to succeed as a regular serial publication, would need to be more than a folder of photographs of men's fashions; it would require sprightly and convincing copy for its text and captions. Smart and Weintraub looked around for writers and editors with experience in the field, but these were not easy to come by. The field of men's fashion writing had not really existed theretofore; when attempts were made to develop the craft on an elevated plane, as in the "What the Well-Dressed Man Will Wear" column of *Vanity Fair*, there were the inevitable snickerings, risqué shafts by vaudeville comedians and convulsive parodies in college humor magazines. "Writing" on this subject was an object of sneers and chuckles.

Several staff writers came and went during the first few years of the existence of *Gentleman's Quarterly*, but none of them really seemed to take the chore seriously. A young man named Dale Fisher, who had written both light verse and refined chitchat for Chicago newspapers, held the job as writer-editor for a few years, but he never really warmed up to the job and Dave Smart was chagrined to find that under no circumstances would Fisher stay in the office a minute after five o'clock. Being a man who could pop with ideas at any hour of the day or night, Smart had a low tolerance for lack of gusto in his hirelings, so that when he had an opportunity to produce for the Hart Schaffner & Marx stores another publication, similar in nature to *Gentleman's Quarterly* (it would be called *Club and Campus*), he began looking around for another copywriter.

As legend has it, or as Dave Smart liked to tell the story over and over again in later years, he selected twenty-five-year-old Arnold Gingrich for the job because he heard the young man's name mentioned favorably three different times on the same day. Gingrich was working at the time as a copywriter for B. Kuppenheimer & Co., a men's clothing manufacturer also located in Chicago. Smart learned that Gingrich was a brilliant copywriter, that he was a graduate of the University of Michigan, and one of his visitors on that day let the fact drop that Gingrich had a rich vocabulary and had been seen reading Aldous Huxley's novel, *Those Barren Leaves*. At the time Gingrich, newly married, and liking his job passing well, had no desire to leave Kuppenheimer, but Dave Smart laid siege to him, calling him day after day over the next several weeks, finally luring him with a promised salary of $6,500 a year, a very tidy sum for 1928. Gingrich would take over as editor and writer not only of *Gentleman's Quarterly* and *Club and Campus* but soon a few other similar publications as well. It was the beginning of a long, fond and intimate relationship with David Smart which would end only with the latter's death in 1952. It was also the beginning of a relationship that a few years later would bring about the finest men's magazine ever to appear in America.

Arnold Gingrich was born in Grand Rapids, Michigan, in 1903. His father, John Gingrich, had come there from Ontario but was descended from a long line of Mennonites who had lived in Pennsylvania since before the American Revolution. John Gingrich emigrated to Michigan because he was a wood carver by trade and the American furniture industry had settled in the state. There were jobs aplenty in Grand Rapids, which had become "the furniture capital of the world." The move to Michigan was traumatic for John Gingrich and his family in more ways than one. He had married a Methodist lady who was inclined to be contemptuous of the ways of the "old order Amish," and when Arnold was a lad he had more than casual contact with his Mennonite uncles and cousins who managed to drape a pall of gloom over the family lifestyle, especially in the summertime when the family returned to "vacation" in Ontario and the "city slicker" Michigan cousins were taken to be a personification of the spirit of Satan.

Clothing, especially all modern fripperies, all displays of ostentation, were anathema to the country Amish, some of whom were called "hook and eye" Mennonites since they refused to wear buttons—buttons had the possibility of becoming pretty and attractive and were therefore sinful. Whether it was the dampening aspect of his Mennonite cousins or some other influence, Arnold Gingrich gravitated during his adult years to a diametrically opposed view of dress—he remained throughout his life fascinated by the decorative and spirit-lifting capacities of clothing, of shoes, hats, suits, overcoats, all of the adornments of the modern man. His later association with David Smart was not brought about precisely by those interests, but it would charmingly fit in with one side of Gingrich's personality.

Gingrich used to say that the "Mennonite influence accounted for the upper fourth of my genes," and he didn't lose any opportunity to fall back on his heritage as a working man's son or as a simple country boy. Some of his friends of later years liked to tell the story of how as both editor and publisher of *Esquire* in the 1950s he was called upon to address a distinguished gathering in a large auditorium. One of his listeners, sitting up in front, was tiny Dorothy Parker, lately a regular *Esquire* contributor, now aged and alcoholic, but not having lost an ounce of her rapier-like wit. At the beginning of this talk, when Gingrich introduced himself as "just a country boy at heart," Dorothy Parker piped up, in her typically malicious stage whisper: "When convenient, when convenient."

And, yes, whatever there was of the country boy in Arnold Gingrich, it existed mostly in a quiescent, residual form, his old Amish cousins nothing but a shimmering memory as he moved freely in the world of writers, artists and city sophisticates during his tenure as editor of several magazines. Leaving school in Grand Rapids he attended the Univeritsy of Michigan in Ann Arbor where he graduated in 1925. He was by no means a playboy in his college years, received a solid education at this renowned land-grant state university, became an omnivorous reader and collector of books. By virtue of his training and self-discipline, his later forays into the field of publishing never had the comic implausibility of the career of Harold Ross.

Like many liberal arts graduates then and since, Gingrich had virtually no firm career objective in mind when he left the University of Michigan in the mid-twenties. Opportunities seemed plentiful in the years of the big bull market, but only an antic twist of fate brought him to his life's work. The fall before his graduation he had secretly married a girl he met in college, but both he and his bride were too frightened to confess the act to the girl's social-climbing mother, who clearly was looking for something better in a prospective son-in-law. Some months after the actual ceremony took place the couple approached the girl's mother to seek her blessing for a "future" union. The mother was not at all pleased with the idea and began setting down as many impediments and roadblocks as her imagination could conjure. After repeated importunings from the young couple, the stubborn but still benighted "mother-in-law" agreed to consider the proposed marriage if Gingrich could get a job that paid fifty dollars a week. This, as it turned out, was easier said than done in 1925.

Laying seige to Chicago, the great metropolis of the Midwest, the place where a fifty-dollar-a-week job might be found if any were available, Gingrich discovered that his youthful energies and manifest abilities earned him many enthusiastic responses from potential employers. But as soon as the figure of fifty dollars a week was mentioned, enthusiasm waned with great suddenness. One of the more than thirty places he visited on his rounds was the Osten Advertising Agency on West Jackson Blvd., where the owner seemed very willing to hire him, but he, too, refused to go anywhere near fifty dollars a week for an inexperienced man. Some time thereafter, however, Gingrich returned to Mr. Osten with a promise to work for nothing as a way of getting his feet wet. He was hired, shortly he was paid a salary, and before long, moving up to other positions, he did attain the fifty-dollar salary necessary to "marry" his wife.

Three years later Gingrich would be offered a salary well over a hundred dollars a week to leave his job as a copywriter at Kuppenheimer Clothes to work for David Smart. By this time he had quite well demonstrated his abilities as an advertising man, but Smart was looking for, and would shortly need, a man with a much greater range of talents than any mere advertising copywriter. Gingrich demonstrated those talents, and those he didn't already possess he picked up on his own. When Smart decided to issue *Apparel Arts* in 1931 and later when he introduced *Esquire,* he was embarking on publishing projects that were foreign to the habitual work of his existing publishing company. Gingrich was not only a brilliant copywriter with a keen sense of the advertising business, he was a man with a wide range of general knowledge, sophisticated in matters of art, literature and current taste. Smart realized that unlike his several earlier copywriters, he had in Gingrich a man of parts, an individual suited for more than the pedestrian chore of churning out fashion booklets. And when the depression fell hard upon his business he put those wider talents to good use—indeed, he had to use them to survive.

The depression brought about a major change in the activities of Dave Smart and Bill Weintraub because orders for fashion booklets to be given away free to customers fell off drastically as money got tight. But the reason the company drifted toward magazine publishing, which eventually led to the founding of both *Apparel Arts* and *Esquire,* is a complex and sometimes humorous story. There had been a certain amount of jealousy in the men's fashion trade over the highly successful booklets produced by the David A. Smart Publishing Co., and sold by the thousands; however, shortly after the depression set in the company got a little needling from the most popular trade journal in the field, *Men's Wear,* which ran an article entitled "Fair Weather Fashion Experts." This choker predicted in sarcastic terms that the whole Smart operation was a "fair weather" outfit, but now with rough weather on the horizon the likes of Smart, Weintraub and Gingrich would be swept overboard and never heard of again. There may have been a tincture of truth in the prediction, but the scoffers had knocked on the wrong door. One day shortly thereafter Arnold Gingrich arrived at the office and found both Smart and Weintraub in high dudgeon—for once not at each other. Being strictly unsinkable types, Smart and Weintraub were determined that somehow or other they were going to turn the tables on these needlers. "How can we ram this down their throats?" asked Smart.

Bill Weintraub had the answer. With a copy of the latest issue of *Fortune* in his lap he suggested that "we can get even with these SOB's." Neither Smart nor Gingrich got the drift immediately, but Weintraub pointed out that *Men's Wear* and all the other trade papers were dismal and unappealing rags. Holding up copies of *Fortune* and *Men's Wear,* Weintraub proclaimed: "Why, *this* is to *that* as chicken salad is to chickenshit." Smart and Gingrich immediately picked up on the idea, and on that day, early in 1931, the concept for *Apparel Arts* was born.

Never having published a magazine before, least of all a large and glamorous magazine like *Fortune,* none of these three realized the full magnitude of the task before them, but all of them got busy at once. In the weeks ahead Weintraub and Gingrich went on the road selling the idea to potential advertisers, and through their efforts a sufficient number of well-heeled advertisers were brought on board. Gingrich eagerly churned out copy week after week, but then one day, showing the material to Smart, who freely admitted it was first rate, the already fatigued Gingrich had dumped on him the biggest load of all. "Well," Smart said, "you've given us an overture, now you'll have to come up with the opera." Gingrich had just assumed that Smart was somehow going to provide the guts of the magazine out of thin air, but now he was informed that he would have to go out and find the art work, the substance, the articles, the meat, or whatever, to make a magazine that would look like *Fortune.* Daunted, staggered by the idea, Gingrich nonetheless plunged forward. He was to learn the craft of magazine editing in a kind of baptism by fire.

And when the first issue of *Apparel Arts* came before the public on October 5, 1931, there is was — a whole opera. There were not only beautiful ads, a distinctive looking cover, but substantive articles on the fashion industry, lush photographs. In this and the succeeding issues Gingrich had somehow scared up some very good features — a piece on the history of Brooks Brothers (there was a full page devoted to a painting of the original establishment of Henry Sands Brooks in 1818), an interesting story, with pictures of silkworms and cocoons, on the making of silk through the ages, a Margaret Bourke-White folio of pictures of a sweatshop on New York's Lower East Side, a story that Gingrich himself researched in Baltimore about the Munsell Color System, which was a means of identifying various shades and hues of color with scientific accuracy. The magazine was clearly a wow, and immediately put all of its competitors in the shade, which is what it had intended to do.

The story of the beginning of *Esquire* was, if anything, even more curious. Although pleased with the success of *Apparel Arts,* none of the founders turned their thoughts to a second magazine, but they came to it by a turning of fortune's wheel. Sometime before Christmas in 1932, with *Apparel Arts* about a year old, a man from the Rogers Peet Company was in the office in

Chicago lamenting to David Smart that many retailers missed the fashion booklets that had been given away to customers. Customers were still asking for them—wouldn't there be a way to come up with something—at least for the Christmas season? Well, of course, it was too late for *this* Christmas, but the idea settled in, and David Smart gave instructions to come up with some attractive little publication that might be distributed to stores, and perhaps sold for a dime, or other small amount. The man from Rogers Peet had thought that maybe it might be possible to get up something that was sliced off *Apparel Arts*, something that would look good and appeal to the man on the street.

In the weeks ahead Smart, Weintraub and Gingrich tossed the idea up, wrote memos about it, played around with dummies, argued the pros and cons. How could they get out an abbreviated edition of *Apparel Arts* for the layman? Something to sell for a dime? From whatever angle they looked at it, the idea seemed an impossibility. Once again, Bill Weintraub, who never pretended to be the idea man of the group, found the fly in the ointment. A general magazine that contained nothing but articles on fashion would not even appeal to a pansy—*Gentleman's Quarterly* and their other booklets, he pointed out, contained a few things besides fashion pages. No, there was no way that you could sell the man on the street a male counterpart of *Vogue* or *Harper's Bazaar*. There would have to be more than articles on fashion.

With this conclusion universally agreed upon, David Smart started to jot down a series of ideas for pieces that might go into the magazine—a few of them eventually materialized in *Esquire*. Some of them were: "Bobby Jones on Golf," "Gene Tunney on Boxing," "Hemingway on Fishing," and "Rudy Vallee on Jazz." The concept of the magazine began to grow, indeed to inflate enormously until the original idea of an inexpensive junior version of *Apparel Arts* disappeared. As Arnold Gingrich recalled, "Each time I came up with another dummy, with more and more features added to make it more and more hairy-chested, Dave would cost out the package and the ante would go up a nickel. To our horror, by the time we had something we all agreed was substantial enough to deodorize the lavender whiff coming from the mere presence of fashion pages, we saw that we had on our hands a magazine that must sell for fifty cents." Fifty cents, of course, was the kiss of death in 1933 when the *Saturday Evening Post* was selling for a nickel. Fifty cents would mean a twin brother to *Apparel Arts*, not a little brother. Could such a magazine be sold to the multitudes? Common sense would say no, but after much soul-searching, Smart, Gingrich and Weintraub gulped, took deep breaths, and agreed to go ahead. A big, expensive, lush man's magazine, as yet unnamed, was now on the drawing boards.

Could there have been a worse time to launch a lavish magazine — the spring of 1933, when Franklin D. Roosevelt, following his inaugural on March 4, had declared a bank holiday to keep people from drawing their money, especially gold, from the banks? It was a time when there was not only a vast army of unemployed, but even those who were employed, even respectable middle-class people, were reluctant to spend what money they had. In cities like New York and Chicago, restaurants were nearly empty in the evening except for the waiters; attendance at movie houses was off by nearly 50 percent. Those in possession of banknotes were hoarding them, and all the coins of the realm were in critically short supply — so was any money available for small purchases. To get coins for small consumer items (all that people were considering), piggy banks were being broken open, streetcar riders were attempting unsuccessfully to get change for dollar bills; even John D. Rockefeller, the richest man in the world, it was said, gave an astonished golf caddy a dollar tip instead of his usual dime — there were no dimes available. Clothing and department stores that had never extended credit before, such as Macy's in New York, opened charge accounts for their customers, not because people had become better credit risks, but because the alternative was not having any business at all.

It was a time that could only have inspired caution, restraint, even downright pessimism in the publisher of a projected penny magazine, let alone the creator of a lush product of fancy like the proposed *Esquire*. Even those who fully appreciated the now legendary selling talents of David Smart and Bill Weintraub doubted that the project could come off. But the publishers had not at this time been thinking of a newsstand magazine at all, had not been thinking of themselves as magazine publishers. The project was at first a spinoff of *Apparel Arts*, and David Smart rationalized the idea by saying that by selling through stores entirely, there ought to be a way to tag along on the present downside of the apparel market. If a men's clothing salesman could sell a customer a fifty-dollar suit — or even if he couldn't — he's got a pretty good chance to sell a fifty-cent item if it looks glamorous and impressive enough. And the motive for the salesman would be there since the plan was to sell the magazine to clothing stores at twenty-five cents a copy. The usually skeptical Weintraub wondered how the publishers could make any money on the deal with that kind of profit to the retailer. "There won't be any," said Smart, "unless we can sell 100,000 copies." And that was the plan. Once again it was an ideal challenge for the super salesmen.

To get off the ground, the magazine would have to offer a great deal to both the stores and to the buyer. The stores could be cozied along by that tidy markup *and* by the fashion inducements and advertising possibilities. The readers would have to be given a really appealing magazine product. Smart and Weintraub set to work on the former problem, Gingrich on the latter. Both tasks would be difficult, but Smart and Weintraub had the easier time of it since they were pawing a turf they had been familiar with for years. But getting up a general-interest magazine was something altogether new. As might be expected, in a matter of only a few months, the boosters attracted enough advertising contracts to get the project off the ground. Gingrich, on the other hand, was scrambling desperately for copy right up to press time.

The magazine was promised for the fall of 1933, and as the weeks and months went by there was still not a firm idea of what the final product would look like, what the editorial mix would be, where contributors in all the arts would come from. Even the name was in doubt up to the very end. At one time the triumvirate had decided upon *Trend*, but they received a letter from a Washington copyright attorney who told them that the name was already taken. So, too, their next three favorites: *Stage*, *Beau*, and *Trim*. Probably with a little whimsey, somebody noticed that the attorney's letter carried the abbreviation "Esq.," so they adopted *Esquire* momentarily as a working title, fully expecting to replace it with something better when the magazine went into final production.

A crude dummy of the projected magazine was gotten up to show potential advertisers. It contained the title *Esquire, The Quarterly for Men* in lettered script and inside some pasted-in clips of fashion drawings mostly taken from pages of old copies of *Apparel Arts*. There were some potential names of departments and some projected titles of articles, such as "Another Cozette" by Alexander Woollcott and "Another Thin Man" by Dashiell Hammett, both of which were distinctly "iffy" when Smart and Weintraub began lugging the dummy around. Such a skeleton dummy was putty in the hands of the master salesmen, however, because they could use it to say, "well, it isn't going to be this, it will be that, etc., or that, or that," perhaps allowing the trial dummy to serve as a Rorschach ink blot to soak up the desires and expectations of potential customers.

While the idea of the magazine was being drummed up around the country by Smart and Weintraub, Gingrich was stuck with the problem of bringing the magazine to concrete realization, and this was no easy chore since the idea itself was indistinct and nebulous. Until very late in the planning stage the image and mix of the magazine were every bit as tentative as its title. It had been decided, for example, that the magazine would have cartoons; but the full-page color cartoons, which later became one of the foundation stones of the magazine's success, and one of its most charming features, were only decided upon at the last minute. But Gingrich knew that he would have to beat the bushes for material and he was every bit as much a "road" man as Smart and Weintraub; accordingly he took several spins around the country to meet with authors, artists and other potential contributors.

Probably the most important early acquisition for *Esquire* was Ernest Hemingway, who would become a regular and devoted contributor to the magazine during its first five years. It seemed essential to everybody concerned that Hemingway be in the magazine: he was a strong masculine writer whose style seemed to be mandatory in any effort to produce a magazine for men that wasn't going to be a mere masculine counterpart of *Vogue*. Fortunately, by a curious set of circumstances, Gingrich was already an acquaintance of Hemingway's and he needed to do little actual arm twisting, even though for several years Hemingway would be letting his material go to *Esquire* at substantially below the going rate.

Gingrich, an avid bibliophile, had been collecting Hemingway for several years — books, first editions, poems, anything he could get his hands on. Among the items in his Hemingway collection were copies of the school paper and the yearbook of Oak Park High School, Class of 1917, containing several Hemingway contributions. The two young men had actually begun corresponding long before the *Esquire* idea was born, Hemingway perhaps having singled out Gingrich's letters from a constant flurry of adulatory missives from readers. Gingrich had also sent copies of *Apparel Arts* to Hemingway in Key West, offering to get him any clothes featured in them that might take his fancy.

In March 1933 Gingrich received a communication from Captain L. H. Cohn of the House of Books in New York that a copy of Hemingway's *Three Stories and Ten Poems*, printed in an edition of only 350 copies in Paris in 1923, was available for seventy-five dollars. The price was steep, of course, for 1933, and Gingrich debated the matter long and hard. On his next trip to New York, the occasion of which was his first roundup of material for *Esquire*, Gingrich stopped by the House of Books determined to buy the book. As he entered the store, he found Ernest Hemingway coming out. The two young men went downtown to have lunch at the Bre-

voort Hotel, and Hemingway immediately agreed to contribute to *Esquire*—
and on a regular basis. He also made some suggestions of other potential
contributors and writers whose stuff would work in *Esquire*, and he punctu-
ated his advice with the remark, "and you can say I sent you."

At lunch, and in later correspondence, Gingrich made it clear to Hemingway that *Esquire* was not yet in a position to pay Hemingway's accustomed rates, and was not expecting to receive his best short fiction. The
agreement on a handshake was that Hemingway would send journalistic casuals on such topics of interest to him as hunting and fishing, for which he
would be paid $250, an amount to be raised later when and if the magazine
flourished. Hemingway, apparently, was more than mildly enthusiastic about
the assignment, especially since Gingrich assured him in follow-up letters that
Esquire would not be a sissy magazine, that it would have "ample hair on its
chest and adequate cojones."

There were apparently several reasons why Hemingway freely and eagerly entered into a relationship with *Esquire* even without seeing the finished
product. It was the depression, after all, and even though he could easily
receive two thousand dollars for a major story, good story material couldn't
be churned out on a monthly basis. Furthermore, editors who paid two
thousand dollars expected a great deal and could afford to make a fuss over
writing that wasn't in strict conformity with their standards. Gingrich, however, made it clear that he would run whatever Hemingway cared to send
before press time, that he would pay for it immediately, and that he wouldn't
tamper with the contents. Accordingly, Hemingway could send along rapidly gotten up (but still usually quite good) journalistic material that would
be published without dispute or friction. In time, *Esquire* would also get
some major Hemingway stories, like the famous "The Snows of Kiliman-
jaro," at much higher rates, but the important thing about the *Esquire* arrangement for Hemingway was that he had an editor ready and willing to
take whatever he cared to send without higgling and without the usual editorial sulphur and brimstone.

Hemingway's regular contributions during the first few years of *Esquire's*
existence gave the magazine the "hairy-chested qualities" the editors believed
were desperately needed. More important, they gave the magazine a high
literary standard to emulate. Hemingway's fact pieces had a hard personal
elegance, brilliantly combining the sportsman's sense of freedom and adventure with a muted metaphysical restraint and seriousness. Here, from *Esquire's* issue of December 1935, were Hemingway's reflections on boxer Joe

Louis after he had demolished Max Baer. They are contained in a piece called "Million Dollar Fright":

Louis is too good to be true and he is absolutely true. He fights out of a geometrically correct, absolutely unhittable bombproof shelter that he shuffles in and out but mostly in. It is easier to go forward flatfooted than to go back. So far everyone has been too afraid of him to try to see how he goes back. If he had no punch he would still be a perfect boxer. The way he carries his hands a hooker can't get around his forearms and elbows and he will punch inside of a hook. He has a beautiful jab that is loose instead of stiff and tight, as most good straight lefts are, and because it is loose he can turn it when it is half way to its target, or perhaps even three quarters of the way, and hook with it after it has started as a jab without there being a break in the motion. That is a miracle of co-ordination.

His reflexes are as fast as those of a bantam-weight and when he has a man going and is hooking both hands to the head he is as fast as any little man you ever saw.

Later, when he slows up, I believe he will hit even harder than he does now. He is not a one punch knocker-out now because he hits so fast he sacrifices something of the paralyzing quality of his blows. It is as though a man had an automatic rifle instead of a double barrelled express and so was not so careful how exactly he called his shots. A lot of his punches to the head are higher on the jaw than the button and he will hit a man with five hooks to the head, any one of which if called a little more carefully, would knock the man out. But he is now so fast that he can afford to do this. And it is the only thing he does that makes him look like a younger fighter.

He has the material to make four or five different kinds of fighters and he may settle into one kind or another when he begins to slow a little. Right now he is all kinds of fighters and there is no flaw you can beat him on. . . .

Some one will beat him finally. Maybe it will be soon, by accident, or maybe it will not be for years until prosperity has softened him up. We who have seen him now, light on his feet, smooth moving as a leopard, a young man with an old man's science, the most beautiful fighting machine that I have ever seen may live to see him fat, slow, old and bald taking a beating from some younger man. But I would like to hazard a prediction that whoever beats Joe Louis in an honest fight in the next fifteen years will have to get up off the floor to do it.

Writing of this sort, of course, went a long way to establishing *Esquire*'s reputation for a mature masculine style and quality.

The presence of Hemingway on a regular basis acted as a magnet for

Esquire, and drew in many other writers who might otherwise have held back. The latitude offered by the editors was also a strong selling point. *Esquire* quickly came to be known as an author's magazine, rather than an editor's magazine, like the *New Yorker*. A *New Yorker* writer had to fit himself into the prescribed mold; he submitted his work expecting flack, editorial argument, sometimes stinging rebukes. Gingrich's editorial policy was completely different. His plan was to assemble a group of well-established authors and allow them to have whatever kind of fun they liked with the magazine. He gave them all the rope they needed. The *New Yorker* was high-intensity business, demanding scrupulous attention to detail; *Esquire* was conceived as a romp, as a playground for writers, most of whom were now harried and harassed by depression economies, and more than a little willing to form an alliance with any magazine that would accept them on their own terms. *Esquire* accordingly never attained the editorial uniformity and near-formulaic consistency of Harold Ross's *New Yorker*, but in its first few years it managed to assemble a large and diverse stable of regulars and irregulars. During the first few years of its existence, *Esquire* was running such well-known writers as F. Scott Fitzgerald, Ring Lardner, John Dos Passos, Erskine Caldwell, Dashiell Hammett, Thomas Mann, George Ade, André Maurois, Irvin S. Cobb, Emil Ludwig, Morley Callaghan, Burton Rascoe, Gilbert Seldes, Langston Hughes and George Jean Nathan. Even the lugubrious and often heavy-handed Theodore Dreiser managed to nudge his way in with a mournful piece about his days as a newspaperman in St. Louis—not at all suitable, it might seem, for a lighthearted smart magazine, but there it was in the July 1934 issue of *Esquire*.

If *Esquire*'s writers didn't provide an easy or obvious uniformity, getting an editorial style in the visual dimension should not have been a superhuman achievement to the publishers of *Apparel Arts*—or so it would seem. On the other hand, *Esquire* was a wholly new venture with no suggestive precedents for guidance. The magazine would have color, that was certain, but in the beginning it was assumed that the only full-color pages would be advertisements for clothing manufacturers and such other space buyers as would take a chance on an untried magazine for men. The magazine was to be light and playful, so there would be cartoons, and a few cartoons in black and white were slotted early. When the magazine came out, however, there would be a number of full-page color cartoons, a brilliant stroke that gave the magazine much of its distinctiveness. There were no American magazines at the time running cartoons in color. Arnold Gingrich had a hazy recollection of a few zesty European magazines that had had color cartoons—he thought of the French *La Vie Parisienne* and the German *Simplicissimus*. He had probably not seen the *Puck* or the *Judge* of the 1880s and 1890s, which ran full-page political cartoons, although they were separately printed chromolithography plates, permitting only one or two such features per issue. In the beginning there was no thought of color cartoons for *Esquire* either, but somewhere along the line, in making up dummies for prospective advertisers, a number of editorial pages in color were provided for, and Gingrich added to his list of chores a search for color cartoons.

When he was on one of his trips to New York, however, a call came through from Smart, saying that the number of color pages had been upped by a third, and that these could not be filled with ads, so that Gingrich had better be on the lookout for more cartoons or other illustrations to take up the space. Gingrich took the news with shock. He hadn't the slightest idea where he was going to find cartoons or other drawings in color to fill up this space—cartoons were especially troublesome: American cartoonists weren't working in color since such work wasn't being bought by commercial magazines, especially in these depression years. He already had a few color illustrations requisitioned—a full-page pictorial feature by Howard Baer called "At the Walkathon," and a color drawing to accompany an article by Gilbert Seldes on burlesque. The situation seemed desperate to Gingrich away from the office, in far-off New York.

And the situation was especially grim since Gingrich had just received Smart's call right after he had suffered a sharp rebuff from a successful New York artist whose stuff he thought would be just right for *Esquire*. The artist in question was Russell Patterson, whose "Patterson Girls" were a regular feature of many Sunday supplements and perhaps as well known at the time as the Ziegfeld girls. Patterson was Gingrich's *beau ideal* in terms of the kind of art work he wanted to see in the magazine, but Patterson laughed at the figure of "one hundred dollars a feature," which Gingrich mentioned as what *Esquire* was able to pay. Patterson also confirmed that no other well-known commercial illustrator would be willing to help out at such prices—writers, it would seem, were going to be easier to come by than artists.

On the other hand, Patterson said that he had a youngster to suggest if Gingrich was not afraid to cross the color line. Gingrich was not in the least afraid to cross any line at this point, so Patterson gave him the address of a "colored kid" up in Harlem whom he believed to be highly talented but who had never been able to get past the receptionist and into the inner sanctum of any editorial offices in New York. The colored kid in question was named E. Simms Campbell, then living with his aunt in a rear flat on Edgecombe

Avenue. When Gingrich took one look at Campbell's drawings, many of which were in color, he almost yelled "Eureka," for this was the very sort of thing that he wanted for *Esquire*. Although Campbell had been a graduate of the Art Institute of Chicago, he had not been able to sell any of his work, except a few sketches or gag ideas that were produced in finished form by other illustrators.

Leaving a small down payment of a hundred dollars—obviously more money than Simms had ever received for anything in his life—Gingrich gathered up a nice sampling of drawings to show to Dave Smart in Chicago, faithfully promising the disbelieving Campbell that *Esquire* would make extensive use of his work, and that he would shortly be back with "real money." When Gingrich returned to the office he showed his cache of drawings and sketches to Smart, who reacted "with awestruck enthusiasm such as Balboa might have had on his first sight of the Pacific." E. Simms Campbell was the answer to their prayers, without a doubt. On his next trip to New York, a few weeks later, Smart also climbed the stairs to Campbell's flat and assured the struggling artist, then a mere twenty-five years old, that his work was just perfect for *Esquire*.

And so it was. The work of E. Simms Campbell would appear in every issue of *Esquire* until the artist's death in 1971, and a few years after the magazine's founding Campbell would be a well-to-do young man, living in a handsome suburban home in White Plains, and receiving commissions from around the globe. The *Esquire* connection would mean the most to him no doubt, because in essence he, as much as anyone else, established the magazine's visual style. His work was highly finished and polished, of course, and he could render a wide variety of curvaceous females—chorus girls, innocents, vamps, supercharged office secretaries—in moods ranging from the voluptuous to the risible. His touch, in any case, fit *Esquire* to perfection. It was slick, jaunty, tongue-in-cheek, stylishly erotic, playfully adult. So apt was the material that it was used eventually in all manner of drawings, not only cartoons—fashion drawings, covers, illustrations for stories and articles, fillers of all sorts.

Campbell was not the only new artist to appear in the first issue of *Esquire* and subsequently to play a pivotal role in the magazine during its early years. In fact, shortly after striking it rich in New York, Gingrich found himself an artist—and an art director—right under his very nose in Chicago. On a warm lovely late spring day, while attending an outdoor art fair in Grant Park, just north of the Art Institute, Gingrich's eye was caught by some speedline drawings that had a kind of droll, elfish and puckish quality.

The artist's studio was located in the vicinity of the old Chicago Water Tower, only a few blocks from *Esquire*'s offices in the Palmolive Building. Wasting no time, since the deadline for the first issue of *Esquire* was only a few months off, Gingrich knocked on the door of one John Groth. The artist turned out to be a blond barefoot boy who looked to be little more than a teenager although in truth he was almost twenty-five.

Unlike Simms Campbell, John Groth had already won a little recognition as an artist, and during the next several months he was to enjoy two one-man shows, one in Milwaukee and the other in Washington at the National Gallery. He had not done caertoons, but Gingrich was very pleased by many of the drawings and was certain that Groth also had the makings of a first-rate cartoonist. More important, his talents could lend themselves beautifully to the *Esquire* style. Of course Groth had the advantage of being nearby, and, joining the staff immediately, he was to play a big role in the layout and design of the magazine as it first appeared. Even more than E. Simms Campbell, he managed to fill up all the gaping holes in the color pages of the magazine's first issue. When the magazine finally emerged, work by Groth — drawings, aquatints, monotypes — appeared on no fewer than seventeen of the magazine's pages. It was such an embarrassment of riches, as Gingrich later recalled, that it was decided to baptize Groth art director — especially since the magazine didn't have one.

Around this same time, Gingrich also discovered another Chicago artist whose name would shortly become even more closely identified with *Esquire* than either Campbell or Groth in the mind of the general public. Driving to work one day, Gingrich had been attracted to some posters for near beer — this in the last year of Prohibition when near bear sales were still significant. The posters contained a very smoothly rendered and curvaceous female that could rivet the attentions of any normal male. Obviously the posters were done by some very skilled illustrator, but Gingrich wasn't sure what the technique was. But that girl — wouldn't it be lovely if she could be worked into an *Esquire* cartoon?

Inquiring of a commercial artist of his acquaintance, Gingrich discovered that the artist did indeed work in Chicago, but his acquaintance merely hooted at the idea that this illustrator, whom he knew, could do cartoons. "For God's sake, he's an airbrush retoucher — you know, does over photographs for catalogues so they don't look like photographs but a sort of bastard blend of photograph and drawing — all smoothed out."

Yes, and that smoothed-out quality was precisely what had attracted Gingrich's attention. He put out a call to the artist, who toiled in a loft nearby with his airbrushes for various commercial clients. His name was George Petty, and he was willing to work for *Esquire* but expressed strong doubts that he could do anything that was funny. Petty had done a lot of poster work, and had recently designed the official poster for the Century of Progress Exposition in Chicago, but he did not see himself as a cartoonist. Gingrich persevered, however, and George Petty did produce a few cartoons with his airbrush—several of them featured a young girl with an old codger. Dave Smart thought they had possibilities, but immediately put his finger on their weakness: "Get rid of that old guy and you've got something." That wouldn't be a cartoon, but it would be a very appealing illustration of a delicious young girl. In the first several issues of *Esquire* Petty cartoons with the old codger would appear, but then suddenly the "Petty Girl" stood out alone in the sunlight in all her pert luminosity. Thus was born one of the great artifacts of American popular culture. Although Smart and Gingrich could not have known it at the time, the "Petty Girl" was going to sell millions of copies of *Esquire* over the next few years, and George Petty, with his lowly airbrush, now raised up to a virtuoso instrument, would become a household name in America.

None of this could have been foretold in the fall of 1933 when the first issue of *Esquire* went to the printers, but the founding fathers of the magazine now knew that they had enough good material on hand to produce a lush men's magazine, and they knew that what they had was good. They had in fact far more material than they needed for the first issue, and this allowed them to start planning for the second issue of the magazine, which was to appear much sooner than they had expected. But all of the material on hand looked splendid, with strong appeal to masculine readers, a veritable feast of visual delights.

Changes were made in the format and in the selection of material right up to the deadline, but one thing that wasn't changed was the title. One day, very near the deadline for printing, Gingrich got a call in his Chicago office from Smart and Weintraub, both in New York. The two combatants, who seldom agreed on anything, had suddenly come to the conclusion that the magazine should be called *Town and Campus*. Gingrich lied, saying he thought this was pretty good, but that the cover, with *Esquire*, was already on the printing press, another lie actually—it was due to go in a day or so. Gingrich had not originally seen much merit in "*Esquire*," but had come to like it, and he came to the defense of the title, reading copy from an eloquent sales brochure he had written. He had his way, and the first issue went to press with the large hand-scripted title, *Esquire*, "The Quarterly for Men," and at the bottom of the cover, also in display type: "Fiction—Sports—Humor—Clothes—Art—Cartoons." The first cover was designed by Edward Wilson, an advertising fashion illustrator, and showed two sportsmen arriving on a wilderness lake in a small seaplane, apparently about to take off with two guides fully equipped with guns, rods and other sporting gear.

The last-minute proposed name change may seem to have been totally misguided in retrospect, but in 1933 the new publication was still conceived of as essentially wedded to the men's fashion industry and to the economy of the clothing business. The plans, after all, were to sell the magazine in clothing stores, perhaps at a rebate, perhaps as a mere afterthought of a cloak and suit deal. The experience of the entrepreneurs had been entirely in the men's fashion field, and they had put together a magazine that would appeal to their traditional and familiar clients. But one minor shift in marketing strategy at the very end completely altered the destiny and fortunes of the magazine in ways that nobody could have predicted in the beginning.

While the plans had been to sell *Esquire* in clothing stores where—so the theory ran—men would come preparing to spend money, and where fifty cents would probably not seem an outlandish expenditure, someone suggested that it might not be a bad idea to have a small newsstand sale. Nobody thought, or cared, whether newsstand copies were actually sold, but only that display on the news racks might make the store clerk's job a little easier—"You know *Esquire*, I guess, probably seen it on the newsstands."

Unfortunately, neither Gingrich nor Smart knew the first thing about newsstand distribution, or how it worked. So they approached Mike Morrissey, head of the American News Company, which then had a virtual monopoly on the distribution of magazines through newsstands. David Smart suggested that an additional 25,000 copies of *Esquire* be printed (above the 100,000 planned for clothing store distribution). With a kindly and paternalistic wave of the hand, Morrisey dashed this expectation in unqualified terms.

"Gentlemen," he said, "there are at this time, in this country, just five thousand places where even *one* copy of any fifty-cent item can be sold on a newsstand. So let us have five thousand, but don't be surprised if you don't sell more than half of them."

Accordingly, when the presses rolled, there were 105,000 copies of *Esquire*—100,000 for clothing stores and 5,000 for newsstands. This calculated ratio turned out to be one of the biggest miscalculations in American publishing history. The day that the magazine hit the newsstands, all copies were sold out within a few hours—at fifty cents. Almost immediately Morrissey was on the phone to David Smart, clamoring for more copies of the issue and insisting that the magazine should become a monthly at once. So great was the newsstand demand that the newly formed Esquire Publishing Company was required to beg back copies from the clothing stores where the magazine was not really experiencing a brisk sale. When the figures were finally in on the first issue of *Esquire*, the originally projected figures had been almost exactly transposed—5,000 copies had been sold in clothing stores, 100,000 on newsstands. In a twinkling, as it were, *Esquire* was no longer a Christmas bauble for the fashion trade but a major mass-circulation magazine.

Having worked assiduously for months, and having made contacts with a large number of contributors, Gingrich was ready to respond to the call for a monthly magazine. The second issue of *Esquire*, originally intended to come out in the spring, landed on the newsstands on December 5, 1933, carrying the monthly date, "January," as well as the words, "Now Issued Every Month." The cover of this issue, which officially arrived on the very day Prohibition came to and end, carried the first picture of the pop-eyed, three-dimensional figure of "Esky," which was regularly repeated (in many different forms of dress) in many future issues, eventually becoming the symbol and trademark of the magazine.

As a publishing venture, *Esquire* did not skyrocket to the top of the circulation charts in a month or two. Many readers availed themselves of the modest subscription price of $1.50 yearly (based on the assumption that the magazine would be a quarterly), so that the second issue sold only 60,000 copies on newsstands. The diminutive subscription department at *Esquire*, geared to trade publications, staggered under the weight of the subscription orders, but every month showed an increase in the number of copies actually printed. New advertising business flooded into the office, nearly obviating the superlative selling skills of Dave Smart and Bill Weintraub, who suddenly found that they were by profession magazine publishers, not salesmen.

And publishers on a grand scale they were. As the depression droned on, *Esquire*, called "the most widely discussed magazine" in America in promotional brochures—and not much in a spirit of exaggeration either—rose steadily in circulation. By the end of 1936 the circulation would be 550,000, and by the end of 1937, a year the depression eased off slightly, 675,000. Advertising revenues were naturally up sharply also, and these years would make wealthy men of the three founders.

The editing and publication of *Esquire* was a streamlined and simplified affair. There was never the large and cumbersome editorial machinery of the kind that developed at the *New Yorker,* nor any large staff to augment it. The management of *Esquire* tended to be a leisurely affair, like the magazine itself. *Esquire*'s offices were located in the Palmolive Building on North Michigan Avenue in Chicago, a very comely art deco skyscrapter that later became, by a grotesque irony of history, the "Playboy Building." On a daily basis when they were in town Arnold Gingrich and David Smart would take their morning coffee at Huyler's Restaurant on the first floor of the Palmolive Building—this ritualistic coffee hour was the magazine's only real editorial conference and jam session. The advertising side of the magazine was run from New York, where the office at 40 East 34th Street was managed by Bill Weintraub. (Weintraub would continue as joint publisher and advertising director until 1941, at which time he left to establish his own advertising agency.)

Probably because of his laid-back and unfussy editorial style, Arnold Gingrich continued to attract new young writers and artists to his magazine throughout its first decade and into the war years. Gingrich also showed a great deal of ingenuity during this same period by writing to editors of other commercial magazines asking to buy material that they considered too daring or offbeat. Often for a few hundred dollars he was able to buy up manuscripts that may have cost thousands in the flush years of the 1920s.

Writers generally liked the freer editorial style at *Esquire*; they liked the fact that David Smart's crew got author's payments out right away. Progressively, as *Esquire* became prosperous, some resented the meagre payments and took their stuff elsewhere. One of those who became disaffected at the end of the thirties was Ernest Hemingway, who had been an old reliable for a long time but who later complained to all who would listen that Gingrich was a "con man." On the other hand, Hemingway had on several occasions been paid in stock—stock that was still in his possession at the time of his death in 1961 and had probably bankrolled a great many safaris and fishing trips in the interim.

Esquire remained a magazine of the first rank until the war years, after which it suffered from the woes of so many of its brethren—diminished resources, paper shortages and the like. Additionally, to curry favor with the War Production Board and get its full share of paper allotments, the magazine strained to produce features that seemed to be in the war effort, and that might demonstrably "enhance the morale of the troops." Accordingly, the magazine took on more the tone and style of a "girlie" magazine, which it had not been before. Now there were big spreads of half-nude females and in time even foldouts of "pinups," many of which almost certainly did wind up on barracks room walls. New and more simpleminded girlie illustrators were added, and even George Petty was once requisitioned to produce one of his girls at almost life size—it had to be folded five times to fit into the magazine.

Some of this wavering in quality may have developed a few years earlier when there was a certain unfortunate dispersion of energies at the Esquire Publishing Company. David Smart, a restless and aggressive publisher, having been enraptured by his success with *Esquire*, was not one to be content with his single success. Unlike Harold Ross who was always threatening in jest to skip out on the *New Yorker* and establish a detective or true story magazine, Smart took his new found eminence as magazine publisher seriously, and, in the late thirties, began looking around for new fields to conquer. He founded a magazine called *Coronet*, a small-format magazine devoted to the arts. It was a modest success. Subsequently he founded a magazine called *Ken*, a political magazine with a kind of muckraking tone. It was a failure. And there were other ventures as well. Unfortunately, fond as he was of Gingrich, Smart insisted that Gingrich be his editor for these magazines as well as *Esquire*, resulting in an unavoidable dilution of authority at the top. By the early war years, when the Esquire Publishing Company was also producing instructional and training films, Gingrich wore out on the editing game. He took a leave of absence from the magazine in the mid-forties, lived abroad for a few years while *Esquire*, still making money hand over fist, languished editorially.

In writing the preface for a volume commemorating the twenty-fifth anniversary of *Esquire* in 1958 — a volume called *The Armchair Esquire*, Gingrich commented that during the 1940s "our grapes weren't being tended as carefully as they had been before. . . . Some of us turned our backs on the vineyard for too long a time, and thought the vines would tend themselves." When Gingrich finally returned to *Esquire* in 1952 he scrapped thousands of dollars worth of manuscript inventory, redesigned the magazine completely, and set it off on a wholly different course. By the early sixties the magazine's new formula, quite different from those of the thirties and forties, had proven highly successful in its own right and had achieved a circulation of over 800,000. The magazine continued to offer "entertainment for men," but it studiously avoided the approaches of the newer adolescent fantasy magazines for men that came to the fore in the fifties.

The Esquire Publishing Company abandoned Chicago for New York in 1950, occupying offices for a time at 488 Madison Avenue, where Gardner Cowles and his giant publishing empire (*Look, Flair*, etc.) were also located.

David Smart died two years later, but he was succeeded as chairman of the board by his younger brother Alfred, who had been active in the company since the founding of *Esquire* in the early thirties. The Esquire Company continued to prosper in the general media field following David Smart's death. The company continued to publish *Esquire*, of course, but it diversified itself, acquiring a broadcasting station in Atlanta, a well-known stamp album company, and other interests. Out of the old *Apparel Arts* magazine grew *Gentleman's Quarterly* in 1957. The company established its own subscription fulfillment center in Boulder, Colorado, which eventually possessed the latest computerized equipment—a far cry from the primitive services of Chicago in the thirties. The Boulder subscription facilities would be servicing twenty-one other magazines by 1963.

Esquire magazine has passed through several editorial evolutions since its founding. Some of its changes have alternatively disappointed or elated its readers, but it has never been an inferior magazine. Most of the time it has been a magazine of the first rank. Nostalgically speaking, perhaps, it has never been quite as good as it was in the 1930s, at which time it was a magazine of irresistible charm and endless good fun.

Looking at the early issues of *Esquire* today is an adventure in culture shock. If issues of the magazine—for, say, 1934, 1935, or 1936—were saved for posterity, perhaps placed in a time capsule, and then presented to historians of some future millennium, these pages, so drenched in jollity, would doubtless impose something of an enigma to an informed historian who had studied the America of the 1930s. These were harsh, parched, implacable, dreary years—the era of the breadline, the soup kitchen, the public dole, a time above all when nobody was said to be spending his change. The first issue of *Esquire* was offered up obviously for the Christmas season, 1933, and it looked like a Christmas catalogue in its gaiety and richness. It looked, too, as if it were a magazine intended for people at leisure, for people whose joys and pastimes had been created in the more ebullient decade of the 1920s and somehow frozen while a grim economic tragedy was being acted out.

It could be that *Esquire* was possible in 1933 precisely because America had not really surrendered to the mood of the depression at all. The "Great Depression," as we now call it, was a term applied by historians of a later day; at the time most people believed that they were slogging through a temporary quagmire in which the pleasures of life were still all there but merely held in suspension, frozen, until the real America should come into the sunlight once again. America was not lame, not moribund, at least it was widely believed at the time—it had just taken to bed to get over a cold. A depression, yes, but not the Great Depression. All we needed was something to make us *feel* better and we would *be* better. The same thing was holding true in the political realm, apparently. President Roosevelt's New Deal had quickly become a popular remedy—yet none of its salves and ointments had any noticeable effect on unemployment until the shadow of war was again on the horizon. Yet people felt better with the New Deal, thought they were beginning to prosper; it seemed as if the nation's malaise had eased, that everything would be all right, that nothing had changed in an essentially affluent and self-confident land.

It is hard to tell what made *Esquire* such an instant and raving success. It was a new concept in men's magazines, an infinitely better concept than all of the existing monthlies for men. It was not a bully bully magazine and it was not an extravagance of adolescent fantasy; there was no overt dependency on the prurient and the lascivious. There was no crass attempt to grab the attention of the boys down at the garage or the backroom of the club house. If and when it glorified any of the hairy-chested virtues it did so with irony, panache and a fey sense of humor.

An advertiser of the day might have paused reflectively if asked who the targeted reader of such a magazine might be. It was clearly not a magazine solely for the affluent, for the "man of society"—none of the smart magazines had ever succeeded with a formula that appealed to plutocrats alone. The *Esquire* man seemed to be prosperous certainly, but, much more important, had discriminating tastes that were not bogus, a choice diversity of interests. *Esquire* had the feel of a generous buffet or smorgasbord, but it entertained not precisely because its rich spread was so well thought out and concocted (it hadn't been really), but because there were so many fresh things to taste— this at a time when the usual magazine menu had become cut down and stereotyped. The prevailing mood of *Esquire* was above all else festive—the first issue looked somehow like a Christmas issue especially gotten up for a one-shot conquest. But then the party just went on and on in subsequent issues. There were other magazines at the time that were slicker, others might have been more intelligent, others more finely crafted, but none seemed to be having such a plain good time—male good fun, but in a high, jaunty style never tinctured with the expected barroom drain on imaginative freedom.

It was the festive mood that seems to have made *Esquire*—this mood of gaiety in the midst of the dark depression. It wasn't just that the magazine yoked together a greater diversity of features than all the earlier magazines for men, and thus was less "specialized." The founders of the magazine had not merely assembled a series of "male-interest" departments—yoking together a "huntin' and fishin' " magazine with a fashion magazine, adding formulaic sex, lusty fiction, cartoons for spice. Nothing was formulaic in *Esquire*. Even articles on hunting and fishing were never specialized or regular departments. That undoubtedly endeared the magazine to a writer like Hemingway, who was interested in such things as matters for subtle reflection and irony.

Part of the appeal of *Esquire*, certainly the appeal to whatever "smart" audience there would have been in the thirties, was that the magazine had a restrained way of dealing with the masculine world. Even the ads were restrained (Bill Weintraub and Arnold Gingrich were especially pleased that the first issue of their magazine contained a lavish color ad for Cadillac—the first automobile ad with no picture of an automobile in it!). To be sure there was always a sense of playfulness, of male fun, but there was a prevailing notion that without restraint, without understatement, all the usual forms of male fun are vapid or boorishly adolescent. *Esquire* was neither of those things.

Undoubtedly, the two magazines that most forcefully influenced the *Esquire* style and format were *Fortune* and *Vanity Fair*. The connection with *Fortune*, with its large format, typography, and so on, was duly noted, and it was also understood in a way that *Esquire* was elbowing in on the province of *Vanity Fair*, which had long cultivated a predominantly masculine readership. And there were other similarities with *Vanity Fair* as well. One was dedication to good art. *Esquire*'s visual appeal was not exhausted by its color cartoons by any means. The first issue of the magazine contained a number of full-page reproductions of paintings, drawings, sketches. A story by John Dos Passos was accompanied by a full-page watercolor by Dos Passos himself—Dos Passos was more than a little talented as an artist apparently. There are a number of paintings and drawings that seem faintly suggestive of the ash can school of painting; then, too, there are subdued black and white photographs—one, reminiscent of *Vanity Fair*'s "We Nominate for the Hall of Fame" series, was of Ring Lardner, Jr., then a student at Princeton whom Alexander Woollcott had suggested to Gingrich might represent a young collegian of distinction. The subdued photograph for *Esquire*, by Gilbert Seehausen, revealed a young man of almost reverential seriousness and intelligent innocence.

The symbolic *Esquire* man was mostly not young, as we see. In his occasional youthful manifestations he seemed to exude the very mood of seriousness found in the portrait of Ring Lardner, Jr. He was not a playboy. The archetypal *Esquire* male, in fact, was tall, distinguished, middle aged, neither athletic nor nonathletic, mostly just well-positioned. Being gray at the temples he could take the world as he found it. And mostly he found the world to be an object of sprightly and bemused contemplation.

A great proportion of the first few issues of *Esquire* was given over to color drawings of the latest fashions, clearly intended for the man of achievement who could presumably afford them. These are all brilliantly executed, of course, since this was one area where all of the magazine's founding fathers had a sure hand. Certainly they are much more alive and vivid than the men's fashion drawings of *Vanity Fair*, which always somehow seemed contrived and silly. It wasn't just the color that had been added, but an atmosphere, a plausible anecdotal element. The *Esquire* man is invariably shown in action at his club, or arguing his case before a jury, strolling on campus, at the racetrack, at the beach, or wherever.

These drawings, in their force and *joie de vivre* provided a great deal of the dash and style to *Esquire*. How much better to have these color drawings than to have used photographs with male models, which is what is always done today. Photographs here would have been a distraction—a boring distraction at that. They would have required the use of male models, and male models never look precisely like real men—they look like male models. Of course the fashion drawings of the commercial illustrators of that day were not real men either—far from it—but they were men rendered in art as a feast for the imagination. So once again they help to sustain the festive atmosphere that *Esquire* was trying to achieve. Once again, too, the drawings carried with them a sense of dignity and restraint in the midst of ever-present celebration.

The same thing can be said about the magazine's cartoons, and the numerous drawings of delicious, pneumatic females that immediately began to appear in its pages. Many of the cartoons are frankly erotic, and there are the usual topics of the battle between the sexes, flirtation, the sex appeal of a glorified but mostly imagined female. The humor is sometimes tart, sometimes cynical, but never quite to be taken seriously. As to the battle of the sexes, the battle goes slightly to the female, as it doubtless almost always must, but only slightly, since the *Esquire* male is mature, unflappable, not totally preoccupied with sex, or with anything for that matter. These beautiful girls, allegedly the male's prey, lounge around elegant bedrooms doing their nails, often making witty and pungent remarks to other young things equally charming in appearance. They seem only half realized, as if living in a kind of perfumed mist. As rendered by George Petty, of course, they could be thought of as "pinups," but they were never really intended to reside anywhere but in the imagination.

That became somewhat less true in the 1940s, when *Esquire* was struggling to find ways to keep up its paper allotments and accordingly drafted a stable of "girlie" artists whose charge was to appeal directly and overtly to adolescent fantasies. In his memoirs, Arnold Gingrich regretted that in the forties *Esquire* moved away from the original Petty Girl, with its decided "class, originality and distinction," and gravitated toward the "meretricious" nudes of Alberto Vargas and other crassly hormonal pictures. Whereas back in 1934 the *Esquire* girl had somehow appealed to the "silvery laughter of the mind," she had now become a product of consumption—a "sex object" as feminist savants like to say.

It was not at all unusual, then, that *Esquire* would eventually have to abandon the *Esquire* girl—she could not hope to make it into the blatantly consumer-oriented world of the postwar era. Indeed the whole original *Esquire* formula would be swamped when the various mammary glandular men's magazines came on the scene in the 1950s. *Playboy*, for example, the best known of this new breed, had also been born in Chicago, founded by Hugh M. Hefner, a failed cartoonist, who had once worked as a fifty-dollar-a-week promotional writer for *Esquire* but who stayed behind when the magazine moved to New York. Just as *Esquire* was retreating from its own preoccupation with sex and titillation in the early fifties, Hefner founded a magazine devoted exclusively to men whose primary concerns were the pleasures of "the great indoors." The *Playboy* girl, soon to be called "Playmate," was photographed, and was marketed solely as a consumer product, mostly for the delayed adolescent. Where the *Esquire* girl had been a creation of wit, the "Playmate" was an object of masturbation.

Hugh M. Hefner himself had great expectations for his new formula, which he regarded as a clear step upward from *Esquire*. And when his magazine became phenomenally successful, for a number of years far more successful financially than *Esquire* had ever been, he fancied that he had crafted his own "smart" magazine, like those of old. He had, he believed, created a new form of light entertainment for the "man-about-town." He painfully aped all the traits of "sophistication" he could find in existing magazine culture. Unfortunately, for all his money, for all his ability to pay top dollar to well-known authors, his magazine couldn't extricate itself from its pubescent fantasies. Hefner tried everything to climb to the same lofty eminence, but he only succeeded on the balance sheet. He even purloined the "editorial we" of the *New Yorker*, a technique of dubious value even among Harold Ross's talented minions. He tried to develop a light, smart touch: he himself was disappointed humorist who for years had struggled to write a massive comic autobiography under the pen name of Goo Heffer. He tried running serious articles on science, culture and morality. He tried to develop himself as a man of high fashion and taste—with little success. When he started pasting up his magazine on his own kitchen table in the early fifties, his sartorial style was that of Joe College—white socks and shiny pants. His haute cuisine was meat and potatoes smothered in gravy and washed down with flagons of Pepsi Cola.

High society had passed *Playboy* by, just as it had passed most new magazines by in the standardized America that has grown up since World War II. *Playboy* in its prime was not a bad magazine, certainly never a boring concoction, but it provides dramatic evidence of the unavoidable truth that nearly all of the attempts to recreate the spirit of the old smart magazines seemed doomed. Perhaps the *Playboy* case is a bit too obvious. The smartness of the old *Esquire* was in the ingenuousness of its style, its atmosphere of unselfconscious jollity and festivity. *Esquire* took nothing seriously—least of all itself, and certainly not seduction and the battle of the sexes. It understood that the way to take everything seriously is to take nothing quite seriously. This was the essential wisdom that turned out great magazine editors like Harold Ross and Arnold Gingrich in the first half of the twentieth century. They and their magazines could be stylish, witty and intelligent without having to posture and pretend. *Esquire* could afford to be youthful without being juvenile.

· NOTES ·

The numbers to the left refer to the text page where the quotation is found.

12 "some three thousand magazines." Mott, *A History of Magazines, 1865–1885*, p. 5.

12 "In 1886 R. Hoe & Co. . . ." Peterson, *Magazines in the Twentieth Century*, p. 5.

13 "S. S. McClure, an Irish immigrant. . . ." Peterson, *Magazines in the Twentieth Century*, p. 6.

17 "If I can get a circulation of 400,000. . . ." Presbrey, *The History and Development of Advertising*, p. 471.

29 "suborned the offices . . . of the Western Union. . . . ," Beebe, *The Big Spenders*, p. 96.

39 "The Americans . . . have not a single comic periodical . . . ," quoted from the *British Quarterly Review*, in White, A Subtreasury of American Humor, preface.

48 "It was necessary that drawings. . . ." Flautz, *Life: The Gentle Satirist*, p. 10.

56 "The purpose of the *Smart Set*. . . ." Dolmetsch, *The Smart Set*, p. 6.

61 "Pay Sydney Porter (O. Henry). . . . Towne, *Adventures in Editing*, p. 64.

63 "a burgundy and gilt reception room. . . ." Dolmetsch, *The Smart Set*, p. 8.

64 "He never hurried. . . ." Towne, *Adventures in Editing*, p. 50.

72 "I'm H. L. Mencken from Baltimore. . . ." Bode, *Mencken*, p. 61.

74 "Men and women have grown tired. . . ." Dolmetsch, *The Smart Set*, p. 35.

85 "There were three that sailed away. . . ." Braley, *New York Sun*, December 6, 1920.

87 "Visitors are kindly requested. . . ."Dolmetsch, *The Smart Set*, p. 75.

89 "I have composed and printed. . . ." The letter of Mencken and Nathan to subscribers when they left the *Smart Set* is in Dolmetsch, p. 87.

96 "*Vanity Fair* has but two major articles in its editorial creed. . . ." Amory, *Vanity Fair: A Cavalcade of the 1920s and 1930s*, p. 13.

99 "F.C.'s interest in the modern French art movement. . . ." Seebohm, *The Man Who Was Vogue: The Life and Times of Condé Nast*, p. 115.

101   "To accomplish it by devoting. . . ." Hellman, "That Was New York: Crowninshield," *New Yorker*, February 14, 1948, p. 72.

111   "In his well-pressed gray suits. . . ." Wilson, *The Twenties*, p. 34.

111   "In spite of the not very attractive. . . ." Wilson, *The Twenties*, p. 39.

127   "We feel confident. . . ." Seabohm, *The Man Who Was Vogue: The Life and Times of Condé Nast*, p. 326.

137   "who had been taught a certain kind of gentility. . . ." Wilson, *The Twenties*, p. 45.

143   "The *New Yorker* will be a reflection. . . ." quoted in Kremer, *Ross and the New Yorker*, pp. 61–62.

150   "Millionaires and peddlars. . . ." *New Yorker*, Nov. 24 1931.

151   "Habitual travellers on Fifth Avenue. . . ." *New Yorker*, December 5, 1931.

164   "I have never seen an adequate account. . . ." quoted in *Letters of E. B. White*, edited by Guth, pp. 73–74, from an article that originally appeared in the *Paris Review*.

180   "Although they were both past masters of persuasion. . . ." Gingrich, *Nothing But People*, p. 26.

186   "Each time I came up with another dummy. . . ." Gingrich, *Nothing But People*, p. 81.

191   "Louis is too good to be true. . . ." Hemingway, *Esquire*, December 1935.

194   "with awestruck enthusiasm. . . ." Gingrich, *Nothing But People*, p. 96

200   "our grapes weren't being tended as carefully. . . ." Gingrich and Hills, *The Armchair Esquire*, preface.

· BIBLIOGRAPHY ·

The principal sources of information about the smart magazines are of course the magazines themselves. Most of the magazines discussed in this book are readily available in most large research collections. Since they were among the most popular and highly respected American magazines, many of them have also been retained by smaller libraries as well.

This bibliography does not pretend to be comprehensive. It merely lists works that the author has found helpful, and which readers in search of further amplification may find useful to consult.

Abel, Bob. "The City Slickers." *Columbia Journalism Review* 7 (Spring, 1968): 11–18.

Adams, Franklin P. *The Diary of Our Own Samuel Pepys*. New York: Simon and Schuster, 1935.

Adams, Samuel Hopkins. *A. Woollcott: His Life and His World*. New York: Reynal & Hitchcock, 1945.

Adler, Betty and Jane Wilhelm. *H. L. M.: The Mencken Bibliography*. Baltimore: Johns Hopkins University Press, 1961.

Allen, Frederick Lewis. "The American Magazine Grows Up." *Atlantic* 180 (November 1947): 77–82.

———. *The Function of a Magazine in America*. University of Missouri Bulletin, Journalism Series 101. Columbia MO: University of Missouri, 1945.

———. *Only Yesterday: An Informal History of the 1920s*. New York: Harper & Row, 1959.

Amory, Cleveland, ed. *Vanity Fair: A Cavalcade of the 1920s and 1930s*. New York: Viking Press, 1960.

———. *Who Killed Society?* New York: Harper & Bros., 1960.

Angoff, Charles, ed., *The World of George Jean Nathan*. New York: Alfred A. Knopf, 1952.

Another Ho Hum, More Newsbreaks from "The New Yorker." Foreword by E. B. White. New York: Farrar and Rinehart, 1932.

Anthony, Norman. *How to Grow Old Disgracefully*. New York: Duell, Sloan and Pearce, 1945.

Arno, Peter. *Peter Arno's Parade*. New York: Horace Liveright, 1929.

————. *Whoops Dearie!* New York: Simon and Schuster, 1927.

Baker, Carlos. *Ernest Hemingway: A Life Story*. New York: Scribners, 1969.

Barnett, Lincoln. *Writing on Life: Sixteen Close-Ups*. New York: William Sloan Associates, 1951.

Baron, Herman. *Author Index to Esquire*. Metuchen NJ: Scarecrow Press, 1976.

Beebe, Lucius. *The Big Spenders*. Garden City NY: Doubleday, 1966.

Beer, Thomas. *The Mauve Decade*. New York: Vintage Books, 1960.

Bender, Marilyn. "The New Yorker: Mannerly Maverick at Fifty." *New York Times* (Feb. 16, 1975): Sec. 3; 1–2.

Bernstein, Burton. *Thurber: A Biography*. New York: Dodd, Mead, 1975.

Blum, Eleanor. *Basic Books in the Mass Media: An Annotated, Selected Checklist*. Urbana IL: University of Illinois Press, 1972.

Bode, Carl. *Mencken*. Carbondale IL: Southern Illinois University Press, 1969.

————. *The Young Mencken*. New York: Dial Press, 1973.

Boorstin, Daniel. *The Americans: The Democratic Experience*. New York: Random House, 1973.

Brosseau, Ray, comp. *Looking Forward: Life in the Twentieth Century as Presented in the Pages of American Magazines from 1895 to 1905*. New York: American Heritage Press, 1970.

Brown, Henry Collins. *In the Golden Nineties*. Hastings-on-Hudson, NY: Valentine's Manual, Inc., 1928.

Brown, John Mason. *The Worlds of Robert E. Sherwood*. New York: Harper & Row, 1962.

Case, Frank. *Feeding the Lions*. New York: Greystone Press, 1942.

————. *Tales of a Wayward Inn*. New York: Frederick A. Stokes, 1938.

Catton, Bruce. "The Restless Decade." *American Heritage* XVI, 5 (August, 1965): 1–20.

Chase, Edna Woolman, and Elka Chase. *Always in Vogue*. Garden City NY: Doubleday, 1954.

Clymer, Floyd. *Scrapbook of Early Advertising Art*. Los Angeles: Floyd Clymer, 1955.

Colman, Carol A. "To the 'Adult Comic Book' Life is Not a Joke." *NYU News Workshop* 27 (Nov. 1972): 1, 6.

Cooke, Alistair. "H. L. Mencken," in *Six Men*, New York: Alfred A. Knopf, 1977.

Cowley, Malcolm. *Exile's Return*. New York: Norton, 1934.

————. *A Second Awakening: Works and Days of the Lost Generation*. New York: Viking Press, 1973.

Creel, George. *How We Advertised America*. New York: Harper & Bros., 1920.

Crowninshield, Francis Welsh. "I Remember Trying." *Vogue*, September 15, 1940.

————. *The Physiology of Taste: Meditations on Transcendental Gastronomy*, by Jean-Anthelme Brillat-Savarin, translated with a foreword by Frank Crownin-shield, New York: Boni & Liveright, 1926.

————. *The Unofficial Palace of New York*. New York: Waldorf-Astoria Hotel, 1939.

Dolmetsch, Carl R. *The Smart Set: A History and Anthology*. New York: Dial Press, 1966.

Douglas, George H. *H. L. Mencken: Critic of American Life*. Hamden CT: Archon Books, 1978.

"Down the Up Staircase." *Newsweek* 81 (April 23, 1973): 48*ff*.

Downey, Fairfax. *Portrait of an Era as Drawn by C. D. Gibson*. New York: Charles Scribner's Sons, 1936.

Drewry, John E. "Magazine Journalism: A Selected Bibliography." *Journalism Quarterly* 25 (September, 1958): 260–77.

Elledge, Scott. *E. B. White: A Biography*. New York: W. W. Norton, 1984.

"Esquire Sans Esquire." *Forbes* 120 (October 1, 1977): 36.

Fadiman, Clifton. *Profiles from the New Yorker*. New York: Alfred A. Knopf, 1938.

Felker, Clay S. "Life Cycles in the Age of Magazines." *Antioch Review* 29 (Spring 1969): 7–13.

Fisher, Edwin, Mort Gerberg and Ron Wolin. *The Art of Cartooning: Seventy-Five Years of American Magazine Cartoons*. New York: Scribner's 1972.

Fishwick, Marshall, W. "Easy Vehicles: Magazines in American Culture." *Magazine Studies Quarterly* (Winter 1976–77): 4–12.

Flanner, Janet. "The Unique Ross." In *Ross, "The New Yorker" and Me*, by Jane Grant. New York: Reynal & Co., 1968.

Flautz, John. *Life: The Gentle Satirist*. Bowling Green OH: Bowling Green University Popular Press, 1972.

Gaines, James R. *Wit's End: Days and Nights of the Algonquin Roundtable*. New York: Harcourt Brace Jovanovich, 1977.

Gale, Zona. "Editors of the Younger Generation." *The Critic* 44 (April 1904): 318–31.

Gibbs, Wolcott. "Time, Fortune, Life, Luce." In *A Subtreasury of American Humor*, edited by E. B. White and Katharine White. New York: Coward McCann, 1941.

Gill, Brendan. *Here at the New Yorker*. New York: Random House, 1975.

Gingrich, Arnold, ed. *The Bedside Esquire*. New York: Tudor, 1940.

————, ed. *The Esquire Treasury*. New York: Simon and Schuster, 1953.

————. "Introduction," *The Esquire Treasury*. New York: Simon and Schuster, 1953, pp. xiii–xv.

————. *Nothing But People: The Early Days of Esquire, 1928–1958*. New York: Crown, 1971.

————. "Some Amplifications of This Issue's Headnotes." *Esquire* 80 (October 1973): 8*ff*.

Gingrich, Arnold and L. Rust Hills, eds. *The Esquire Reader*. New York: Dial Press, 1960.

————. "Preface," *The Armchair Esquire*. New York: Putnam, 1958.

Grant, Jane. *Ross, "The New Yorker" and Me*. New York: Reynal & Co., 1968.

Hageman, E. R. and James E. Marsh. "Contributions of Literary Import to Esquire, 1933–1941, An Annotated Checklist." *Bulletin of Bibliography* 22 (Jan.–April 1957): 33*ff*; (May–Aug. 1957): 69*ff*.

Halsey, Louis. "The Talk of the Town and the Country: E. B. White." *Connecticut Review* 5 (October 1971): 37–45.

Hancock, La Touche. "The Poets of Printing House Square." *The Bookman* 15 (May 1902): 268–73.

Harriman, Margaret Case. *Blessed Are the Debonair*. New York: Rinehart & Co., 1956.

————. *The Vicious Circle*. New York: Rinehart & Co., 1951.

Hayes, Harold T. P. "Arnold Gingrich, Esquire." *New Republic* 175 (4 Sept. 1976): 33*ff*.

Hellman, Geoffrey. "Last of the Species" [Frank Crowninshield]. *New Yorker*, Sept. 19 and 26, 1942.

————. "That Was New York: Crowninshield," *New Yorker* 23 (February 14, 1948): 72*ff*.

Hoffman, Frederick J. *The Twenties*. New York: Viking, 1955.

Holbrook, Stewart. *The Age of Moguls*. New York: Doubleday, 1953.

Holmes, Charles S. *The Clocks of Columbus: The Literary Career of James Thurber*. New York: Atheneum, 1972.

Hooper, Roy. *Ralph Ingersoll: A Biography*. New York: Atheneum, 1985.

Hope, Anthony. "Mr. C. D. Gibson on Love and Life." *McClure's*, Sept. 1897.

Hoyt, Edwin P. *Alexander Woollcott, The Man Who Came to Dinner: A Biography*. New York: Abelard-Schuman, 1968.

Hyman, Stanely Edgar. "The Urban New Yorker." *New Republic* (July 20, 1942): 90–92.

Ingersoll, Ralph. "The New Yorker." *Fortune* 10 (August 1934): pp. 72–86; 90, 92, 97, 150, 152.

————. *Point of Departure*. New York: Harcourt, Brace & World, 1961.

Johnson, Robert Owne, comp. *An Index to Literature in The New Yorker*. Metuchen NJ: Scarecrow Press, 1969.

Johnson, Robert Underwood. *Remembered Yesterdays*. Boston: Little, Brown, 1923.

Kahn, E. J. *About the New Yorker and Me*. New York: G. P. Putnam's Sons, 1979.

Kanner, Bernice. "March 'Esquire' Takes on the Clay Felker Look." *Advertising Age* 49 (Jan. 9, 1978): 4.

Kutz, Bill, and Barry G. Richards. *Magazines for Libraries*. 3d ed. New York: R. R. Bowker, 1978.

Kaufman, Beatrice, and Joseph Hennessy. *The Letters of Alexander Woollcott*. New York: Viking Press, 1944.

Keats, John. *You Might as Well Live: The Life and Times of Dorothy Parker*. New York: Simon and Schuster, 1970.

Kimball, Penn T. "The Non Editing of Esquire." *Columbia Journalism Review* 3 (Fall 1964): 32–34.

Kramer, Dale. *Ross and the New Yorker*. Garden City NY: Doubleday, 1951.

Kramer, Hilton. "Harold Ross' New Yorker." *Commentary* 28 (August 1959): 122–27.

Krutch, Joseph Wood. "The Profession of a New Yorker." *Saturday Review of Literature* (January 20, 1954): 15–16.

Lardner, Ring, Jr. *The Lardners: My Family Remembered*. New York: Harper & Row, 1976.

Lawrenson, Helen. *Stranger at the Party*. New York: Random House, 1975.

Lazarsfeld, Paul F., and Rowena West. "Magazines in 90 Cities: Who Reads What?" *Public Opinion Quarterly* 1 (October 1957): 35–36.

Life: A Humorous Weekly, Andover Mass: Fieldstone Prsss, 1971.

"Life with Esquire." *Forbes* 101 (February 1, 1968): 42.

Logan, Andy. *The Man Who Robbed the Robber Barons*. New York: W. W. Norton, 1962.

Lord, Walter. *The Good Years*. New York: Harper, 1960.

Lyon, Peter. *Success Story: The Life and Times of S. S. McClure*. New York: Scribner's, 1963.

Macdonald, Dwight. "Laugh and Lie Down." *Partisan Review* 4 (December 1937): 44–53.

MacDougall, A. Kent. " 'Esquire' Keeps Thriving by Deflating Heroes, Backing the Unpopular." *Wall Street Journal* (May 8, 1968): 1ff.

McClure, S. S. *My Autobiography*. New York: Unger, 1963.

Mahan, Gigi. *The Last Days of the New Yorker*. New York: McGraw-Hill, 1988.

Maloff, Saul, ed. *Esquire's All About Women*. New York: Harper & Row, 1963.

Maloney, Russell. "A Profile of the New Yorker." *Saturday Review of Literature* 30 (August 30, 1947): p. 7ff.

————. "Tilly the Toiler." *Saturday Review of Literature* 30 (August 30, 1947): 7–10; 29–32.

Manchester, William. *Disturber of the Peace: The Life of H. L. Mencken*. New York: Harper & Bros., 1950.

————. "The Last Years of H. L. Mencken." *Atlantic* 236 (October 1975): 82–90.

Martin, E. S. "John Ames Mitchell." *Harvard Graduates Magazine*, September 1918.

May, Henry F. *The End of American Innocence*. New York: Alfred A. Knopf, 1959.

Mencken, H. L. *A Gang of Pecksniffs*. Edited by Theo Lippman, Jr. New Rochelle NY: Arlington House, 1975.

———. "A Personal Word," brochure on the *Smart Set*, New York, n.d.

———. *Pistols for Two*, by Owen Hatteras (pseud.), New York: Alfred A. Knopf, 1917.

———. *Prejudices: A Selection*. Edited by James T. Farrell. New York: Vintage Books, 1959.

———. *The Vintage Mencken*. Edited by Alistair Cooke. New York: Vintage Books, 1955.

Mitchell, John Ames. "Contemporary American Caricature." *Scribner's Magazine*, December 1899.

Morton, Charles W. "A Try for 'The New Yorker,' " and "A Brief Interlude at 'The New Yorker,' " *Atlantic*, April, May 1963, pp. 45–49; 81–85.

Mott, Frank Luther. *American Journalism*. New York: Macmillan, 1969.

———. "Fifty Years of Life: The Story of a Satirical Weekly." *Journalism Quarterly* 25 (Sept. 1948): 226ff.

———. *A History of American Magazines, 1865–1885*, Cambridge: Harvard University Press, 1938.

———. *A History of American Magazines, 1885–1905*, Cambridge: Harvard University Press, 1957.

———. *A History of American Magazines, 1905–1930*, Cambridge: Harvard University Press, 1968.

———. "The Magazine Revolution and Popular Ideas in the '90s." *American Antiquarian Society Proceedings* 64 (April 1954): 195–215.

Mussey, J. B., ed. *The Cream of the Jesters*. New York: Albert and Charles Boni, 1931.

Nathan, George Jean. *The Intimate Notebooks of George Jean Nathan*. New York: Alfred A. Knopf, 1932.

———. "Litany for Magazine Editors." *Smart Set*, February 1915.

———. "Suggestions to Our Visitors." *Smart Set*, n.d.

"New Politics, New New Yorker." *Time* 99 (May 1, 1972): 34ff.

"The New Yorker." *Fortune* 10 (August 1934): 73ff.

The New Yorker Album, 1925–1950, New York: Harper & Bros., 1951.

"The New Yorker: An Outline of Its History." Booklet published by the business office of *The New Yorker*, 1946.

"The New Yorker at 40." *Newsweek* 45 (March 1, 1965): 62–64.

Nolte, William H. *H. L. Mencken: Literary Critic*. Middletown CT: Wesleyan University Press, 1966.

Nolte, William H., ed. *H. L. Mencken's Smart Set Criticism*. Ithaca NY: Cornell University Press, 1968.

O'Gara, Jim. " 'New Yorker' at 40, Prospers, Also Retains Character as Choosy Magazine." *Advertising Age* 36 (Feb. 15, 1965): 144–47.

Parker, Dorothy. *Constant Reader*. New York: Viking Press, 1970.

Peterson, Thane. "Arnold Gingrich, Esquire." *Northliner* (January 1979): 15*ff*.

Peterson, Theodore. "The American Magazine: An Assessment." *Cresset* 24 (September 1961): 7–10.

———. *Magazines in the Twentieth Century*. Urbana IL: Univ. of Illinois Press, 1964.

Phillips, Cabell. *From the Crash to the Blitz, 1929–1939*. New York: Macmillan, 1969.

Presbrey, Frank. *The History and Development of Advertising*. Garden City NY: Doubleday, 1929.

Pringle, Henry L. "Sex, Esq." *Scribner's* 103 (March 1938): 33*ff*.

Pulitizer, Ralph. *New York Society on Parade*. New York: Harper & Bros., 1910.

Rascoe, Burton. *Before I Forget*. New York: Doubleday, 1937.

Rascoe, Burton, and Groff Conklin. *The Smart Set Anthology*. New York: Reynal & Hitchcock, 1954.

Richardson, Lyon A. *A History of Early American Magazines*. New York: Thomas Nelson & Sons, 1931.

Rogers, Agnes, and Frederick Lewis Allen. *I Remember Distinctly*. New York: Harper & Bros., 1947.

Rosmond, Babette. *Robert Benchley: His Life and Good Times*. Garden City NY: Doubleday, 1970.

Russell, Isabel. *Katharine and E. B. White: An Affectionate Memoir*. New York: W. W. Norton, 1988.

Salmon, Peter. " 'The New Yorker's' Golden Age." *New Republic* 140 (June 29, 1949): 19–20.

Sampson, Edward C. *E. B. White*. New York: Twayne, 1974.

Seebohm, Caroline. *The Man Who Was Vogue: The Life and Times of Condé Nast*. New York: Viking Press, 1982.

Seldes, George. " 'Ken,' The Inside Story." *Nation* 146 (April 30, 1938): 497–500.

Sheed, Wilfred. *Clare Boothe Luce*. New York: E. P. Dutton, 1982.

Shuttleworth, Jack. "John Held, Jr. and His World." *American Heritage* 16:5 (August 1965): 28–32.

Singleton, M. K. *H. L. Mencken and the American Mercury Adventure*, Durham NC: Duke University Press, 1962.

The Social Comedy, New York: Life Publishing Company, 1906.

"Some Words and Pictures About Arnold Gingrich." *Esquire* 86 (October 1976): 65–70.

Stenerson, Douglas C. *H. L. Mencken: Iconoclast From Baltimore*. Chicago: University of Chicago Press, 1971.

Stewart, Donald Ogden. *By A Stroke of Luck: An Autobiography*. New York: Paddington Press, 1975.

———. *Perfect Behavior*. New York: George H. Doran, 1922.

Strunk, William, Jr., and E. B. White. *The Elements of Style*. New York: Macmillan, 1959.

Sullivan, Mark. *Our Times*, Vol. I–V, New York: Scribner's, 1926–33.

Tassin, Algernon. *The Magazine in America*. New York: Dodd, Mead, 1916.

Tebbel, John. *The American Magazine, A Compact History*. New York: Hawthorne Books, 1969.

Teichman, Howard. *The Wit, World and Life of Alexander Woollcott*. New York: Wilhain Morrow, 1976.

"Thirty Years Hath Esquire." *Esquire* 30 (October 1963): 8*ff.*

Thurber, James. "E. B. W." *Saturday Review of Literature* (October 15, 1938): 8–9.

———. *The Years With Ross*. New York: Grosset and Dunlap, 1957.

Titus, Edna Brown, ed. *Union List of Serials in the United States and Canada*. New York: H. W. Wilson, 1965.

Towne, Charles Hanson. *Adventures in Editing*. New York: D. Appleton, 1926.

———. *So Far So Good*. New York: Morrow, 1945.

———. *This New York of Mine*. New York: Cosmopolitan Book Corp., 1931.

Ulrich's International Periodical Directory, Annual Serial.

Watt, William W., and Robert W. Bradford. *An E. B. White Reader*. New York: Harper & Row, 1966.

Wecter, Dixon. *The Saga of American Society*. New York: Scribner's, 1937.

Weeks, Edward. *My Green Age: A Memoir*. Boston: Little, Brown, 1973.

———. "The Place of Magazines in America." *Quill* 50 (September 1926): 14–16.

Welty, Eudora. "Dateless Vintner." *New York Times Book Review* (September 25, 1977): 7; 43.

White, E. B. *Letters of E. B. White*. Edited by Dorothy Lobrano Guth. New York: Harper & Bros., 1976.

———. "Ross, Harold Wallace," *Encyclopedia Britannica*, 1964 ed.

White, E. B. and Katharine White, eds. *A Subtreasury of American Humor*. New York: Coward McCann, 1941.

Wilson, Edmund. *The Shores of Light: A Literary Chronicle of the Twenties and Thirites*. New York: Farrar, Straus & Giroux, 1952.

———. *The Twenties*. New York: Farrar, Straus & Giroux, 1975.

Winterich, John T., ed. *Squads Write!* New York: Harper & Bros., 1931.

Wolfe, Tom. "Lost in a Whichy Thicket." *New York Herald Tribune Magazine* (April 18, 1965): 16*ff.*

————. "The New Journalism à la Recherche des Whichy Thickets." *New York* (February 21, 1972): 39–48.

————. "Tiny Mummies." *New York Herald Tribune Magazine* (April 11, 1965): 7*ff*.

Wolseley, Roland, E. *The Magazine World: An Introduction to Magazine Journalism.* New York: Prentice-Hall, 1951.

————. *Understanding Magazines.* Ames IA: Iowa State University Press, 1965.

Wood, James Playsted. *Magazines in the United States.* 2d ed. New York: Ronald Press, 1956.

————. *The Story of Advertising.* New York: Ronald Press, 1958.

The World in Vogue: An Anthology. New York: Viking, 1963.

Yardley, Jonathan. *Ring: A Biography of Ring Lardner.* New York: Random House, 1977.

· ACKNOWLEDGMENTS ·

I should like to thank Theodore Peterson, author of *Magazines in the Twentieth Century*, for his careful and painstaking reading of the manuscript of this book. I should also like to thank the various libraries whose collections allowed me to study the smart magazines and assemble anecdotal and pictorial material about them over a period of ten years and more. I am especially grateful to Diane Carothers, Communication Librarian of the University of Illinois for her assistance during the planning stages of this project. My deepest appreciation goes to the staffs of the following libraries: New York Public Library; the Enoch Pratt Public Library of Baltimore; the New-York Historical Society; the Chicago Historical Society Library; the Newberry Library; the Library of Congress; the Library of the New-York Historical Society; the Library of Smithsonian Institution; and the University of Michigan Library.

For permission to quote extensively, I am grateful to the following sources: pages 80*ff.*, "Undeveloped Notes," by George Jean Nathan, courtesy of *the Smart Set*, September 1922; pages 150*ff.*, "Up in the Air," from the November 14, 1931, issue and "Bus Stop," from the December 5, 1931 issue, both courtesy of the *New Yorker* magazine, © 1931, © 1959; pp. 191*ff.*, "The Million Dollar Fright," from *Esquire*, December 1935, courtesy of the estate of Ernest Hemingway, © 1935.

PICTURE CREDITS
Smart Set cover: University of Illinois Library; Charles Hanson Towne: New-York Historical Society; Col. William D'Alton Mann: Brown Brothers; Frank Crowninshield: George Eastman House; Nathan and Mencken: Alfred A. Knopf, Enoch Pratt Public Library collection; Daniel's Motor Co. ad: University of Illinois Library; *Vanity Fair* cover and drawing: University of Illinois Library; Edmund Wilson: Princeton University Library; Robert E. Sherwood: Library of Congress; Claire Boothe Brokaw: Cecil Beaton photo, George Eastman House; Algonquin Round Table: Al Hirschfeld drawing, Smithsonian collection; Dorothy Parker: Culver Pictures; Harold Ross: George Eastman House; Rea Irvin: New York Public Library; *New Yorker* mastheads: author's collection; *New Yorker* cover: University of Illinois Library; Robert Benchley: Brown Brothers; Katharine White: Culver

Pictures; Peter Arno: George Eastman House; Wolcott Gibbs: Library of Congress; E. B. White and James Thurber: Library of Congress; *Judge* parody of the *New Yorker*: author's collection; *Esquire* cover: University of Illinois Library; George Petty: Chicago Historical Society; *Esquire* drawing: University of Illinois Library; *Esquire* men's fashion ad: University of Illinois Library; David A. Smart and Arnold Gingrich: Chicago Historical Society.

· INDEX ·

*The main page references to the smart magazines are given here in **boldface** type.*